6 96

Believers

SPIRITUAL LEADERS OF THE WORLD

Believers

SPIRITUAL LEADERS OF THE WORLD

ELIZABETH GOLDMAN

OXFORD UNIVERSITY PRESS
NEW YORK · OXFORD

For Gabe and Jake

Oxford University Press
Oxford   New York
Athens   Auckland   Bangkok   Bombay
Calcutta   Cape Town   Dar es Salaam   Delhi
Florence   Hong Kong   Istanbul   Karachi
Kuala Lumpur   Madras   Madrid   Melbourne
Mexico City   Nairobi   Paris   Singapore
Taipei   Tokyo   Toronto

and associated companies in
Berlin   Ibadan

Copyright © 1995 by Elizabeth Goldman

Published by Oxford University Press, Inc.,
198 Madison Avenue, New York, New York 10016

Oxford is a registered trademark of Oxford University Press, Inc.

Library of Congress Cataloging-in-Publication Data

Goldman, Elizabeth.
Believers : spiritual leaders of the world / by Elizabeth Goldman.
p. cm. — (Oxford Profiles)
Includes bibliographical references and index.
ISBN 0-19-508240-0
1. Religious biography—Juvenile literature. 2. Religions—Juvenile literature.
[1. Religious leaders. 2. Religions.]
I. Title. II. Series.
BL72.G65 1995
200'.92'2—dc20   94-41673
[B]   CIP
                                                                                                              AC

1 3 5 7 9 8 6 4 2
Printed in the United States of America
on acid-free paper

On the cover: (clockwise from top left) Confucius, Martin
Luther King, Jr., Cotton Mather, and Mother Teresa
Frontispiece: An early 16th-century French sculpture in
stone shows Saint Anne teaching Mary to read.

Design: Sandy Kaufman
Layout: Valerie Sauers

Contents

Preface 7

Moses 11

Zarathushtra 15

Mahavira 18

Siddhārtha Gautama 21

Lao Tzu 25

Confucius 28

Mencius 32

Chuang Tzu 34

Aśoka Maurya 37

Mary 40

Jesus of Nazareth 43

Paul of Tarsus 48

Mani 52

Augustine of Hippo 54

Muhammad 58

Rābi'ah of Basra 64

Hildegard of Bingen 66

Moses Maimonides 70

Francis of Assisi 73

Joan of Arc 76

Guru Nānak 80

Thomas More 83

Martin Luther 87

Ignatius of Loyola 91

John Calvin 95

Isaac Luria 99

Anne Hutchinson 102

William Penn 106

Cotton Mather 110

Junípero Serra 114

Ann Lee 118

Richard Allen 122

Elizabeth Ann Seton 126

Handsome Lake 129

Joseph Smith 132

Isaac Mayer Wise 137

Mary Baker Eddy 140

Mohandas Gandhi 145

Pope John XXIII 150

Elijah Muhammad 154

Teresa of Calcutta 157

Malcolm X 161

Martin Luther King, Jr. 165

Desmond Tutu 171

Tenzin Gyatso 175

Further Reading 180

Index of Religious Leaders by Tradition 185

Index of Religious Leaders by Place of Birth 187

Index 188

Preface

Who are we and why are we here? This is the question the world's religions seek to answer. Although all societies have some kind of religion, their answers to life's questions do not form a single body of knowledge.

Religion is not a discipline, like science, that steadily provides new knowledge, filling in our picture of the world. In some cases, religion is opposed to science because it is rooted more strongly in belief than in reason. The truths of religion cannot be measured or counted because we cannot stand outside of religion to study it.

Although in our imaginations, we can live in the past, visit other planets, or journey to the center of the earth, in reality we are limited. We can live only in the bodies we were born with, shaped by our particular strengths and weaknesses; we can live in only one place and one time. Students of religion call this limited reality that we experience *conditioned reality*. Our age, size, sex, and nationality are all conditions. All people know the world only from their own, limited points of view. But nearly all peoples believe that an unconditioned reality—infinite, eternal, and absolute—must also exist.

Such an unconditioned reality goes by many names. People in the West usually call it God, or Allah, or Jesus. But to a Taoist, it is Tao, and to a Confucian, Heaven. Hindus call it Brahman; Buddhists call it nirvana. In many Native American traditions, it is known as the Great, or Mysterious, Spirit.

The word *religion* comes to us from the Latin. Its root *lig* seems linked to "tying" and "binding"; *religio,* for the Romans, meant an "obligation" or "oath." The theologian Paul Tillich defined religion as "ultimate concern"— whatever commands a person's most serious attention, whether that is God or money, Mozart or basketball. Other scholars speak of religion as the "encounter with the sacred," or with the Holy, the Ultimate.

These definitions suggest that religion may be a private matter. Sometimes it is, but more often, religion is social and involves other people. We might say, therefore, that religion is a community's response to what it experiences as sacred. That response is typically in the form of shared beliefs, prayers, rituals, and codes of behavior.

Religions have always arisen, and they continue to arise, from specific places, people, and problems. Each religion has a particular history and way of looking at the world. In this way religions are much like languages, with distinct qualities, histories, and points of view. Languages grow as cultures change, and so do religions. A conquering army may impose a new language on a people. One language may evolve into another, or two languages may grow into a third. So it is with religions.

There is another, more dangerous, way in which religions are like languages. Just as speakers of one language often misunderstand speakers of another language, followers of one religion may find another one comical or grotesque. And similarly, as people who speak one language may exclude people who do not, followers of one religion may use religious differences as a reason to dislike or distrust followers of another religion. Our inability to understand one another may magnify our differences.

Most of the traditions treated in this book began as changing times made new demands on people. Some religions, such as Buddhism and Islam, seem to have arisen as people began living in cities: the rural codes that had suited people for centuries were suddenly inadequate. Technological changes have influenced religions as well. The invention of farming in the ancient Near East called a new set of gods and goddesses into being in ancient Babylonia. The printing press played a pivotal role in the Protestant revolution of the 16th century by permitting radical ideas to reach a very large number of people.

Throughout their histories, religions have often been identified with the people who played roles in them. To many people, Christianity is inseparable from Jesus, and Buddhism is linked to the Buddha, for instance. We call these leaders founders of their traditions.

Not all religions are associated with founders, of course. The religions of Native Americans, of tribal peoples in Africa and Australia, of ancient Egypt, India, Europe, Greece, and Mesopotamia, and the Shinto religion in Japan all evolved without founders. Scholars call these religions, which arose communally rather than through a founder, *basic*. In some cases, the founder religions grew out of basic religions. For example, Buddhism and Jainism, both founder religions, grew out of earlier Indian traditions not associated with founders. Basic religions continue to be the living tradition in many parts of the world.

Because the focus of this book is on individuals who made a difference in various religions, these basic religions are touched on only in passing. They are fascinating in their own right, and you are encouraged to investigate them. Some sources for further reading are listed at the end of each profile; general sources are listed at the end of the book.

And what of the people profiled in this book? Coming up with a list was a struggle. The editors and I tried to cover the world's major religions—noting, as I have mentioned, that basic religions would be slighted. We aimed for a mix of people, trying to include some who would be new as well as those who would be familiar. *Believers* thus leans heavily toward Europe and the United States. By no means do I want to suggest that the people included here make a definitive list of religious leaders.

This collection begins with Zarathushtra (also known by his Greek name Zoroaster) and ends with Tenzin Gyatso, the Dalai Lama of Tibet, and so spans nearly 4,000 years. Some of the unfamiliar figures included in this volume are female. Given women's long and involuntary silence about the world and religion, where it has been possible to tell the story of a religious woman's life, I have. Throughout, I have tried to be balanced, which means nearly everyone may take offense at one point or another.

Some of the more contemporary figures will seem more "political" than earlier figures. This is an illusion based on our nearness to contemporary figures. Most religious changes grew out of political and social crises in their countries of origin. Mahavira, for example, was repelled by the organization of Indian society into castes, or rigid classes; Jesus lived during a foreign occupation of his country; Muhammad was shaped by the growing chasm between rich and poor Mecca. Eventually, the political urgencies that forced religious change faded, leaving only the ethical and spiritual teachings connected to that change. In our own time, the political urgencies are still with us.

These biographies are arranged chronologically because that seemed the clearest way to approach this subject. Although religions do not build on accumulated knowledge the way sciences do, earlier religious ideas constantly influence later ones, and ideas from one tradition influence people in another. To divide these biographies by tradition or geography seemed to violate this interrelation among religions.

Some rough categories of the religions treated here may be useful, all the same. I use three categories.

Monotheism refers to religions whose believers worship a single god, or ultimate power. Judaism, Christianity, Islam, and Sikhism are all monotheistic religions. They are linked to Zoroastrianism, the ancient monotheistic religion that is still practiced today by a small number of people.

Polytheism refers to religions based on the worship of many gods, although one god may rule over the others. The Hindu and Jain religions of India are polytheistic, as are African and Native American traditions.

Finally, there are religions that do not have an explicit god or group of gods at their core but still have belief systems, codes of behavior, rituals, and prayers. Buddhism and Confucianism are examples of this kind of religion.

There are a number of ways to use this book. One, certainly, is simply to read the biographies of people you are interested in or curious about. Another method might be to read the book from beginning to end to get a feeling for how religious ideas have evolved. At the back of the book, you will find an index of the biographical subjects arranged according to nationality and to religious tradition. You might read all the Indian biographies, for example, or all the Catholic ones. As you begin to read, I think, some common themes may stand out.

For instance, nonviolence—called *ahimsa*—appears as a strong ideal in the teachings of Mahavira, founder of the Jain religion. The Indian prince Aśoka Maurya embraces it; Muhammad and Saint Augustine do not. The Shaker founder Ann Lee expands the concept of nonviolence to include noncooperation with government. Gandhi—through the Russian writer Leo Tolstoy—builds on Ann Lee's ideas, in turn encouraging Martin Luther King, Jr., who in turn strengthens the nonviolent ideas of Desmond Tutu.

Theocracy, the idea that rulers should be guided by religion, can also be traced, through figures as dissimilar as Lao Tzu, John Calvin, and Junípero Serra. Or you might follow a thread within a tradition, such as the Christian ideal of faith as understood by Saint Paul, Saint Augustine, Martin Luther, and Anne Hutchinson.

Similar themes also emerge among the subjects' lives themselves. While a few, such as Mother Teresa, modeled their lives on their parents' faith and actions, many had deep, lifelong conflicts with their parents. Martin Luther and Saint Francis struggled with their fathers, Saint Augustine with his mother. It seems clear that religious ideas are connected, at least in part, with our feelings about our parents.

Another thing binds these figures together. Most of them lived in troubled times, and they took sides. Fully a quarter of these biographical subjects died violent deaths as a result of their beliefs. The political element of religion is easier to see as we approach the figures of the 20th century: Gandhi, espousing the twin gospels of equality and nonviolence, forged a political movement, as did King and Tutu. The specific political circumstances that gave rise to a Confucius, a Martin Luther, or a Richard Allen are eroded by time, but they existed nonetheless.

Finally, we might note that many of these subjects felt misunderstood by their peers and their society. Zarathushtra was rejected by his people; Ann Lee was jailed. Some, like Moses or Muhammad, felt confused and anxious, reluctant to do the difficult work they felt called to do. Others, such as Isaac Mayer Wise and Ignatius Loyola, found their lives made sense only after they adopted a religious path.

What is striking is how human these figures were, how various and far from flawless. What they have in common is not perfection so much as courage. To them, questions of who we are and why we are here really mattered. I hope this book will be an opportunity for you to explore the answers they found.

Elizabeth Goldman
Dover, New Hampshire

Moses

THE LAWGIVER

Alarmed by how quickly his population of Hebrew slaves was increasing, the pharaoh, king of Egypt, ordered all male Hebrew babies destroyed. But one mother placed her son in a basket of reeds and slipped it into the river. He was later found, unharmed, by an Egyptian princess who raised him as her own. She called him "Moses," for "I drew him out."

Moses is regarded by his tradition as a great hero, whose life was extraordinary from the beginning. He is credited with writing the Torah, the first five books of the Hebrew Bible—Genesis, Exodus, Leviticus, Numbers, and Deuteronomy. The Torah details the laws and early history of the Jewish people.

The historical Moses, however, is lost to us. Scholars conclude that because this Jewish man had an Egyptian name (actually meaning "son"), he probably did exist. Apart from the biblical account, there is no record of a successful revolt by the Hebrew slaves in Egypt, although perhaps Egyptians chose not to record it.

In the Bible, the book of Exodus describes how the Red Sea was parted as Moses led the Jews out of captivity in Egypt: "Moses stretched his hand over the sea; and the Lord drove the sea back by a strong east wind all night, and made the sea dry land, and the waters were divided."

The title page of a Haggadah published in Amsterdam in 1695 shows Moses (right), holding the tablets with the Ten Commandments, and his brother Aaron, the high priest. A Haggadah is a guide for celebrating a seder, the festive meal at Passover, the festival that commemorates the exodus of the Jews from Egypt.

The Hebrew Bible (what Christians call the Old Testament) does not seem to be the work of a single writer; it contains many points of view from different periods in history. Because the names it uses for God vary, some scholars have suggested that the Bible had several authors. One, probably writing in the 10th century B.C.E., calls God Yahweh (Jehovah) and is named the J author by modern scholars. Another writer, the E author, writing some 200 years later, calls God Elohim. (Some scholars think that J and E are the same author, whom they call JE.) Deuteronomy is said to be the work of yet another writer, or group of writers, D, who wrote about 100 years after E. The work of all three writers seems to have been edited by P, a priestly writer who lived in the 6th century B.C.E. There are, however, other theories about how and when the Bible came into being.

The biblical story of Moses is probably a creation from the 7th or 8th century B.C.E. As a young man, Moses made a sharp break from his sheltered past in the pharaoh's palace; he killed an Egyptian guard for mistreating a Hebrew slave and fled from Egypt. Moses settled in Midian, on the far side of the Sinai Peninsula and the Gulf of Aqaba. There, he worked as a shepherd and married a Midianite woman named Zipporah. They had two sons, whom Moses named Gershom, "stranger in a strange land," and Eliezer, "my God is a help."

One day in the rocky desert wilderness of the Sinai, Moses saw a burning thornbush that was not consumed by its flames. A voice, which Moses understood to be that of God, spoke from the flames and told him to return to Egypt and free his people. Moses resisted. He was not capable, he said. He wanted to know who he should say had sent him; he did not think the Hebrews would listen to him; he was a poor speaker.

The voice promised to accompany Moses and to help him. To persuade the Hebrews of Moses' powers, God worked wonders, turning Moses' stick into a snake and back, making Moses' hand diseased and then well again, and turning water into blood. It revealed its name: YHWH (pronounced Yahweh), meaning "I am [who] I am." Deliberately vague about his name, YHWH was very different from the other gods and goddesses of Moses' time, who represented powers symbolized by particular mountains or animals.

The patriarchs, or fathers, of Judaism—Abraham, Isaac, and Jacob—had called their supreme being Adonai (my Lord) and Elohim (God of gods). But in the encounter with the burning bush, the God of the Hebrews revealed the name YHWH for the first time. This event marked the new way the Hebrew people would know God. God would make himself known not just to selected individuals, as he had to Abraham, Isaac, and Jacob, but to a whole people.

When Moses returned to Egypt, he advised the pharaoh that YHWH wanted his people to go into the wilderness for a three-day spring festival. The pharaoh not only refused but increased the Hebrews' workload. In response, YHWH brought a series of 10 plagues on the Egyptians, ending with the death of all first-born sons and first-born animals. YHWH commanded the Hebrews to make an animal sacrifice to him and daub blood on their doorposts and lintels. This mark would be a signal for him to "pass over" their homes and spare their sons; this became the basis for the Jewish festival of Passover, during which Jews celebrate their deliverance from slavery in Egypt.

Devastated by the last plague, and conceding that his own gods were powerless before YHWH, the pharaoh let the Hebrews go. When he realized, however, that Moses meant to lead his people to freedom, he sent an army after them. In the biblical account, YHWH dried up the Red Sea for the Hebrews but drowned the Egyptian soldiers. This event occasioned perhaps the earliest poem in the Bible, the Song of Miriam (Exodus 15), which rejoices in YHWH's triumph.

According to traditional biblical reckoning, three months after the Exodus, or flight from Egypt, Moses climbed Mount Sinai to receive the Ten Commandments. Like a marriage contract, they established a new relationship between the Hebrew people and God.

The Hebrews are to recognize YHWH as their only God. They may make no images—pictures, statues, or idols—of anything to worship. They may not misuse God's name, to do magic or harm to others; they may not kill, commit adultery, steal, lie, or want things that belong to others. YHWH's command to keep the Sabbath holy—to save every seventh day to rest and remember God—linked the human world to God.

When Moses descended from Mount Sinai with God's words inscribed on two tablets, he found his

Moses

BORN

14th century B.C.E.
Egypt

DIED

13th century B.C.E.
Mount Nebo, present-day Jordan

TRADITION

Judaism

ACCOMPLISHMENT

Hebrew prophet and lawgiver who organized the religious community of Jews and established its judicial traditions

> *"But I am slow of speech, and of tongue."*
>
> —Exodus 4:10

people worshiping and dancing before a statue of a golden calf. Having been deprived of Moses as their visible connection to YHWH while he had been on Mount Sinai, they had lost their faith and had made an idol to worship. Furious, Moses shattered the tablets and ground the calf to dust. Then he returned to God to ask forgiveness for his wayward people and offered to die if God would not forgive them.

God called Moses to climb the mountain again and replaced the tablets. On this occasion, God further allowed Moses, uniquely among all Jews, to experience God's divinity— God made his "goodness pass before" Moses and let Moses see his back.

Moses was the central figure in the formation of the relationship between God (YHWH) and the Hebrew people as a community. At the heart of this new relationship was the experience of freedom from Egyptian slavery. Because the Hebrew people had been freed, God would require that they help others in need. Throughout the Hebrew Bible, God repeatedly prompts them to "remember the stranger, because you were strangers in Egypt."

After four decades of wandering, according to the Bible, Moses led his people out of the wilderness to the land they would occupy: Canaan (present-day Israel). Although Moses saw the new land from the top of

Mount Nebo, he did not enter it himself. The great hero who navigated the way from slavery to freedom, and from magic to monotheism, did not taste the final fruits of his work.

Although Moses is centrally important to Judaism, he was buried in an unmarked grave so that no cult of worship would grow up around him. For all his power as a spiritual and political leader, and as a model for Jewish people, Moses' success in his mission is reflected in his being viewed by his people as a hero, not a god.

FURTHER READING

De Graaf, Anne. *Moses: God's Chosen Leader*. Grand Rapids, Mich.: Eerdmans, 1991.

Johnson, Slyvia A. *Moses*. Minneapolis, Minn.: Lerner, 1983.

Plaut, W. Gunther. *The Torah: A Modern Commentary*. New York: Union of American Hebrew Congregations, 1981.

Zarathushtra

THE STRUGGLE AGAINST EVIL

According to tradition, light from Zarathushtra's body shone through his mother from the womb. He is said to have smiled at birth instead of crying, as other babies do.

Stories of an extraordinary birth and childhood are common to many founders of the world's great religions. Lao Tzu was born after gestating 60 years; the infant Moses was saved by a princess from drowning; the Buddha was fathered by an elephant the size of a seed. Such stories serve to remind their listeners that these figures are set apart, extraordinary, holy.

The 7th-century-B.C.E. prophet Zarathushtra is no exception. Stories of his early gifts mark him as exceptional, and indeed, he was one of the world's great religious innovators. In his teachings, two powerful ideas about God and humankind emerged clearly for the first time in history. These were the ideas of dualistic monotheism and transfiguration. *Dualistic monotheism* refers to the idea that a single (mono) god created the universe but that a struggle goes on here, in the world, between the two (dual) forces of good and evil. *Transfiguration* refers to the idea that each person and the world itself can be changed for the better through religious acts.

A Zoroastrian devil (right) tempts the first humans with fruit in this counterpart to the Judeo-Christian story of Adam and Eve's temptation by a serpent. Zarathushtra believed that both good and evil powers existed in the world but that good would eventually triumph.

> *"Give ear to the highest truths. Let each of you, one by one, consider them with an illumined mind, before deciding which of two paths to tread."*
>
> —from the *Gathas*

The religion Zarathushtra founded is known as Zoroastrianism, from the name Zoroaster, by which he is often called. *Zoroaster* is derived from the Greek from of Zarathushtra, his Persian name.

Zarathushtra developed his ideas over time and, like other religious founders, in response to the circumstances of his era. Scholars disagree on the dates, but he was probably born around 628 B.C.E to a priestly family of the Iranian steppes, the treeless plains of present-day Afghanistan and Iran. The names of his father, Pourushaspa ("owner of grey horses"), and his mother, Dughdova ("one who has milked"), have been preserved, but little else is known about his life. His parents practiced a religion known as Mazdayasni, which had a ruler god, known as Mazda, as well as many other gods and spirits. By Zarathushtra's time, most people worshiped the lesser deities, devoting special effort to keeping evil spirits at bay.

As a young man, Zarathushtra left his family and friends to go on a religious quest. Wandering across the steppes, he meditated and prayed. Around the age of 30, he received the first of a series of visions of a supreme being. He called this being Ahura Mazda—"lord of light," God of all wisdom and creation, saver of souls and the source of all goodness. Although his people worshiped a range of lower gods, Zarathushtra recognized a single God above all of them. This idea of a single God is the basis of all monotheistic religions.

Ahura Mazda did not rule the world alone, however. Allied with him were angelic beings, the Amesha Spentas, "the immortal holy ones," who represented aspects of Ahura Mazda, such as strength and goodness. The greatest of these was Asha, righteousness.

In cosmic opposition to Ahura Mazda was the evil spirit Angra Mainyu. Aided by their lesser spirits, the forces of good and evil were in constant struggle with one another. Scholars call religions of such warring, opposed forces dualistic.

Zarathushtra understood humankind's role as not merely to avoid evil but to fight it. The possibility that people can redeem themselves through fighting evil is key to the idea of transfiguration. Zarathushtra taught that at the end of time, when good finally prevails over evil, the souls of the dead will rejoin their resurrected bodies for a Last Judgment. The blessed will live forever.

Although he saw evil as an independent force in the universe, Zarathushtra believed that men and women are free and responsible for their own choices of good or evil. He offered his followers both a way to behave in this world and a promise of reward in the next. This would prove more compelling than worshiping and placating evil spirits, but not immediately.

At first, Zarathushtra's people rejected him. He taught that Ahura Mazda was the true God, while other gods, such as those of his parents, were false. Ten years passed before Zarathushtra made his first convert. Treated as a heretic and an outcast, particularly by his people's priests, Zarathushtra finally left his homeland. It was only on traveling east that he found favor when King Vishtashpa of Bactria, in present-day Afghanistan, granted him an audience. Persuaded of Zarathushtra's vision, Vishtashpa publicly embraced the religion of Ahura Mazda, and his court followed.

In practical terms, Zarathushtra urged his followers to live the "good life": to exercise self-discipline, sexual faithfulness, honesty, and charity. He stressed the central importance of both moral and physical purity, or cleanliness. Death, to him, was particularly unclean, so Zoroastrian dead are not buried, burned, or set upon the water. Their bodies are carried to the tops of sacred towers and left for the sun to purify and the birds to devour.

Worship of Ahura Mazda spread throughout the region of present-day Iran, western India, Afghanistan, and Iraq. Once Zarathushtra was imprisoned on charges of sorcery, or witchcraft, but he was released. He continued to preach until his death at 77, when he was killed by a priest of the old tradition.

Zarathushtra's teachings were collected in holy books known as *Avestas*. The oldest part of the *Avestas* is the *Gathas*, hymns and poems said to have been composed by Zarathushtra himself. They form the basis of Zoroastrian religious service.

Some scholars suggest that Judaism may have absorbed some Zoroastrian ideas during the Babylonian Exile, beginning in 586 B.C.E., when the Jews were held in captivity by the Babylonian Empire. Zarathushtra found admirers among Greek thinkers, including Pythagoras, and early Christians regarded him as a herald of Christ. A mystery cult, or secret religious society, centered on Mithra, the Persian sun god, spread rapidly through the Roman Empire in the first centuries of the common era. It reached as far north as Britain. Christianity was not officially adopted over Mithraism until the 4th century C.E., when the emperor Constantine made Christianity the state religion. After that, Christians regarded Zarathushtra as a heretic.

Zarathushtra's decline among Western thinkers reversed during the 14th century Renaissance for a time and again during the 18th century Enlightenment, when philosophers revived the classical Greek interest in him. In a widely influential work, *Thus Spake Zarathushtra*, the 19th-century German philosopher Friedrich

Nietzsche credited Zarathushtra with first identifying the true nature of life as a struggle between good and evil. Contemporary followers of Zarathushtra include the Parsis (Persians) of western India and the Bodin or Gabar people of predominantly Muslim Iran. Together, they number around 100,000 people.

FURTHER READING

Farhang, Mehr. *The Zoroastrian Tradition.* Boston, Mass.: Amity House, 1988.

Hinnells, John R. *Persian Mythology.* New York: Hamlyn, 1973.

Masani, Rustom. *Zoroastrianism: The Religion of the Good Life.* New York: Macmillan, 1968.

Mehta, P. D. *Zarathushtra: The Transcendental Vision.* Shaftesbury, England: Element Books, 1985.

BELIEVERS

Zarathushtra

BORN

about 628 B.C.E.
Persia (present-day Iran)

DIED

about 551 B.C.E.
Persia

TRADITION

Zoroastrianism

ACCOMPLISHMENTS

Persian religious prophet and founder of Zoroastrianism; his followers collected his hymns, the *Gathas*, and other teachings in the *Avestas*

Mahavira

THE ONE WHO TURNED THE WORLD AWAY

Many religious seekers consider the body a prison: it is, after all, subject to pain, illness, accident, and age. They discipline and deny their bodies in order to free their spirits from this prison. This practice of discipline and self-denial is known as asceticism. Perhaps no religious seeker has ever embraced asceticism more fiercely than the founder of India's Jain tradition, Nataputta Vardhamāna.

Little is known about Vardhamāna's life. One story told after his death says that he was so peaceful in his mother's womb, that he did not kick her for fear of hurting her. Another tells how, as a boy, he calmed a poisonous snake by his gentleness alone.

Vardhamāna was probably the son of a wealthy chieftain in Magadha (present-day Bihar) in India's rich Middle Country, between the Ganges Delta and the foothills of the Himalayas. Born a little before Siddhārtha Gautama, the Buddha, Vardhamāna was also revered by his followers. They called him Mahavira ("great hero") or Jaina or Jina ("conqueror"). The religion of Vardhamāna is therefore known as Jainism.

Like the Buddha, Mahavira rebelled against the ancient Indian religion of Brahmanism and the Indian society of his day. Both men rejected the arrangement of society into classes, or castes. Both turned away from the creator god celebrated in the sacred stories of the Vedas and from the animal sacrifices and fire-worshiping rituals of Brahmanism.

Vardhamāna's parents were followers of Parshva, a Jina, or holy man, who lived some 300 years before Mahavira. Parshva was known as a spiritual ford-finder, one who makes a way for others to cross a river. (In this case, the river was a metaphor for life and the far shore was salvation.) Mahavira is considered the 24th, and last, such ford-finder in the Jain tradition. Vardhamāna joined an order of Parshva monks when he was 30 but found their form of asceticism too lax. So he gave away everything he owned, even his begging bowl, pulled his hair out by the roots, and set out to travel northern India as a naked, begging monk.

There are two traditions of stories about Mahavira, which are often called the strict and the lenient. In the lenient version, Mahavira married and fathered a daughter before he renounced the world. He did not give away his clothes and lived naked, or "sky-clad," only because his robe fell from him and he did not notice. In the strict version, Mahavira never married and cast his clothing off at his renunciation. In this tradition, only naked monks can achieve enlightenment.

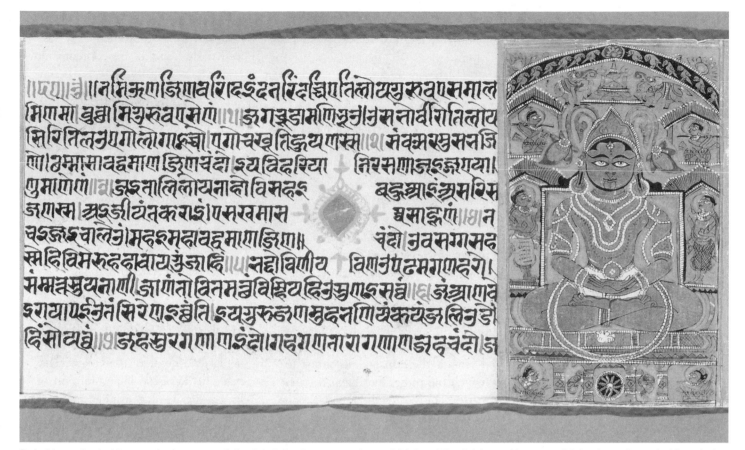

Rishabhanatha in Heaven depicts one of the 24 *tirthankaras,* or saints, of Jainism. The 24th, and last, was Mahavira—the only historical figure. This Indian painting dates from about 1500 and shows Rishabhanatha waiting to be reborn as a *tirthankara.*

In the stories of both traditions, Mahavira wandered for more than 12 years, meditating and imposing harsh ordeals on his body. He lived without clothing or a house and went without food for weeks at a time. He endured insults, injuries, and insect bites without complaint. In one story, some herdsmen set fire to Mahavira's feet and drove nails into his ears as he meditated, but he did not flinch.

Another story tells of a farmer who saw Mahavira meditating near a field. Assuming he was not busy, the farmer asked him to watch his cattle. Mahavira took no notice of the farmer, the cows, or the request. That evening when the farmer returned, his cows

"Oh man, refrain from evil, for life must come to an end.
Only men foolish and uncontrolled are plunged in the habit
of pleasure....
'Not I alone am the sufferer—all things in the universe
suffer!'
Thus should man think and be patient, not giving way to
his passions.
As old plaster flakes from a wall, a monk should make thin
his body by fasting
And he should injure nothing."

—from *The Book of Sermons*

Mahavira

BORN

About 599 B.C.E.
Probably Bihar, India

DIED

About 527 B.C.E.
City unknown, India

TRADITION

Jainism

ACCOMPLISHMENTS

Founder of Jainism; his teachings, not collected until 200 years after his death, include *The Book of Sermons* and some 45 other texts

were missing. Beating Mahavira angrily, he accused him of stealing them.

Mahavira endured these ordeals in order to achieve nirvana—a state of bliss and cessation of desire—and *moksha,* or liberation from repeating the cycle of death and rebirth, which all souls, in traditional Indian religion, are doomed to experience. He differed from other seekers, including religious people of his own time, in refusing to believe in a personal God who acted in people's lives to save them. He insisted that freeing the spirit from its bodily limits was a purely human task. This task, however, is subject to the traditional Indian religious law of *karma* (Sanskrit for "action" or "deed"). Karma is the principle according to which the things that happen to a person are the results of past actions, either in the same lifetime or a previous one.

Mahavira believed that the absolute truth could never be fully known. For this reason, it was never right to harm another. He preached and practiced *ahimsa,* nonviolence toward all things. Though he traveled constantly, he stopped during the monsoon season, so as not to harm the new vegetation that the rains produced.

Finally, after 12 years, he reached the end of his labors. He achieved *kevala,* or separation, in which the soul is liberated from the body's needs and constraints. Now freed from matter, his soul would live forever at the top of the universe. His followers called him an *arhat,* one worthy of worship.

Out of compassion for others, Mahavira continued to travel and preach in the Ganges Valley for 30 more years. A gifted organizer, he enlarged his following to more than 50,000 monks and nuns and 450,000 lay members.

Like other religions that arose to challenge traditional Indian Brahmanism, Mahavira's teachings stressed asceticism and nonviolence. He seems, however, to have taken these ideas further than any of his contemporaries. Mahavira's dedication to asceticism was so strong that some of his followers went naked rather than accept the comfort of clothing. Others starved to death in the name of asceticism. Even today, devout Jains wear cheesecloth masks to avoid accidentally breathing in insects and sweep their paths clear of living creatures before they walk so as not to harm them.

At the age of 72, Mahavira died a *siddha,* one liberated, in Indian thought, from the curse of rebirth into another body. Mahavira was not, by any account, a charming, personable man, but his example of fierce self-denial and absolute nonviolence has made his ideals an important part of Indian life. He has inspired many Indian leaders, from Aśoka Maurya to Mahatma Gandhi.

FURTHER READING

Dundas, Paul. *The Jains.* New York: Routledge, Chapman & Hall, 1992.

Jaini, Padmanabh S. *The Jaina Path of Purification.* Berkeley: University of California Press, 1979.

Tobias, Michael. *Life Force: The World of Jainism.* Fremont, Calif.: Jain Publishing, 1991.

Warren, H. *Jainism.* Flushing, N.Y.: Asia Book Company, 1988.

Siddhārtha Gautama

THE BUDDHA, OR AWAKENED ONE

The Buddha's mother had a strange dream before he was born. A huge white elephant was falling from the sky toward her, becoming smaller and smaller as it neared. When it reached the size of a seed, it entered her side and formed a perfect baby.

The baby was born painlessly, bathed by golden light, in a peaceful forest grove in Lumbini, in present-day Nepal. The newborn's hair was thick and perfectly curled, a sign of spiritual perfection. So goes the most popular legend about the birth of the founder of Buddhism. It reflects an impulse common to many followers of religious leaders—the urge to make a god or superhuman hero out of a remarkable man.

The man whom people would come to call Buddha was the son of a raja, or ruler, of the Shakya tribe of northeastern

A 10th-century sculpture depicts the birth of the Buddha, who, according to tradition, entered the world bathed in golden light in the middle of a forest.

"You yourself must make an effort; the Buddhas are only preachers."

—from *The Dhammapada* (Pali canon)

A 14th-century Siamese stone head of the Buddha. At age 29, Siddhārtha Gautama left his family and his privileged existence and went out into the world to unravel the mystery of human suffering.

India, near the foothills of the Himalayas. His father had political and military aspirations for the boy and named him Siddhārtha (victorious one). The Gautama family lived in present-day Bihar, India's Middle Country—the flat, broad floodplain of the Ganges River. There, centuries earlier, a civilization dominated and defined by priests known as Brahmans had arisen.

The land was rich. By the time of Siddhārtha's birth, in the 5th century B.C.E., it supported vast farmlands, a growing population, and bustling cities. Many older practices, such as animal sacrifice, began to conflict with the wholly different pressures and freedoms of city life.

Some scholars have suggested that Siddhārtha's teachings are aimed in part at addressing the sense of disconnection that people in this new kind of society may have felt; his followers tell a more dramatic story. In the most famous legend of Siddhārtha's youth, his father tried to prevent the young man from learning about human suffering. He arranged Siddhārtha's marriage to a beautiful young woman, who bore Siddhārtha a son, Rāhula. Siddhārtha's father built him an enclosed compound, known as the "garden of happiness," in the country.

But Siddhārtha felt impelled to know something more of the world, and he ventured outside the garden into the village and surrounding country. His explorations introduced him to the awful facts of existence: old age, illness, and death itself. Shaken, the prince is said to have cried, "I have been living in a graveyard!" Finally, Siddhārtha met a monk. With his head shaved and a bowl for begging food in his hand, the monk clearly cared little for worldly things. To Siddhārtha, the monk represented another way to live, free from *dukkha*, life's pain and apparent meaninglessness. At the age of 29,

Siddhārtha left his comfortable life, his weeping parents, his wife, and his newborn son. "In the prime of my youth I cut off my hair and beard and went forth from a house to a houseless life," he later remarked. Buddhist tradition calls this decision the Great Renunciation.

Many *shramanas*, or teachers, wandered the Middle Country, teaching ways to reach enlightenment, or spiritual understanding. Siddhārtha followed several spiritual paths, and decided to be an ascetic, one who disciplines his body and practices self-denial in order to reach spiritual understanding. In the company of five disciples, he set off on his own.

According to tradition, Siddhārtha became so weak from his ascetic practice that he nearly died. When he accepted a bowl of milk from a young girl, his disciples abandoned him, but Siddhārtha concluded that asceticism was not the answer. He decided to sit still until he understood the way out of human misery—the discomfort, disappointment, and pain of being alive. Buddhist tradition says he sat for 49 days at the foot of a tree known today as the *bo* tree, the tree of wisdom. Demons tempted and threatened him, but he remained unmoved. As he sat, Siddhārtha's awareness passed beyond the world of the senses to that of thought; he went beyond knowledge of life and death, good and evil. At last he reached nirvana—freedom from ignorance, blind desire, and human limitation. He likened it to the "coolness" of health that follows a fever.

At this point Siddhārtha could have, according to traditional Indian thinking, left his earthly life behind and entered permanently into nirvana, freed forever from the cycle of births and rebirths each person is condemned by his or her karma to endure. Moved by the suffering of others, however, the Buddha elected to stay in the world and teach his truth, or *dharma*, to others.

The Buddha called his new understanding the Middle Way, a way of living between the extremes of asceticism and mindless luxury. Rejoining his disciples near the city of Benares, he taught them the essence of his *dharma*—his four Noble Truths. These are

> Life is full of misery (*dukkha*).
> Misery is rooted in self-centered desire.
> Misery can be ended.
> The way to end misery is to follow the Eightfold path.

The Eightfold path guides the seeker in living a pure life through such measures as right intentions, right actions, right work, and right speech. Elsewhere, the Buddha also detailed what not to do: take life wantonly, steal, lie, act immorally, take alcohol or drugs. And he named five evil trades: dealing in weapons, poisons, intoxicants, slaves, and prostitution.

Siddhārtha did not intend to create a religion. His message was anti-religion, if anything. He opposed ritual sacrifices and the godlike role the Brahmans assumed. Nor did he accept the common people's beliefs in witchcraft, spirits, and omens. Now a Buddha, or "awakened one," Siddhārtha offered a message focused on moral effort and clear thinking rather than worship. Aimed at the situation of actual men and women, it celebrated compassion, nonviolence, charity, and self-restraint.

India's traditional Brahmanic religion equated the indestructible human soul with the creative force of the universe. But the Buddha taught that there was no unchanging, independent eternal soul—only misery and its alternative, nirvana. He rejected fatalism, the belief that events are predetermined and beyond the control of humans, and taught that people are masters of their fate. Believing that all men are equal, he rejected the Hindu caste system, which separated members

Siddhārtha Gautama

BORN

About 560 B.C.E.
Lumbini, India

DIED

About 480 B.C.E.
Kushinagara, India

TRADITION

Buddhism

ACCOMPLISHMENTS

Founder of Buddhism

"All that we are is the result of what we have thought: it is founded on our thoughts, it is made up of our thoughts."

—from *The Dhammapada* (Pali canon)

of society into different classes according to their status at birth. (It took much longer, however, for women to be treated as the equals of men.)

The Buddha spent the last 45 years of his life in the cities of the Ganges River plain, such as Benares and Sarnath. At one point he returned to Kapilavastu, where he grew up. There, to the sorrow of his father, Siddhārtha converted his brother, his son, and his wife. His early followers became the nucleus of the *Sangha*, or assembly of Buddhists. Unlike caste-based religions, Buddhism was open to all.

The Buddha lived to be nearly 80 years old. As he sensed his approaching death, he returned to the little village of Kushinagara, near where he had been born. His last words were said to be, "My brothers! Everything that has a beginning must have an end. Work out your salvation with diligence."

After his death the Buddha was treated as important rulers were: he was cremated and his remains divided and buried in memorial mounds, or *stupas*. These *stupas* eventually became objects of religious worship, as later, statues of the Buddha himself did.

For centuries, the Buddha's teachings were preserved orally. By the time his teachings were collected, they included many later stories and traditions. Today, the complete Buddhist teachings fill hundreds of volumes. Perhaps the best-known collection of Buddhist teachings in the Western Hemisphere is the Pali canon, assembled in 25 C.E.

FURTHER READING

Kelen, Betty. *Gautama Buddha In Life and Legend*. New York: Lothrop, Lee & Shepard, 1967.

Landaw, Jonathan. *The Story of the Buddha*. Pomona, Calif.: Auromere, 1979.

Landaw, Jonathan, and Janet Brooke. *Prince Siddhartha*. Boston: Wisdom, 1984.

Ling, Trevor. *The Buddha*. New York: Scribners, 1973.

———. *A Dictionary of Buddhism*. New York: Scribners, 1972.

Stewart, Whitney. *To the Lion Throne*. Ithaca, N.Y.: Snow Lion, 1990.

Wangu, Madhu B. *Buddhism*. New York: Facts on File, 1992.

Lao Tzu

THE UNCARVED
BLOCK

Some 2,600 years ago, it is said, a Chinese woman leaned heavily against a plum tree and bore a baby fathered by a falling star. The baby had been in her womb for 60 years and therefore could speak at birth. He named himself after the plum tree and his own large ears: Li Erh ("plum ear"). People called him Lao Tzu ("old man" or "old master").

Lao Tzu is said to have married and fathered a son, Tsung, who became a soldier. At one time, Lao Tzu served as palace secretary and later was keeper of the archives in the Chinese imperial capital.

According to Taoist tradition, Confucius visited him and reported, "I understand how birds can fly, how fishes can swim, and how four-footed beasts can run.... But when it comes to the dragon, I am unable to conceive how he can

Regarded as a sage by some, a divinity by others, Lao Tzu is shown here riding a water buffalo. He is believed to have written the ancient *Tao Te Ching*.

Buddha, Confucius, and Lao Tzu (from left to right) as depicted in a Chinese scroll painting from the Ming dynasty. These three are revered as the founders of the three major religions of the Far East—Buddhism, Confucianism, and Taoism.

soar into the sky riding upon the wind and clouds. Today I have seen Lao Tzu and can only liken him to a dragon."

At the legendary age of 160, disgusted by office corruption, Lao Tzu left the capital in a chariot pulled by a black ox. Alerted by the weather that a sage was approaching him, the guard of the Western Pass, who met all travelers going west, asked Lao Tzu to leave him some wisdom. Lao Tzu immediately wrote the 5,000 characters that make up the *Tao Te Ching (The Book of the Way and Power)* and departed, never to be heard from again.

These are the legends about Lao Tzu. There is perhaps more uncertainty about him than about any other major religious figure in the world. Even the first Chinese historian, Ssu-ma Ch'ien, writing nearly 2,000 years ago, could not document Lao Tzu's life. Some scholars deny that Lao Tzu ever existed; others attribute his book to several people and his ideas to a general school of thought from his time. But others find evidence in the *Tao Te Ching* of a single mind at work. They call this author, whoever he was and whenever he wrote, Lao Tzu.

Provocative, puzzling, and tantalizingly brief, the *Tao Te Ching* has been translated into English more often than any book except the Bible. Written at a time of violence, warfare, and unrest, the *Tao Te Ching* was designed as a handbook for rulers, but it has also always been considered as a guide to the moral life. The *Tao Te Ching* asks how to make people moral. Its answer startles: by acting indirectly, as nature does.

Lao Tzu's word for this process was *wu-wei*, consciously suspending one's impulses and expectations. It is better, he said, to be like the stick that bends with the wind rather than the rigid one that breaks.

Lao Tzu's most often used symbol is water. "Water," he says, "of all

"The Way (Tao) that can be known is not the true Way (Tao)."

—from *Tao Te Ching*

BELIEVERS

Lao Tzu

BORN

6th century B.C.E.
China

DIED

6th century B.C.E.
China

TRADITION

Taoism

ACCOMPLISHMENTS

Founder of Taoism; his teachings are known as the *Tao Te Ching*

things the most yielding, can wear down rock, which is the most hard." As water preserves its nature in all circumstances by always yielding to its environment, the wise person accepts destiny with continual flexibility. The space inside a bowl, in another example, is normally not considered in its own right, yet that is what gives the bowl its useful shape. In the same way, all things and events receive their purpose and value from the Tao, which also works in the world unseen. The wise person will likewise seek to work humbly and unrecognized but will be supremely useful and influential.

Lao Tzu urged people to be strong by being weak and urged leaders to lead by seeming not to. Much of the *Tao Te Ching* is based on paradoxes of this nature. The book's opening lines state, "The Way (*Tao*) that can be known is not the true Way (*Tao*). The name that can be named is not the true name." To try to name the elusive power that animates the cosmos, he thought, is to limit and reduce it, to be untrue to its nature.

Lao Tzu celebrated a nonverbal, natural, and simple way of being in the world. Another image that occurs frequently in the *Tao Te Ching* is that of an infant in its mother's arms. "All of the others," he said, "are making their mark in the world, while I, pigheaded, awkward, different, am only an infant nursing at the breast." It would be best, he said, if people lived so simply that they did not even keep written records but only remembered things by making knots in a rope.

Lao Tzu believed that people's original nature is good. Insisting that people be good backfires, he taught: to *try* to do good invites only failure. His ideal person was like an "uncarved block," a piece of wood before the artist shapes it, or like "raw silk," the cloth before it is dyed.

The Taoist tradition that emerged from Lao Tzu and a later Taoist, Chuang Tzu, served in some senses as a counterpart to Confucianism—Taoism was a personal, rather than a social, "way."

Lao Tzu himself was later venerated as a god. Taoism eventually evolved into a very popular religion, complete with gods, priests, magical charms, and quests for immortality. In the 7th century C.E., a Taoist-influenced form of Buddhism arose, known in China as Ch'an and in Japan as Zen.

FURTHER READING

Brown, Stephen F. *Taoism*. New York: Facts on File, 1992.

Kaltenmark, Max. *Lao Tzu and Taoism*. Stanford, Calif.: Stanford University Press, 1969.

Lao Tzu. *Tao Te Ching*. New York: Viking Penguin, 1964.

Sims, Bennett B. *Lao Tzu and the Tao Te Ching*. New York: Franklin Watts, 1971.

Waley, Arthur. *The Way and its Power: A Study of the Tao Te Ching and its Place in Chinese Thought*. 1958. Reprint. New York: Grove/Atlantic, 1988.

Welch, Holmes. *Taoism: The Parting of the Way*. Boston: Beacon Press, 1957.

Confucius

CHINA'S UNCROWNED KING

onfucius died a failure. His family life had been unhappy, and he had accomplished almost none of the things that he had set out to do. Yet perhaps no other person has had such a profound and lasting influence on Chinese thought, culture, and life as Confucius.

Confucius was born in northeastern China in about 551 B.C.E. His name is a transliteration by Jesuit missionaries of K'ung-Fu-tzu, or Master Kung. According to legend, he was descended from kings, but he was probably the younger son of a fading aristocratic family. His father died when Confucius was three years old, and his mother raised him. She arranged for Confucius to be educated, and he was apparently an outstanding student, excelling at a range of subjects, from music (playing the lute) to history and archery. When she died, Confucius mourned her for more than the traditional two years and three months.

At 19, Confucius married and began working, first guarding storehouses and later tending pastures. His wife bore him a son and perhaps also two daughters.

In Confucius's day, China was ruled by the first-born sons of the aristocracy. Few of these rulers were trained for government; some had simply seized power and kept it by force. It was a time of war, lawless violence, and intrigue. These hardships shook the people's faith in the "Will of Heaven," the orderly relationship between rulers and the ancient Chinese god Shang-Ti, or "lord on high." To improve this dismal state of affairs, Confucius opened a school. The first person in China to offer higher education, he taught a curriculum that became a model for later Chinese education: it included history, poetry, government, manners, music, and foretelling the future.

Confucius flourished as a teacher. He is said to have attracted several thousand students and never to have turned one away, "even if he came to me with nothing more to offer as tuition than a package of dried meat." He asked much of his students, however: "If, when I give the student one corner of the subject, he cannot find the other three for himself, I do not repeat my lesson."

Confucius looked to the past to repair the present. Accepting many of China's conventional ideas, he discarded what was stale. People and actions must fulfill their names, he insisted. For example, he showed that high birth did not make a man a gentleman; conduct and character did. In this and other teachings, Confucius helped break down the system of inherited kingships so that it could be replaced with government by men of merit.

As a teacher, Confucius offered a way of understanding the world that focused on the mutual obligations within social relationships.

What Confucius did for the idea of the gentleman he also did for the idea of being human. He taught that only society shapes people into truly human beings and that, in turn, people shape society. Many associate Confucius with strict rules about how people should behave, but his goal was respect, rather than rigidity. For Confucius, the essence of being human is maintaining respectful relationships with other people.

Confucius believed that the power of the universe itself—the Tao—expresses itself through respectful relationships. He taught that the important relationships to nurture are those between ruler and subject, father and son, husband and wife, elder and younger brother, and friend and friend. Of all these, he felt the father-son relationship, which extends to include respect for all elders and ancestors, is the most important.

Confucius also saw ritual as essential to social life. Rituals and other ceremonies shape our lives, from simple handshakes and greetings to

> *"I transmit, I do not invent."*
>
> —from *Analects*

> *"When a cornered vessel no longer has any corner, should it be called a cornered vessel? Should it?"*
>
> —from *Analects*

business promises and marriage vows. If, on any one of these occasions, people merely pretend to be sincere, they rob the event of meaning. Confucius believed that emotions should correspond to actions, that beliefs should match behaviors.

Several of Confucius's students earned government positions, but Confucius himself never did. A student once compared Confucius's insight about governing to a gemstone. "Should I store it or seek a good price and sell it?" the student asked. "Sell it!" said Confucius, "*I am just waiting for the right price.*" In reality he was too blunt-spoken and high-principled for any ruler to engage his services.

At the age of 56, disgusted by his lack of opportunity in government, Confucius left his home in Lu. Un-daunted by his age and prior failure, he traveled through China for 10 years, seeking a ruler wise enough to listen to him. Many gave him money and support, but no one would hire the old, outspoken man. He spent his last years teaching and died at the age of 72.

After the death of their mentor, Confucius's followers collected his ideas in a text called the *Analects (Conversations)*. These ideas gradually worked their way into Chinese culture. As China endured invasions and shifts in population, Confucius's teachings served as a primer for people who were struggling to maintain their cultural identity as Chinese.

Confucius did not found a religion (although later Chinese worshiped him as a god), and he did not believe in spirits, an afterlife, or a human-looking god. All of his teachings, however, are based on the existence of a benevolent force in the universe.

Confucian ideas, particularly concerning government by merit rather than heredity, influenced European thinkers during the 18th-century Enlightenment, an era that fostered a rational and scientific approach to politics, religion, and society. The Confucian models of both government and education prevailed in China until the Maoist Revolution of the 1930s.

FURTHER READING

Creel, H. G. *Confucius: The Man and the Myth*. New York: John Day, 1949.

Dawson, Raymond Stanley. *Confucius*. New York: Hill & Wang, 1982.

Fingarette, Herbert. *Confucius—The Secular as Sacred*. New York: Harper & Row, 1972.

Hoobler, Thomas. *Confucianism*. New York: Facts on File, 1993.

Kelen, Betty. *Confucius: In Life and Legend*. Nashville, Tenn.: T. Nelson, 1971.

Lau, D. C., trans. *The Analects (Lun yü) of Confucius*. New York: Penguin, 1979.

Sims, Bennett B. *Confucius*. New York: Franklin Watts, 1968.

Smith, D. Howard. *Confucius*. New York: Scribners, 1973.

Two scenes of Confucius (seated, at right, and in the center, at left) with his disciples. Perhaps no other figure has had so enduring an influence on Chinese thought and culture.

BELIEVERS

Confucius

BORN

About 551 B.C.E.
Lu (modern Shantung Province), China

DIED

About 479 B.C.E.
Lu, China

TRADITION

Confucianism

ACCOMPLISHMENTS

Major shaper of Chinese culture and civilization; the *Wu Ching*, or Five Classics of Chinese literature, are attributed to him as author, or compiler, and include *The Classics of Poetry*, *The History*, *The Book of Changes*, *The Spring and Autumn Annals*, and *The Rites*; his teachings, or sayings, were collected by his students in the *Analects*

Mencius

PHILOSOPHER OF GOODNESS

The Chinese philosopher Meng K'o—known in the West by the Latinized form of his name, Mencius—followed in the footsteps of China's first great teacher, Confucius. Mencius was born about 371 B.C.E. near Confucius's birthplace in northern China and led a similar life as an itinerant teacher. Both men were raised by their widowed mothers, and both apparently also showed an early interest in rituals. Like Confucius, Mencius lived in troubled times and wanted to reform society and government. Mencius, too, tried to interest rulers in his ideas, and he also died an apparent failure.

From his teachings, collected by his followers after his death and known as the *Mencius,* it seems likely that, like Confucius, Mencius traveled in search of employment as an adviser and, when that failed, turned to teaching to support himself. Mencius based his teachings on Confucian ideas, but he developed those ideas so fully that some scholars credit him with cofounding Chinese Confucianism.

Confucius had taught that people can be good; they lack only proper models. Thus Confucius concerned himself with how people should conduct themselves. Mencius taught that human nature is originally good, naturally good.

Mencius struggled to keep Confucian ideals—compassion, justice, and the maintenance of proper rituals and relationships—alive in the face of China's continuing social unrest. Two schools of philosophy, Moism and Egoism, had gained favor in the century after Confucius's death. Moism, linked to the thinker Mo Tzu, valued things and ideas for their usefulness alone. Egoism, identified with the philosopher Yang Chu,

Often credited as the cofounder of Chinese Confucianism, Mencius—depicted here in an illustration from a 17th-century book—emphasized the inherent goodness of human nature.

> *"Humanity subdues inhumanity as water subdues fire."*
>
> —from *Mencius*

taught that self-interest should be the measure of all things. Mencius steered a middle, Confucian, path.

Everyone shares feelings of "sympathy, shame and dislike, reverence and respect, right and wrong," he said. When people see a baby in danger, Mencius observed, they instinctively try to save it, but not because of the baby's usefulness (the Moist position) or because others will think better of them for it (the Egoist position). We do it because it is our nature to be compassionate, just as it is water's nature to flow downhill.

In contrast to the Egoists, who taught that *i*, honor, is bestowed on us by others, Mencius taught that *i* was a person's own sense of rightness. The Moists asserted that people should behave morally, even when alone, because spirits are watching them. Mencius maintained that people should always behave morally because human actions, good or bad, shape character. The Moists also believed that one should love everyone equally, but Mencius argued that people feel, and should show, more love for those close to them.

Because he believed that people are essentially good, Mencius saw the true role of education as uncovering, or drawing out, the goodness within each student. Just as taste in food and beauty can be developed, he taught, the teacher should cultivate the student's innate taste for goodness. In answer to why some people behave badly, Mencius suggested that people are like seeds sown in a variety of fields. Those who fall on good soil grow compassionate, while those who fall on rocky soil do not.

Mencius's ideas of how to develop goodness in students differed from those of Confucius, who had preferred to teach observation and critical thinking. Mencius added controlled breathing and meditation to his training. His remark that "all things are complete within us" suggests that he thought human nature represents or contains the nature of all things. Meditation would have been an avenue to such an understanding.

He developed his ideas on economics and justice from this notion of natural human goodness. "Hungry people cannot be expected to be moral," he remarked. Mencius proposed a *wang tao*, a "kingly way," for rulers to care compassionately for their people. It involved removing certain taxes, guaranteeing care for the aged, and granting land directly to the people. He spelled out this last proposal in a plan to divide each section of land into nine equal squares. Eight families would farm one square each, and all would farm the center square communally. Produce from the center square would be paid to the ruler as taxes. Mencius argued for rotating crops in order to avoid exhausting the soil. He was also one of the earliest voices in China to champion the conservation of lakes and forests.

Because Mencius believed that "all things are complete in us," it followed that no person was better or more deserving than another. One of China's earliest advocates of democracy, he taught that people have the right to rise up against unjust rulers. Because of his emphasis on the goodness of human nature, Mencius's thinking is often called idealistic Confucianism.

FURTHER READING

Waley, Arthur. *Three Ways of Thought in Ancient China*. London: George Allen & Unwin, 1963.

Mencius

BORN

371 B.C.E.
China

DIED

289 B.C.E.
China

TRADITION

Confucianism

ACCOMPLISHMENTS

Chief early exponent of Confucian ideals and shaper of later Confucian philosophy; his teachings were collected as the *Mencius*

Chuang Tzu

BUTTERFLY MAN

The Taoist philosopher Chuang Tzu once dreamed that he was a butterfly, drifting over a river and fields. When he awoke and saw his reflection in the river, he laughed. "Now how do I know," he wondered, "whether I am a man who dreamed he was a butterfly—or a butterfly dreaming he is a man?"

Very little is known about the life of Chuang Tzu. The earliest historian of China, Ssu-ma Ch'ien, writing in about 100 B.C.E., mentions Chuang Tzu (the title *Tzu* means "master") as a government official of the southern state Sung, in the present-day province of Hunan. In his writings, Chuang Tzu appears familiar with the major ideas and debates of his time, so he may well have worked in an official position.

During Chuang Tzu's lifetime, China was gripped by social turmoil and political instability. The great Chinese philosopher Confucius had lived in equally troubled times 200 years before Chuang Tzu. Faced with similar circumstances, the two men took different approaches to improving Chinese society. Confucius believed that people needed a strong government ruled by officials trained in virtue, which they could acquire by revering the examples of their ancestors. In contrast, Chuang Tzu proposed freedom, advocating that people try to change their minds rather than change their world.

Using mockery, surprise, and humor to make his point, Chuang Tzu praised things that most people would find ugly or useless. Unlike Confucius, he shunned the idea of being useful. In one story, a messenger invited Chuang Tzu to serve as an official in the Ch'u court. Chuang Tzu roared with laughter. "Have you ever seen the ox being led to the sacrifice?" he asked. "After being fattened up for several years, it's decked out in embroidery and led to the great temple. At that point it would no doubt prefer to be an uncared-for piglet, but it's too late, isn't it? Go on! I'd rather play in the mud than be harnessed to a ruler!"

Most people see the world in terms of opposites, Chuang Tzu realized—a person or thing seems good or bad, beautiful or ugly, right or wrong. But the true nature of things goes far beyond these slippery labels, he believed. Underlying all the world as it seems is the Tao (Way), or the power of the universe, which embraces all opposites in its ultimate unity. When we judge something, we prove only that we have an incomplete view of it. A harmonious wholeness is always behind one-sided appearances.

The idea of the Tao runs through all early Chinese thinking. The Taoist Chuang Tzu, and Lao Tzu before him,

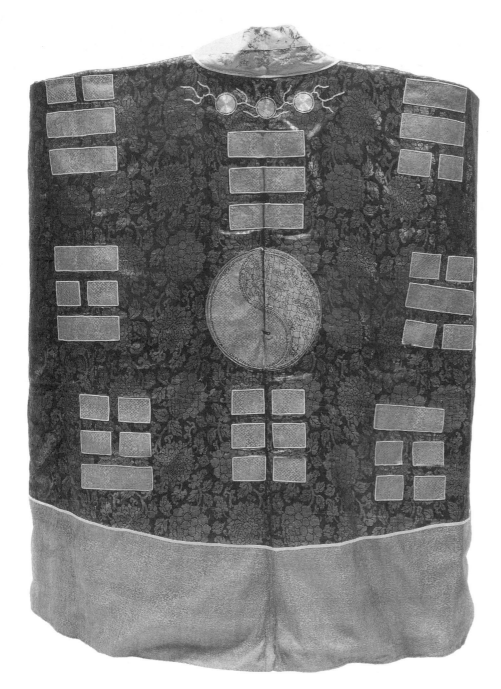

The blue brocaded robe of a Taoist priest from late 18th-century China displays a red satin yin-yang symbol in the middle. This symbol suggests the balance and interaction between yin forces (dark, cool, passive) and yang (light, warm, active). In the Chinese way of thinking, everything in the universe contains both yin and yang. For example, the bright side of a hill is yang; its shadowed side, yin.

Chuang Tzu

BORN

about 369 B.C.E.
China

DIED

about 286 B.C.E.
China

TRADITION

Taoism

ACCOMPLISHMENTS

With Lao Tzu, he was a founder and central figure of Taoism; his teachings were collected as the *Chuang Tzu*

talked about the Tao in a special way, however. They said that words cannot convey its meaning. Because the same words mean different things to different people, they cannot truly describe reality.

Lao Tzu had compared the Tao to water or to the space inside a bowl.

Chuang Tzu, however, did not try to give an example of the Tao; he merely pointed to it:

"Where is this Tao?" asked a student.

> *"All men know the advantage of being useful, but they do not know the advantage of being useless."*
>
> —from the *Chuang Tzu*

"There's no place it doesn't exist, " Chuang Tzu said.

"Come! Be more specific!"

"It's in the ant."

"Such a low thing?"

"It's in the grass."

"That's lower still!"

"It's in the pottery shards."

"How can it be so low?"

"It's in the manure."

For Chuang Tzu, the ideal of life was *wu wei*, action without purposeful gain or effort. One of his favorite examples of *wu wei* was the master artist or craftsperson whose skill is second nature. The artist does not ponder every move but simply acts *naturally*, with Tao, the power of the universe.

The *Chuang Tzu*, as his collected teachings are known, is regarded as a masterpiece of Chinese literature. Chuang Tzu's influence on Chinese culture was stronger on philosophy and the arts than it was on religion, however. Taoist religion took a very different direction than Chuang Tzu had pointed to. Though Lao Tzu and Chuang Tzu had spoken about the Tao in symbolic language, some of their followers tried to apply their words literally. This effort coincided with an interest in alchemy, a quasi-scientific attempt to convert common metals into gold. A tradition of Taoist alchemy, aimed at reaching immortality through meditation and other practices, arose. Many Taoist followers turned to the outright worship of Lao Tzu and other Taoist sages whose wisdom had earned them the title of Immortals.

Chuang Tzu had a more significant impact on Ch'an, or Meditation Buddhism, founded around the 6th century C.E. Known as Zen Buddhism in Japan, Ch'an Buddhism emphasizes, as Chuang Tzu did, intuition and direct experience over knowledge and words.

FURTHER READING

Chuang Tzu. *The Complete Works of Chuang Tzu.* Translated by Burton Watson. New York: Columbia University Press, 1968.

Kaltenmark, Max. *Lao Tzu and Taoism.* Stanford, Calif.: Stanford University Press, 1969.

Merton, Thomas. *The Way of Chuang Tzu.* New York: New Directions, 1965.

Aśoka Maurya

THE PRINCE OF KINDNESS

The young prince surveyed the scene of his first major military victory. Before him, dead or injured, lay the people of his new kingdom, Kalinga. This should have been a joyful moment for Prince Aśoka. He was the grandson of Chandragupta Maurya, who, in the 4th century B.C.E., had liberated northern India from the Greeks to create a unified country. Aśoka was no stranger to force or bloodshed.

But Aśoka's victory impressed on him the human cost of war. "If only one thousandth the number of Kalingans who suffered were to suffer similarly, it would weigh heavily on my mind," he later wrote. Appalled by the misery that he had caused, he decided to use his immense power as a force for good.

In India, this stone pillar inscribed with maxims is one of hundreds of such structures that Prince Aśoka Maurya erected around his kingdom after his conversion to Buddhism.

This elephant carving in rock marks another site of inscriptions credited to Aśoka Maurya. In his day, Aśoka was the most powerful man in the world.

As a boy, Prince Aśoka had absorbed the somewhat ruthless theory of statecraft practiced by his grandfather Chandragupta. His parents raised the prince in the traditional Vedic Indian religion, centered around sacred stories known as the Vedas and animal sacrifices and fire-worshiping rituals led by Brahman priests. But they were also attracted to newer movements, such as those of the ascetic, or self-denying, Ajivakas and the Jains. One story says that Aśoka's father even tried to increase the family's knowledge by purchasing a Greek philosopher.

The little known about Prince Aśoka suggests that he was an awkward, homely man, although intelligent and sensitive. When he was 18, his father sent him to rule the city of Ujjain. There, he married a pious woman of Buddhist leanings named Devi. Soon after, Aśoka's father sent him to another city, Taxila, where Aśoka's older brother Sumana had proved himself to be a tactless and inept ruler. Replacing Sumana, Aśoka quelled a rebellion.

After their father's death, in about 274 B.C.E., Sumana and Aśoka appear to have fought over the kingship. According to Buddhist tradition,

Aśoka murdered Sumana and his 99 other brothers, wading to the throne through their blood. The story of this violence may have been intended to dramatize the contrast with his later embrace of Buddhism.

Aśoka celebrated his coronation according to custom, with ritual sacrifices and huge feasts. His people celebrated with *samajas*, elaborate festivals of dancing, singing, fighting contests, and feasting. In time, Aśoka would ban both the sacrifices and the festivals, becoming a convert to Buddhism, pacifism, and vegetarianism.

"All men are my children."

—from the Thirteenth Rock Edict

Some stories claim that Nigrodha, the son of his slain brother Sumana, converted Aśoka. Aśoka may also have been inspired by his wife's interest in Buddhism. He merely said, "After a lapse of ten years I began to realize the true pattern of my life." He had probably been interested in Buddhism for some time, and the Kalinga massacre made him decide firmly on a Buddhist course.

Although Aśoka did not abandon his throne for the spiritual life, he bent his government to spiritual ends. Unlike his grandfather, he tried to create a government based on loyalty rather than fear.

On a practical level, Aśoka improved the roads by installing wells, roadside seating, and shade-giving trees. He also built hospitals, both for people and for animals, and sponsored research into medicinal herbs and plants. Exhorting his citizens to practice morality, he made nonviolence a keystone of his empire. Even more radically, he guaranteed all his citizens equal protection under the law. He directed his local governments to distribute charity, protect the aged, and fight injustice.

Such an ambitious program required a complex bureaucracy. In about 256 B.C.E., Aśoka appointed a cadre of morality officers to oversee his officials. His pilgrimages to the major sites of the Buddha's life both increased his piety and provided an opportunity for him to check on his officials. During these journeys he also enlarged the *stupas*, or mounded earth shrines of the Buddha's relics, and built new ones. Aśoka also built hundreds of stone pillars carved with edicts, or messages, addressed to his people. Much of the current knowledge about Aśoka and early Indian history comes from these edicts.

Although during his lifetime Aśoka succeeded in uniting most of the Indian subcontinent under his rule, less than 50 years after his death, in 232 B.C.E., the Mauryan Empire collapsed. The Buddhist experiment in government slowly ended. When they regained power, India's Brahman priests took care to minimize Buddhist political influence. At the same time, popular worship of the *stupas* meant that the Buddha was increasingly regarded as a god rather than as a model for civic rulers.

Aśoka's son Mahinda and daughter Sanghamitra both took monastic vows and spread Buddhism to Sri Lanka. Although Buddhism died out by the 11th century in India—absorbed by Hinduism and erased by Islam—other missionaries carried Buddhism to Southeast Asia, China, and Japan.

BORN

About 292 B.C.E.
Maghada (northern Bihar), India

DIED

About 238 or 232 B.C.E.
Maghada (northern Bihar), India

TRADITION

Buddhism

ACCOMPLISHMENTS

King of northern India (the Mauryan Empire) who modeled his government on Buddhist ideals of righteousness

FURTHER READING

Gokhale, Balkrishna Govind. *Asoka Maurya*. New York: Twayne, 1966.

Kanitkar, Helen, and Hemant Kanitkar. *Asoka and Indian Civilization*. Edited by Malcolm Yapp et al. San Diego, Calif.: Greenhaven, 1980.

Ling, Trevor. *The Buddha*. New York: Scribners, 1973.

Smith, Vincent A. *Asoka: The Buddhist Emperor of India*. Reprint. Columbia, Mo.: South Asia Books, 1990.

Mary

✝

VIRGIN AND MOTHER

In the Christian tradition, the miracle of God's incarnation as Jesus is linked to the miracle of his being born of a virgin, Mary. She assumes religious significance as the mother of Jesus.

There are other instances of wondrous births among the world's religious traditions. The Buddha's mother, for instance, was said to have been impregnated by a tiny airborne seed. Mary's motherhood took on special importance in Christianity because Jesus was seen as both man and God.

The 15th-century Florentine Fra Filippo Lippi was just one of many Italian Renaissance artists who painted the Madonna and child. Veneration of the Virgin Mary is one of the hallmarks of Roman Catholicism.

Mary's place in Christian thought and worship developed gradually, however. In the first surviving written account of Jesus, Saint Paul describes him simply as "born of woman." In the Christian New Testament book of Mark, composed about 70 C.E. and considered the oldest Gospel, or "good news," Jesus' own people recognized him only as "the carpenter, the son of Mary and brother of James." Only the Gospels of Luke and Matthew, written around 95 C.E., describe him as being born of a virgin.

Although Mary eventually became an important figure in Christianity, she and her family seem not to have understood Jesus well in his lifetime. In the Book of Mark, Jesus' family wishes him to stop preaching because people have said he is "beside himself"—disturbed or insane. They either fear for him or simply disagree with what he is doing. When his mother and brothers come to take him home from preaching, Jesus dismisses them, suggesting that his true mother and brothers "are those who hear the word of God and do it." He seems to have chosen the family of his followers over his own family.

Later accounts elaborate on Mary's place in the story of Jesus. The books of Luke and Matthew both describe Mary as conceiving Jesus without Joseph, her husband. This may have been a way of showing that Jesus was indeed divine or that he was the fulfillment of an earlier prophecy. Luke portrays Mary as a faithful woman who accepts what must have seemed to her an incredible role: when an angel tells her that she will bear a child through a divine act, she responds with a burst of poetry. This poem, known as the "Magnificat," marvels at God's strength and goodness.

Other references to Mary in the Christian New Testament are tantalizingly few. The Book of John, probably written at the end of the first century C.E., portrays the relationship between Jesus and Mary as both tense and tender. At a wedding feast in Cana, Mary prompts Jesus to perform a miracle when she notes that the guests have no wine. Jesus then turns the water into wine, though he seems angry with her. "Woman, what have you to do with me?" he asks. Later, however, John includes Mary among the very few of Jesus' disciples who attend him in his last moments. In John's account, Jesus directs one of his disciples to care for Mary and asks her to treat the disciple as her son. After Jesus' death, John writes that Mary joined Jesus' disciples in prayer, placing her among his most intimate followers.

A richer account of Mary appears in the 2nd-century book called the *Protoevangelium of St. James*, which, though influential, is not part of the official New Testament. In *St. James*, Mary is the long-awaited child of Anne and Joachim, a couple who had previously been unable to have children. James paints Mary as, miraculously, a virgin both before and after Jesus' painless birth.

The development of Mary's image from the Gospels to the book of Saint James suggests that she assumed increasing importance among early Christians as time went on. By the second century C.E., Christians identified Mary as the "new Eve." Chapter 3 of Genesis tells how Adam and Eve earned God's curse upon humanity by tasting the forbidden fruit of the Tree of Knowledge in the Garden of Eden. Christians began to see Mary's redemptive role, as the mother of Jesus, offsetting Eve's transgression.

Controversy raged in the early Christian church over Jesus' nature. Was he wholly God and not a man, or simply a man whom God adopted at his baptism? In the 4th century, Arius of Alexandria proposed that Christ was neither wholly divine nor wholly

Mary

BORN

About 22 B.C.E.
City unknown, Judea (present-day Israel)

DIED

First century C.E.
Probably Judea

TRADITION

Christianity

ACCOMPLISHMENTS

Mother of Jesus; object of veneration in the Christian church

> "My soul magnifies the Lord, and my spirit rejoices in God my Savior."
>
> —Luke 1: 46-47

human but something in between. This deepened the controversy. The Christian emperor Constantine called a church council in Nicaea in 325 to try to settle the matter. After much debate, the council concluded that Jesus was both man and God in one being. Reaffirming this position at a later council, called in Ephesus in 431, church leaders also declared Mary *Theotokos*, God-bearer, or Mother of God, to great popular acclaim.

This secured Mary's position in the Christian Church and the liturgy, or worship service. Feast days and celebrations, such as the Annunciation and Nativity, and prayers such as the *Ave Maria*, "Hail Mary," were devoted to her. Mary's own Immaculate Conception, or virgin birth, and ascension to heaven later became part of Catholic teaching.

Some scholars suggest that the celebration of Mary has parallels in the ancient (4000 B.C.E. and earlier) Near Eastern worship of a virgin goddess who controlled life, death, and rebirth. Traces of such a worship tradition are evident in Judaism. In the Hebrew Bible, for instance, a female divinity, Wisdom, sometimes appears alongside God.

One component of the Protestant Reformation in the 16th century was the deflation of the cult of Mary. In Roman and Eastern Catholicism, however, Mary remains a magnet for religious feeling. In some Eastern Orthodox traditions (which separated from the Roman Catholic Church in the 11th century), she is even seen as co-redeemer of the world with Christ.

FURTHER READING

Ashe, Geoffrey. *The Virgin*. London: Routledge & Kegan Paul, 1976.

Bodker, Cecil. *Mary of Nazareth*. New York: Farrar, Straus & Giroux, 1989.

Hiutze, Barbara. *Mother of Jesus*. Nashville, Tenn.: Broadman, 1977.

Warner, Marina. *Alone of All Her Sex*. New York: Knopf, 1976.

Jesus of Nazareth

✝

THE GOSPEL OF LOVE

Jesus of Nazareth is recognized by Christians as the Son of God and is nearly universally acknowledged as a spiritual and moral leader of the highest order. Nevertheless, very little is known about his life.

In its barest outline, the story of Jesus tells of a man born in Galilee, a region under Roman rule in present-day Israel, to a Jewish woman named Mary. Around the age of 30, after he was baptized, or ritually purified, by the prophet John, he began healing the sick and preaching universal love. His public career probably lasted no longer than two or three years before Roman officials arrested, tried, and executed him. He appeared after death to several of his disciples and to Saint Paul.

No firsthand accounts of Jesus' life and ministry exist. The earliest record is that of Saint Paul, who did not know him. Paul began writing his letters on Christianity in 48

This print by Rembrandt depicts Jesus of Nazareth raising Lazarus from the dead, one of many miracles attributed to Jesus in the New Testament.

According to Christian tradition, at the Last Supper Jesus foretold his betrayal and death and instituted the sacrament of the Eucharist. The scene is depicted here by the 14th-century Sienese artist Ugolino.

C.E., almost 20 years after Jesus had been put to death. The Gospel, or "good news," accounts that came later were based on orally transmitted stories. Mark's Gospel dates to about 70 C.E., and the Gospels of Matthew and Luke date to about 95 C.E. These three books are known as the Synoptic Gospels because they present a common (*syn*) view (*optic*) of Jesus. The Gospel of John, which presents a somewhat different view, identifies Jesus as the incarnated Word, or Logos, of God. It was probably written near the end of the 1st century C.E.

For centuries, students of Christianity regarded the search for information about the personal life of Jesus, as distinct from his role as a religious leader, as fruitless. In the last two centuries, however, interest has been renewed. Scholars have compared the Gospel accounts and studied the

political realities of the era in which Jesus lived. They have analyzed other religious stories from the Middle East and examined writings from the time of Jesus, particularly the Gnostic Gospels and the Dead Sea Scrolls.

The Gnostic Gospels, discovered in Nag Hammadi, Egypt, in 1945, are a collection of religious writings by a Greco-Roman philosophical and religious sect known as the Gnostics, who saw the world as mired in an evil that only spiritual knowledge (*gnosis*) could defeat. Discovered near Qumram, Palestine, in 1947, the Dead Sea Scrolls contain copies of much of the Hebrew Bible from about 100 B.C.E., giving scholars insight into Jewish thought at the time of Jesus. From all these scholarly efforts a fuller picture of the life and times of Jesus of Nazareth has emerged.

"Therefore I tell you, do not worry about your life, what you will eat or what you will drink, or about your body, what you will wear. Is not life more than food, and the body more than clothing? Look at the birds of the air, they neither sow nor reap nor gather into barns, and yet your heavenly Father feeds them. Are you not of more value than they? And can any of you by worrying add a single hour to your span of life?"

—Matthew 6:25–28

The Roman Empire had absorbed the tiny country of Judea (Israel) by the time Jesus was born. The Jewish people had been dominated by foreign powers before, but the Roman rule seems to have been especially harsh. Destructively high taxes drove many people into poverty. The Romans punished defiance with crucifixion—binding or nailing the lawbreaker to a cross until he died an agonizing death. Only a few years before Jesus' birth, some 2,000 Jews were crucified for rebellious activities.

Intense social stresses divided the Jews into religious sects. A wealthier group, called the Sadducees, allied itself with Rome. The Sadducees believed in strict observance of the Torah, or Jewish law, and rejected the idea of resurrection, or life after death. They thought that Jews should be led by hereditary high priests and preferred a form of worship based on prayer and animal sacrifice in the Jerusalem Temple. (The Temple, built to biblical specifications and dating to King Solomon, was the center of Jewish religious life.) The more liberal-minded Pharisees, in contrast, believed that Jewish law could be interpreted and adapted, and they accepted the idea of resurrection. They favored leadership by "wisdom teachers" (later known as rabbis). In addition to rituals in the Jerusalem Temple, they prac-

ticed prayer-based worship in less formal synagogues.

Two other groups contributed to the religious divisions. The Essenes were an ascetic, or self-denying, monastic group who had withdrawn from the world to live communally in simplicity and moral purity. John the Baptist may have come from this movement. The Zealots were a loosely organized Jewish nationalist party of anti-Roman revolutionaries.

Into this potentially explosive situation came Jesus, a charismatic faith healer who talked about "a kingdom" in such a way that some Jews thought he meant the coming kingdom of God. Other people, including the Romans, thought he meant the restoration of the Jewish nation.

Very little is known about Jesus' upbringing or his life before he began preaching. He may have been born in Bethlehem, but the story of his birth there may also have been written to make his life correspond with Jewish prophecies about a coming Messiah, or king, who would end the misery of the Jews and return the world to Paradise.

Jesus (the name is a Greek form of the Hebrew name Joshua, which means "the Lord saves") probably trained to be a carpenter like his father, but the Aramaic word *naggar* could also have meant "scholar." Certainly, Jesus knew the Hebrew

scriptures well and quoted them with ease. In the Gospel accounts, an early sign of his spiritual mission was his baptism by John the Baptist. John was a radical preacher, a hermit who survived on locusts and wild honey and taught that people should prepare for the coming Messiah and the end of the world by reforming their lives. (His moral criticisms eventually got him killed.) Central to John's preparations was baptism, or ritual washing. His baptism of Jesus, according to the Gospels, was marked by the presence of a dove, a Hebrew symbol of God.

When Jesus began preaching, he, too, announced that the "kingdom of God" was at hand and that people had to change their way of living. Jesus' teachings, such as the Sermon on the Mount—recorded in Matthew 5, 6, and 7—exhort justice for the poor, love for one's neighbor, and leaving the punishment of evil to God. All of these things had been said earlier in the Hebrew Bible.

And yet, Jesus presented Jewish ideas in such a stunning way that he excited extremes of emotion among the people who heard him. In accepting baptism, working miracles, and healing, he seemed to mock the authority of Sadducee Judaism. In embracing the lives of the poor and associating with sinners and criminals, he seemed to overturn the natural

"You shall love the Lord your God with all your heart, and with all your soul, and with all your mind. This is the great and first commandment. And a second is like it, You shall love your neighbor as yourself. On these two commandments depend all the law and the prophets."

—Matthew 22:37–40

order of the social classes. He took his meals with social outcasts, shared what he had freely, and healed people without charge. In speaking out as a Jew, however, he also invited Roman animosity.

Although in the Gospels, Jesus refers to himself as the "Son of Man," which could be interpreted as "Messiah," no one is certain how Jesus saw himself. He may have served for a time as a Pharisee "wisdom teacher," or rabbi, but at some point he seems to have taken on a wider role. Although he preached alone at first, Jesus eventually gathered 12 close followers, or disciples, during his brief time of preaching. These men identified Jesus as the Messiah (in Greek, *Christos*), and two of them shared a vision of Jesus in the company of Moses and the Hebrew prophet Elijah.

In accepting the title of Messiah, Jesus may have seen himself as a latter-day David (the use of *messiah* for "king" dates to around 1000 B.C.E., to the reign of the Jewish king David), a sign that God would soon act for Israel. Or he may have seen himself as the Messiah who would usher in the kingdom of God. Certainly, there was

a feverish intensity to the expectations that he raised.

When Jesus rode into Jerusalem on the back of a donkey, exactly as a Jewish prophecy had predicted the Messiah would arrive, the crowds cheered him with loud cries of "Hosanna" (save us!). He approached the Jewish Temple, a marvel of the ancient world, destroyed once by the Babylonians and rebuilt by the Roman-appointed King Herod. Inside the Temple, Jesus angrily denounced the men who were changing money and doing business there and knocked over their tables, in order to restore the Temple to its original religious purpose. During the following week, he preached from the Temple compound and celebrated a ritual meal with his 12 disciples.

Some of Jesus' disciples seem to have been political revolutionaries. Judas Iscariot's name, for example, came from the word *scarius*, which refers to a dagger-wielding assassin. Jesus' disciples Simon, Peter, James, and John may also have been linked to the Zealot cause. It seems unlikely that Jesus himself was a political revolutionary, however. He was a

religious prophet whose message, in those tormented times, necessarily had a political tone. He was too dangerous to live, the Romans believed. Betrayed by his disciple Judas, Jesus was taken prisoner in the garden of Gethsemane.

Jesus' disciples fled, and most were later put to death by Romans for what seem to be political reasons. The Roman procurator, or governor, Pilate, condemned Jesus to death by crucifixion, a painful punishment reserved for rebel slaves and revolutionaries.

According to the Gospels, after his death, the body of Jesus was taken down from the cross by his disciples and laid in a tomb. Three days later, his female supporter Mary Magdalene and one or two other women went to prepare his body for burial and found the tomb empty. When told that Jesus had been resurrected, or restored to life, they ran away in fear. A number of his disciples reported seeing the resurrected Jesus after his death. Christianity, as a religious movement, dates from those reports.

In places, the Gospel accounts suggest that the Jews sought to kill Jesus for heresy, but this seems un-

This terra-cotta bust of Christ was produced by an anonymous Florentine sculptor in the early 16th century.

BELIEVERS

Jesus of Nazareth

BORN

About 6 B.C.E.
Bethlehem, Israel

DIED

About 33
Jerusalem, Israel

TRADITION

Christianity; Judaism; Muslims acknowledge him as a prophet and Hindus as an avatar

ACCOMPLISHMENTS

Jewish teacher and prophet whom Christians consider to be the Messiah; his sayings and teachings were collected by Christian followers in the New Testament

likely. It is more probable that anti-Jewish sentiments found their way into the Gospels in versions written for Roman readers. Jesus found little support among the Sadducee class, but the Pharisees may well have mourned him.

Jesus' brother James seems to have carried on his work after his death among a group of Jews, known as Nazarenes, who embraced Jesus' teachings. This movement combined traditional observances of Jewish law with belief in the Messiah Jesus. They practiced vegetarianism and celebrated the Eucharist, or Last Supper, in memory of Jesus. Within the 1st century they came into conflict with another group of Christians who followed Saint Paul in rejecting much of Jewish law. The religion of Christianity evolved from these Pauline Christians. Rejected by the Jews as heretical, the Nazarene movement died out by the 4th century, when Christianity was proclaimed the state religion of the Roman Empire. Christianity grew to prominence in Europe in the Middle Ages and in its various forms has about 1.5 billion followers around the world today.

FURTHER READING

Backhouse, Halcyon. *The Incredible Journey.* Nashville, Tenn.: Nelson, 1993.

Crossan, John Dominic. *The Historical Jesus: The Life of a Mediterranean Jewish Peasant.* New York: HarperCollins, 1991.

Davies, J. G. *The Early Christian Church.* Westport, Conn.: Greenwood Press, 1965.

Lynch, Patricia A. *Christianity.* New York: Facts on File, 1991.

Maccoby, Hyam. *Revolution in Judea: Jesus and the Jewish Resistance.* New York: Taplinger, 1973.

McManners, John, ed. *The Oxford Illustrated History of Christianity.* New York: Oxford University Press, 1992.

Monk, Robert C., and Joseph D. Stamey. *Exploring Christianity: An Introduction.* Englewood Cliffs, N.J.: Prentice-Hall, 1984.

Riches, John. *The World of Jesus: First Century Judaism in Crisis.* New York: Cambridge University Press, 1990.

Sanders, E. P. *Jesus and Judaism.* Philadelphia: Fortress Press, 1985.

Wilson, A. N. *Jesus.* New York: Norton, 1992.

Paul of Tarsus

PROPHET OF THE END-TIME

The theology of Christianity is largely the product of a brilliant, argumentative Jewish theologian known as Paul of Tarsus. Paul never met or saw Jesus in his lifetime. Rather, his ideas grew out of a mystical encounter with what he understood to be Christ.

Initially, however, Paul wanted nothing to do with Christ or Christians. He was born Saul to an educated, Greek-speaking Jewish family of leather workers in Tarsus, southern Turkey. (He changed his name to Paul when he became a follower of Christ.) His family was part of the Jewish Diaspora—the movement of Jews away from Judea (present-day Israel) and into the larger Roman Empire. Saul was raised in the Jewish tradition, although, because Tarsus was a center of Greek philosophy, he probably knew something of the Greek mystery religions that celebrated the death and rebirth of certain gods and goddesses.

When Jesus died, about 33 C.E., some Jews accepted him as the Messiah, or savior, and a Jewish-Christian movement began. As a devout Jew—he was in Judea to train to become a rabbi—Saul abhorred these Jewish Christians. He chased them from public places and broke up their meetings; in the New Testament Book of Acts, Saul is described as guarding the coats of Jews who stoned to death a young man preaching the gospel of Jesus. According to tradition, in about 34 C.E., he was traveling to Damascus, Syria, to chase some Jewish Christians back to Jerusalem when something extraordinary happened.

In the Book of Acts, written by the Apostle Luke, Saul is said to have seen a flash of light and been knocked to the ground. Then he heard a voice that he understood to be that of Jesus ask, "Saul, Saul, why do you persecute me?... I am Jesus whom you are persecuting." Temporarily blinded, Saul had to be led to Damascus, where a Jewish-Christian leader baptized him. His own account, in Corinthians and Galatians, is quieter, but similar: Christ called him and nothing was ever the same again. Paul may have had this experience on the road to or in the city of Damascus. It may have been sudden or gradual, but it set him on an utterly new path. The former persecutor of Christians became their greatest missionary.

In appearance, Paul was ungainly, perhaps even ugly. He seems to have been an intense, excitable man who easily agitated and upset people. He boasted but also belittled himself. Unlike most other Jewish men of his time, Paul seems not to have married and to have remained celibate. He may well have also adopted the disheveled

"When I was a child, I spoke like a child, I thought like a child, I reasoned like a child; when I became a man, I gave up childish ways. For now we see in a mirror dimly, but then face to face. Now I know in part; then I shall understand fully, even as I have been fully understood. So faith, hope, love abide, these three; but the greatest of these is love."

—I Corinthians 13:11–13

El Greco's portrait of Paul of Tarsus, who was a persecutor of the first Christians and later became the most important theologian of early Christianity.

dress and erratic behavior of the Greek philosophers who called themselves Cynics, who disdained convention and custom.

Paul called himself the last apostle. *Apostle,* a Greek word meaning "messenger," took on religious significance when early Christians applied it to Jesus' close disciples. Paul had not known Jesus, as the original apostles had, but his vision of Christ was real to him. With justification, he called himself the hardest-working apostle. Given his former hatred of Christianity, he had come the longest way. He claimed to be weak, nervous, a poor speaker, and plagued by a chronic but unspecified illness. Nevertheless he walked hundreds of miles for his cause and brought his considerable intelligence to bear on the religious dilemmas posed by God born as a man.

After his conversion, Paul spent several years in Arabia with other Christians. Then he took the first of three journeys, traveling 10 years in Syria and Cilicia (present-day Sicily).

*"Lo! I tell you a mystery.
We shall not all sleep,
but we shall all be changed,
in a moment, in the
twinkling of an eye,
at the last trumpet.
For the trumpet will
sound, and the dead
will be raised imperishable,
and we shall be changed."*

—I Corinthians
15:51–52

Portrayed here on a bronze medallion, the Christian apostles, or witnesses, Peter and Paul were the leading figures in the early Christian church. Both men were later declared saints by the Roman Catholic Church.

He intended to convert Jews, but he had better luck with Gentiles (non-Jews). The Jewish Christians in Jerusalem believed that Christians must follow not only the spirit of Christ but also the ritual laws of Moses. These included practicing male circumcision, following a special diet, and observing every seventh day as a Sabbath, a day of rest and worship. Paul rejected these laws, reasoning that if such ritual observances had been enough to save humankind, then Christ's resurrection and his own conversion experience would not have been necessary. "If Christ has not been raised, then our preaching is in vain and your faith is in vain," he wrote in I Corinthians 15:14. Paul replaced

adherence to ritual laws with faith in Christ. This idea—known as justification, or salvation, by faith alone—would strongly influence later Christian thinkers, notably Martin Luther.

Paul spoke to Christians through the epistles, or letters, that he wrote to his parishioners and future converts—such as the Thessalonians, Galatians, Corinthians, and Romans.

His basic message, he said, was that Jesus Christ freely suffered and died out of love for human beings. By describing Jesus as Christ—from the Greek word *Christos*, meaning "the anointed one"—Paul identified him as the Messiah, or savior king whom the Jews were awaiting to deliver the world from suffering. To Paul, Jesus' death by

crucifixion (a particularly painful death that involved hanging by one's outstretched arms from a wooden cross) implied the spirit's triumph over the body, with its pains and passions. Jesus' resurrection, or reappearance after death, promised eternal life to those who accepted Christ's sacrificial death and embraced his teachings, Paul believed.

To Paul and other Jews of his time, the appearance of the Messiah signaled the end of the world. The Messiah was to usher in the Day of Judgment. Paul's personal experience of Christ led him to believe that salvation, or eternal life in a resurrected spirit, lay in having faith in Christ. By faith, Paul did not mean merely believing in certain values or simply observing certain practices; faith to him meant putting one's whole trust in Christ.

Sometimes Paul argued that faith in Christ made people perfect. But he also condemned actual practices, such as divorce and prostitution. Because he felt that the end of the world was approaching, Paul thought it was best not to make major life changes: the married should stay married, and widows should not remarry, for example.

Paul's theology arose from specific challenges. In Corinth, the Christian community prided itself on what was considered a kind of divinely inspired speech known as speaking in tongues. During worship services, some believers would become so moved that they would begin making sounds that neither they nor their listeners could always interpret. Paul, too, spoke in tongues, but he promised to show the Corinthians "a higher way," the way of love, as he outlined in Chapter 13 of his first Epistle to the Corinthians.

Paul made three journeys in all, touring the cities of Greece, modern-day Turkey, Syria, and Judea. After his third journey, he returned to Jerusalem around 58 C.E. to deliver money that he had collected for the poor members of the Jerusalem church. There he caused a small riot by bringing a Gentile, or non-Jew, farther into the Jerusalem Temple than was allowed. Roman troops had to put down the melee that followed.

Jailed in Jerusalem for two years, Paul was finally allowed to stand trial in Rome. But he was shipwrecked en route, and he spent the winter on the island of Malta. In Rome he was held under house arrest for two years and then imprisoned. He was probably executed in 64 C.E., one of many Christians killed by the Roman emperor Nero, although he may have reached Spain, continued his missionary work, and died there.

Christianity might have died with Paul, except that in 66 C.E., the Jews of Judea rose against the Roman Empire. Judea was crushed. More than a million Jews died, the Temple in Jerusalem was destroyed, and the Jews were again dispersed. The Jewish-Christian movement died out, but Paul's Gentile Christianity survived. His writings were first collected about 90 C.E.

Paul's struggle to wrest a universal system of beliefs out of his own Jewish experience and his vision of Christ resurrected was heroic. The context in which he wrote has changed, but the questions about human destiny that he addressed have not. Christian thinkers have turned to him time and again for inspiration, guidance, and the example of his faith.

FURTHER READING

Ham, Wayne. *Paul's First Missionary Journey*. Independence, Mo.: Herald House, 1989.

Sanders, E. P. *Paul*. New York: Oxford University Press, 1991.

Vos Wezeman, Phyllis, and Colleen A. Wiessner. *Saul to Paul: Enlightened to Serve*. Prescott, Ariz.: Educational Ministries, 1989.

BELIEVERS

Paul of Tarsus

BORN
1st century C.E.
Tarsus (present-day Turkey)

DIED
About 62–64
Probably Rome

TRADITION
Christianity

ACCOMPLISHMENTS
Apostle to the Gentiles; his Epistles are collected in the New Testament

Mani

BATTLE OF THE LIGHT AND DARKNESS

ani was born April 14, 216, in Ctesiphon, which was located southeast of Baghdad, in what is now Iraq. His father was a member of a religious sect led by a Jewish Christian, that is, a Jew who believed that Jesus was divine, and who probably practiced a combination of traditional Jewish and early Christian rituals. Mani broke from this sect at age 24, apparently over an element of ritual washing. He traveled to Media, in present-day Iran, and founded his own religious sect, which came to be known as Manichaeism.

Mani's teachings have as their main theme a permanent, cosmic struggle between Light (goodness) and Dark (evil). When the two warring elements mix, he taught, suffering results. Mani believed that earth was the troubled result of a collision between Light and Dark and that the Dark had overpowered the Light. For Mani, evil and Dark dominated the world; only tiny particles of Light shone here and there.

Manichaean scribes are depicted here in a fragment of a Persian manuscript. Mani and his followers believed life to be an eternal struggle between Light and Dark, Good and Evil, Spirit and Flesh. A pessimist, Mani emphasized humankind's essentially sinful nature.

"Man must not believe until he has seen the object with his own eyes."

—from *Kephalaia*

And as evil and Dark controlled the world, so, too, did they control the human body.

Mani believed knowledge could free the Light from the grip of the Dark. Each person, he taught, has a reasoning ability trapped in his body. He urged his followers to discipline their bodies—by abstaining from sex and by not eating meat, harvesting grains, or drinking alcohol—in order to free this power. Mani had two classes of followers—the higher, or elect, members and the Mere Hearers, or auditors. By following Mani's strict regimen and by preaching and teaching, the elect acquired a resource of light that would ensure their immediate entry into paradise after death. The auditors, who were allowed to marry and did not follow such an austere plan, administered to the elect and hoped to be reborn as elect members.

Taking his religion through Persia (present-day Iran) and India, Mani converted the Persian king Sapor I, who permitted him to preach Manichaeism throughout his kingdom. A missionary religion from the beginning, Manichaeism spread rapidly in the Middle East.

Mani saw his teachings as the culmination of "many rivers" of thought. He saw Zarathustra, the Buddha, and Jesus as his forerunners but gave major importance to Jesus. He called himself the Apostle, or messenger, of Jesus. Mani did not, however, regard Jesus as a man of flesh or treat his death by crucifixion as a historical event. Jesus was instead a symbol of light, he said, and the Crucifixion a symbol of suffering. Mani rejected the Hebrew Bible (the Christian Old Testament) and all traces of Jewish thought in the New Testament because of Judaism's insistence that the human body and the physical world, as God's creations, are good.

Mani's success finally made him the target of a powerful Zoroastrian priest; it was probably on the instructions of this priest that he was tortured and executed by the Persian king who succeeded Sapor I. After his death, Mani's followers were persecuted as well.

Manichaeism reached as far east as China and Inner Mongolia and as far west as Egypt. Despite being banned by both the Roman Catholic Church and Chinese authorities, Mani's ideas have drawn adherents throughout history. Perhaps his most famous convert was Saint Augustine of Hippo, who followed Manichaeism as a Mere Hearer for nine years before converting to Christianity.

FURTHER READING

Chadwick, Henry. "Augustine." In *Founders of Thought: Plato, Aristotle, Augustine.* New York: Oxford University Press, 1991.

Klimkeit, Hans-Joachim. *Gnosis on the Silk Road: Gnostic Parables, Hymns, and Prayers from Central Asia.* San Francisco: Harper, 1993.

Mani

BORN
April 14, 216
Ctesiphon, Iraq

DIED
About 277
Probably Iran

TRADITION
Manichaeism

ACCOMPLISHMENTS
Founder of Manichaeism; author of numerous texts, most now fragmented, including the *Shaburagan* (from about 250), *The Image,* and *Kephalaia*

Augustine of Hippo

ARCHITECT OF THE "CITY OF GOD"

The great Christian philosopher Augustine of Hippo converted to Christianity only after exploring other ways of understanding the world, such as Manichaeism and Platonic philosophy. His masterful blending of Greek and Biblical ideas influenced all later Christian thought.

He was born Aurelius Augustinus in Tasgate (present-day Souk-Ahras), Algeria, the son of a Roman father, Patricius, and a Christian mother, Monica. His devout mother registered him as a Christian but did not have him baptized. Later, Augustine wrote that he knew Christians, "men who prayed," as he put it, at school, and he prayed,

Giovanni di Paolo's portrait of Augustine, the Christian saint whose search for spiritual understanding led him first to embrace Manichaeism. Augustine's *Confessions,* his account of his spiritual struggle, remains a classic of Christian literature.

too—not to be whipped. He was apparently a good student but easily distracted.

As a young man, Augustine was drawn to literature, especially the works of the Roman poet Virgil. When he was 12, his father sent him away to study. He returned home at 16 and remained there a year because his family could not afford any further education.

During that year of idleness he joined a youthful gang. One of the gang's exploits that impressed him very deeply was the nighttime theft of pears from a neighboring orchard. Later in his life he puzzled over this. "I stole a thing of which I had plenty of my own and of much better quality," he wrote in his *Confessions*. "Nor did I wish to enjoy [the pears], but rather to enjoy the actual theft and the sin of theft." He would struggle his whole life to understand where the impulse to do such wrong comes from.

At 17, Augustine went to Carthage for advanced study in law and rhetoric, the art of argument and persuasion. There he fell in love with a young woman. Though they never married, their relationship lasted 15 years and together they had a son, Adeodatus (literally "gift from God"). But Augustine felt a terrible unease. He sought peace with "vehement passion," he said.

His first refuge was the religion of Mani. A 3rd-century Persian prophet, Mani taught that the universe was the battleground for a cosmic struggle between Light and Dark, good and evil. Augustine may have found comfort in the Manichaean idea that evil originated from outside humans.

When he returned to Tasgate to teach rhetoric, Augustine's embrace of Manichaeism alienated his mother: she would not let him in her house. She later recounted a dream to Augustine in which he told her, "Where you are, I am." He took it to mean that she would convert to Manichaeism; she thought it meant he would join her in Christianity.

In reality, Augustine was beginning to find Manichaeism inadequate. It was better at attacking Christianity, he said, than in offering a vision of its own. He did not break fully with the Manichaeans, however. When he decided to leave northern Africa for Rome, he relied on Manichaean associates to get settled there.

In Rome, Augustine was quickly recognized as a gifted teacher and was promoted to a post in Milan. His widowed mother, common-law wife, his son, and fellow North African students joined him there. In Milan Augustine first encountered the ideas of Plotinus, a 3rd-century Greek philosopher. A follower of Plato, Plotinus saw God as the Absolute Good, the perfect center from which all intelligence flows. This idea would assume an important place in Augustine's own thought.

Augustine also began attending the sermons of Milan's Catholic bishop, Ambrose, and was fascinated by Ambrose's use of chanting and song in worship services. Augustine had read the Bible but had dismissed it as crude; Ambrose awakened the young man's interest by showing him how to read the biblical stories as fables or parables rather than as literal truths.

Probably to rise in Milanese society, Augustine dismissed his common-law wife and arranged to marry a wealthy heiress. Meanwhile, he took a mistress. Tormented by the gap between his ideals and his actions, he sought counsel from Ambrose and other Christians.

In August 386, the various pressures on Augustine created a personal crisis. Feeling "overcome by violent anger" with himself for not accepting God's will, he escaped to his garden. In the midst of his anguish he heard a child's voice, probably from a nearby

"There is no salvation outside the church."

—from *On Baptism* (A.D. 400)

> *"That which began in time is consummated in eternity."*
>
> —from *City of God*
> (A.D. 426)

courtyard, chanting, "Take it, read it; take it, read it." Augustine opened the Bible at random. His eye fell on Saint Paul's commandment in Romans 13: "Put on the Lord Jesus Christ, and make no provision for the flesh, to gratify its desires."

After years of wrestling with his spiritual dilemmas, Augustine submitted completely to God. He broke his marriage engagement and retreated with his mother, son, and fellow students to the countryside. There he wrote two books, *On the Happy Life* and *On Order*. Within the year, in 387, Augustine, his son, and fellow student Alypius were baptized by Bishop Ambrose himself.

Augustine started back to Africa with his mother. Near Rome, the two shared a profound and moving vision of God. His mother died soon after, and Augustine continued to write and study in Rome for two years before returning to Tasgate. There, he set up a monastery, the first in Latin-speaking Africa.

During a chance visit to Hippo Regius (present-day Annaba, Algeria), Augustine was impressed into the priesthood. Four years later, in 395, he was named bishop of Hippo. In Hippo, Augustine established a monastery to train future priests and bishops. For the rest of his life he would hold himself and his priestly brothers to a strict standard of morality. It was also in Hippo that Augustine began writing his *Confessions*, a frank account of

his personal life and his spiritual growth.

Augustine's tenure as a religious leader was as tumultuous as his earlier intellectual struggles. His first battle was against his former colleagues, the Manichaeans. He condemned them as heretics for making God the origin of evil as well as good. Augustine saw God as wholly good, the Light of all lights. He believed people are free to choose good or evil, though usually, out of ignorance, they choose sin, or "evil"— excessive love of the self and its pleasures. Only God moves people to turn away from sin, he thought.

Another movement predating Augustine's conversion also caught his attention. The Donatists, a native Arab Christian movement, believed that church officeholders, such as priests, must themselves be pure and good for their religious actions to be effective. The church's view, and Augustine's, which prevailed, was that the church office itself conferred grace, whatever the officeholder's moral state.

A more serious threat was Pelagianism. A contemporary of Augustine, the British monk Pelagius taught that people are free to choose good or evil and can make themselves perfect. To Augustine this was pride at its worst. God's grace alone, not human nature, he argued, frees humankind from sin.

Augustine began writing his masterwork, *City of God*, in 411, in response to the fall of Rome to barbar-

"Will is to grace as the horse is to the rider."

—from *On Free Will* (A.D. 395)

ians in 410. In it, he wrote that humanity was engaged in building two cities, symbolically named Jerusalem and Babylon. Babylon was "the earthly [city], which is built up by the love of self to the contempt of God." Jerusalem was "the heavenly [city], which is built up by love of God to contempt of self." In part, he was coping with the reality of invasion. He was trying to show that Rome's fall was not the result of discarding the old gods in favor of Christianity, and he was describing an eternal world far above immediate chaos in the Roman Empire.

Augustine thought that God's purpose for humankind is carried out through history. History, as Augustine described it, is a drama written and produced by God and enacted by humankind. It is the setting for the struggle between the love of the eternal good and love of momentary pleasure.

In 429, barbarians from Spain invaded North Africa. Augustine died the next year, just before the Vandals, a tribe of Germanic warriors that had overrun Spain, reached Hippo.

The Catholic Church later named Augustine and his mother saints.

Augustine set the tone for the next thousand years of Western Christian culture. The first great autobiographer in the Western Hemisphere, Augustine has fascinated psychologists as well as theologians. His profound influence on the Protestant Reformation can be seen in the works of both Martin Luther and John Calvin.

FURTHER READING

Augustine. *The Confessions of St. Augustine.* Translated and with an introduction by Henry Chadwick. New York: Oxford University Press, 1991.

Battenhouse, Roy Wesley, ed. *A Companion to the Study of St. Augustine.* New York: Oxford University Press, 1955.

Chadwick, Henry. "Augustine." In *Founders of Thought: Plato, Aristotle, Augustine.* New York: Oxford University Press, 1991.

Dawson, Christopher. "St. Augustine and His Age." In *St. Augustine: His Age, His Life, and Thought.* New York: Meridian, 1957.

Hansel, Robert R. *The Life of St. Augustine.* New York: Franklin Watts, 1969.

Willard, Barbara. *Augustine Came to Kent.* New York: Doubleday, 1963.

Augustine of Hippo

BORN

November 13, 354
Tasgate (present-day Souk-Ahras), Algeria

DIED

August 28, 430
Tasgate, Algeria

TRADITION

Christianity (Roman Catholic)

ACCOMPLISHMENTS

Major shaper of medieval Christianity; major works include *On Free Will* (395); *Confessions* (400); *On the Trinity* (416); and *City of God* (426)

Muhammad

PROPHET OF ISLAM

There is no god but Allah and Muhammad is his prophet." Islam's central creed affirms Muhammad's essential role in his tradition.

Born into a poor family in 6th-century Mecca, Muhammad ibn Abdallah lost his father before birth and his mother before he reached the age of six. Like other religious leaders, Muhammad's early life is associated with a miracle: two angels opened his breast and washed his heart in snow, removing from it a black clot. This was a sign that through a divine act, this man had become extraordinary.

After his mother's death, Muhammad was cared for by his grandfather; when he died, Muhammad was raised by his merchant uncle Abu Talib. Because he was orphaned while still a minor, Muhammad inherited nothing from his father or grandfather, according to Arab custom of his time. Although he had no resources with which to begin business for himself, the young man accompanied his uncle on trading expeditions. He quickly earned a reputation in Mecca as a bright and honest man. Other men called him al-Amin, "the honest, reliable one."

Originally a religious sanctuary where people could meet in peace, Mecca gradually evolved into a trading center as well. By the 6th century, Mecca had become a prosperous city on the major route between the Mediterranean Sea and the Indian Ocean. (War between the Persian and Byzantine empires made routes through Iraq impassable.) Because it was an important trading center, and because its rocky soil discouraged farming, merchants gradually accumulated wealth and power in Mecca.

As the city grew, however, the traditional morality of its early settlers began to break down. The nomadic tribespeople who settled Mecca had brought their tribal protector gods from the rocky wilderness. Among these were nature and fertility gods, all of them under the loose guidance of a single sky god named Allah (The God).

Public prayer and worship in Mecca were centered on the Black Rock, the Ka'aba. Possibly a meteorite, it was said to have been taken to Mecca by the Judeo-Christian patriarch Abraham and his son Ishmael. By Muhammad's time, the Black Rock was surrounded by some 360 different god-idols. These idols may have been linked to Babylonia (present-day Iraq) to the east, where the gods corresponded to the number of days in the calendar. Zoroastrianism, Judaism, and Christianity also had followers in Mecca. Muhammad's own wife, Khadija, had a Christian cousin.

Khadija was originally Muhammad's employer. A successful merchant, she hired him to manage her caravans.

This illustration from a 16th-century Persian manuscript portrays the angel Gabriel (far left) leading Muhammad, astride a magical horse, to Paradise. Because Muhammad is believed to have set out on this journey from Jerusalem, that city is considered holy by Muslims.

Despite the difference in their ages—he was 25 and she was 40 when they wed—the two enjoyed a long and companionable marriage and raised four daughters. Although Muhammad later took several wives, during Khadija's lifetime, she was his only wife.

Scholars disagree on the details of Muhammad's life in Mecca. It is possible that later writers compressed events that developed over time and that some of the accounts of Muhammad's life are legends. Muhammad does seem always to have been a religious and generous man. According to tradition, he and his family lived frugally, sharing their wealth with the poor, and they prayed together regularly. He is said to have retreated to a cave in Mount Hira above Mecca each spring. There he would fast, pray, and consider the affairs of his city.

It was near this cave, in his 40th year, that Islamic tradition says Muhammad was confronted by a being who called himself an angel. "Recite!"

The Prophet's Mosque in Medina is the second holiest site in the Islamic religion, after the Ka'aba in Mecca. Muhammad is buried under the dome.

the angel commanded. Stricken, Muhammad replied that he had no words. The angel pressed him, holding him so tightly that Muhammad thought he would die, until words finally came. They are considered the first lines of the Koran: "Recite in the name of your Lord who has created / Created man out of a germ-cell."

Although Muslims would later call it the Night of Power and Excellence, Muhammad was terrified. He feared he was in the company of a *jinn*, or magical spirit, rather than an angel, a messenger from God. His wife Khadija comforted him and believed he was indeed speaking the word of God. She was the first person to recognize Muhammad as an authentic prophet. Her Christian cousin, Waraqa, confirmed her view.

Muhammad became convinced that the messages he had received had indeed come from outside himself. (And later tradition even portrays Muhammad as illiterate.) Muhammad understood that he had been called by the God of Jews and Christians. God had called the Arab people in their own language and Muhammad was to be God's messenger.

Muhammad's earliest messages celebrated God's power and goodness. He called on people to acknowledge their dependence on God, to pray often, to live chastely, and to be generous with their wealth, especially to the weak. He spoke out against the love of money and condemned cheating. His concerns appear directed at least in part at the ruling merchant Quraysh clan of Mecca, although he also condemned the practice of poorer families who left newborn girls in the desert to die.

At first, Muhammad preached only to his own household and a small circle of followers. In 613, he began preaching publicly. Muhammad does not seem to have intended to found a new religion; he spoke merely as a "warner." But his message was religious. He warned people of their need to create a just and generous society, and he warned them that there was only one God, Allah, who would judge them. And the day of judgment, he warned as well, was approaching. Both aspects of his message—justice and monotheism, or belief in a single God—earned him powerful enemies among the powerful Quraysh. Muhammad was protected by his uncle Abu Talib, a clan chief, but followers who lacked such protection suffered abuse and bodily harm. Some of Muhammad's followers felt so unsafe that they left Mecca for a time to live among Christians in Abyssinia.

Abu Talib died in 619, followed soon after by Khadija. Without his uncle's protection, Muhammad and his followers were more vulnerable. The account of Muhammad's famous Night Journey seems to be linked to this low point in his life. One night, it is said, a magical horse transported Muhammad from Mecca to Jerusalem, where he led Hebrew and Christian prophets in prayer. Then, from a rock (now surrounded by the Dome of the Rock Mosque in Jerusalem) he rose to heaven. The angel Gabriel led him through six more levels of heaven

(from which was coined the expression "seventh heaven") to Paradise, the place of ultimate reward, and back to Mecca. It is for this reason that Jerusalem, as well as the cities of Mecca and Medina, is holy in the Islamic faith.

Perhaps strengthened by this experience—accepted by some as real, by others as a dream or vision—Muhammad began to consider leaving Mecca. Many of his followers had gone to Yathrib (it was renamed Medina, "city of the Prophet," to honor Muhammad), an agricultural center 250 miles north of Mecca. Eventually, after all of his followers had fled Mecca, Muhammad, too, in the company of his chief adviser, Abu Bakr, left the city. They reached Medina on September 24, 622. This emigration, or *hijra*—breaking of relationships—was a pivotal moment in Islam, comparable to the Exodus in Judaism. Islamic history and the Islamic calendar date from it.

Medina was split among various religious factions, and some evidence suggests that Muhammad was invited to Medina to mediate a peace. His political leadership quickly showed itself. He forged an alliance among eight Arab clans, their Jewish dependents, and the emigrants from Mecca. The alliance recognized Muhammad as a prophet; all parties to the agreement were known as Muslims. This was the first Islamic community, or *umma.*

For the next 10 years, the Muslims engaged in expeditions, ranging from raiding parties and punitive skirmishes to strategic attacks. These campaigns

were aimed largely at the ruling Quraysh tribe of Mecca and ultimately led to war with them. The Battle of Badr, in 624, was Muhammad's first significant military victory. In 627, some 10,000 Meccans marched on Medina, but Muhammad had surrounded the main city with a moat. The attack failed.

A year later, the Meccans and the Muslims agreed to a 10-year cease-fire. Breaches by Meccan allies, however, prompted Muhammad to march on Mecca with a large army. He met no resistance, and the leaders and people of Mecca joined behind him; in time, they converted to Islam.

One of the first things Muhammad did when he returned to Mecca was to visit the Ka'aba. He ordered the destruction of all the images and idols there. Soon after, Muhammad's army defeated a tribal group that threatened Mecca, and he was accepted as the unquestioned leader of the Arab people. During the last two and half years of his life Muhammad converted most of the nomadic Arab tribes to Islam. He also made treaties with Jewish and Christian enclaves on the Gulf of Aqaba.

Like Moses and Zarathushtra before him, Muhammad saw himself as a prophet of the almighty God, sweeping away the idols of polytheism (the worship of many gods). He did not see himself as the founder of a new religion, but as an "unveiler," the restorer of Jewish and Christian tradition. He called Muslims to worship the same God that Jews and Christians did. *Islam* means "surrender to God's will," and a Muslim is "one who surrenders or follows God's will."

Although his teachings grew out of the Jewish and Christian traditions, Muhammad also challenged those traditions. He saw Jews and Christians as having fallen away from God's original revelations. The Jews erred, he said, in seeing themselves as "chosen people." Christians, he thought, had distorted God's meaning with their conception of the Trinity. He saw this belief in God as Father, Son, and Holy Spirit as a return to polytheism.

Muhammad initially expected the Jews to embrace Islam because it shared profound roots with Judaism. The first Muslims prayed facing Jerusalem, the holy city of the Jews. But by the Battle of Badr, it was clear to Muhammad that the Jews would not accept his new religion. Mecca became the *qiblah*, the direction Muslims faced during prayer.

By the time of his farewell sermon, in 632, Muhammad could address his followers as a single people: "Know ye that every Muslim is a brother to every other Muslim and that ye are now one brotherhood." He urged Muslims to respect each other and to live in peace, to practice charity and protect the weak.

On June 8, 632, three months after his last sermon, Muhammad died. Abu Bakr, who would be named Islam's first caliph, or leader, after Muhammad, reminded the Muslims, "If you worshiped Muhammad, know he is dead. But if you worshiped God, know God is living and will never die."

For 20 years Muhammad had received and recited revelations, often stopping whatever he was doing to let the words flow. They are regarded as the actual words of God, transmitted through Muhammad. After Muhammad's death, they were compiled in the Koran, the holy book of Islam. Muhammad's own life and actions would also be studied as a guide to proper living. The traditions of the prophet are known as *ahadith*.

Like the Jewish and Christian traditions, Islam is a religion of both revelation and a book. Islam's sacred text, the Koran, is written as a long poem composed of many parts. Each part, called a *sura*, is intended to be recited. The art of recording the Koran in beautiful calligraphy is another aspect of Islamic devotion, particularly because other artistic representations of God are forbidden.

The Koran is a book about God. It tells how God created three levels of reality: heaven, earth, and hell, with humankind as the special stewards of earth. Other beings populate the universe as well: angels, *jinns*, and devils. Angels are immortal guardians created out of light. *Jinns* are made from fire and, like people, can be good or bad. Satan (from the Old Testament Hebrew name *Shaytan*, meaning "enemy") and his devils are fallen angels.

The Garden of Eden story in the Koran shows Satan tempting Adam rather than Eve to first disobey God and eat the fruit of the Tree of Knowledge of Good and Evil. It portrays Adam's sin as his own. This sin, however, is not passed down through generations of humanity; there is no original sin in the Islamic tradition. Each individual's acts, however, have cosmic consequences. As God's representatives on earth, people are expected to follow the straight path of God's will, which requires tolerance, justice, and prayer. A final Day of Reckoning will grant eternal reward or punishment.

Islam requires no agreement with a creed, or set of beliefs. It requires only righteous action: prayer and charity. The Five Pillars of Islam are: faith in Allah and Muhammad, regular prayer, almsgiving or charity, ritual fasting, and a pilgrimage to Mecca, if practicable.

Although legends of miracle working grew up around him, Muslims do not revere Muhammad as a god. He has two roles, neither of which is divine. One is as bringer of the literal word of God, and the other is as a model of how to live. In Muhammad's time, Arabic people were shifting from a nomadic life to an urban one, and his reforms provided the ground for a personal morality to replace the eroding communal one.

These reforms affected not only social values—protecting the weak, for instance—but also social practices. The Koran prohibits drinking alcohol, gambling, and eating pork. Muhammad also encouraged his followers to give up the violent kinds of revenge that tribes often took on each other as payment for injuries. Muhammad's teachings also affected family life. Where earlier Arabic society was structured loosely around women (a clan leader was typically the brother of the most important woman), under Islam, husbands became more important figures. Before Muhammad, a woman might take several husbands; after his teachings were widely adopted, a woman usually married only one man. Islamic men, by contrast, were encouraged to have as many as four wives at once. This seems to have been aimed at providing women more protection than they had enjoyed in pre-Islamic Arabia.

The first four caliphs, who ruled from 632 to 661 C.E., were all known to Muhammad and chosen by group agreement. But with the fourth caliph, Ali, husband of Muhammad's daughter Fatima, the idea of inherited leadership split the Islamic community. Ali's followers broke off into the Shia movement (today, about 15 percent of all Muslims). The majority of Muslims were and are known as Sunni.

As the founder of Islam, Muhammad was also the unifier of the Arab peoples. The Arab state that formed under his adept leadership would, within 100 years of his death, spread Islamic culture to Iraq, Persia, Palestine, Syria, and Egypt. By the 8th century the Islamic empire stretched from India to Spain and North Africa.

During Europe's Dark Ages, when Christian culture rejected classical Greek civilization as godless, Islamic culture preserved Greek thought, from science and mathematics to literature and philosophy. Today, Islam is the fastest growing of all religions.

FURTHER READING

Ahmad, Fazl. *Muhammad the Prophet of Islam*. Chicago: Kazi, 1984.

Alladin, Bilzik. *The Story of Mohammad the Prophet*. Pomona, Calif.: Auromere, 1979.

Armstrong, Karen. *Muhammad: A Biography of the Prophet*. San Francisco: Harper San Francisco, 1972.

Bakhtiar, Laleh. *Muhammad's Companions: Essays on Those Who Bore Witness*. Parts 1 and 2. Chicago: Kazi, 1993.

Esposito, John L. *Islam: The Straight Path*. New York: Macmillan, 1987.

Hasim, A. S. *Life of Prophet Muhammad*. Chicago: Kazi, n.d.

Hood, Abdul Latif Al. *Islam*. New York: Franklin Watts, 1987.

Karim, F. *Heroes of Islam*. Book 1, *Muhammad*. Chicago: Kazi, n.d.

Pike, E. Royston. *Mohammad: Prophet of the Religion of Islam*. New York: Praeger, 1969.

Muhammad

BORN

About 570
Mecca (present-day Saudi Arabia)

DIED

June 8, 632
Medina (present-day Saudi Arabia)

TRADITION

Islam

ACCOMPLISHMENTS

Founder of Islam; Allah's revelations to him through the angel Gabriel were collected by his followers in the Koran

Rābi'ah of Basra

LOVING GOD

"I ask forgiveness of God for my lack of sincerity when I say 'I ask forgiveness of God.'"

—quoted in *Lives of Good Women* (13th century) by Taqi al-Din al-Hisni

The Islamic mystic Rābi'ah al'Adawiyah is said to have walked the streets of her native Basra, in present-day Iraq, carrying a torch and a pitcher of water. According to legend, she explained: "I want to pour water on Hell and throw fire into Paradise! When those two disappear we will see who worships God out of love, not out of fear of Hell or hope of Paradise!" Rābi'ah, who lived a century and a half after the death of Muhammad, infused later Islamic mysticism with her powerful message of love. Mystics believe that, through contemplation and self-surrender, they can reach God or ultimate reality. Rābi'ah is notable for insisting that the aim of mystical devotion should be the pure love of God in addition to union with God. She expressed this love in poems and prayers of exceptional piety.

A mystical form of Islamic worship arose during the early centuries after the prophet Muhammad's death in 632 C.E. Adopting woolen cloaks like those of the Christian mystics of the desert and Muhammad himself, the Sufis (from *suf*, meaning "wool") willingly endured hardship and sacrificed comfort in order to try to experience God directly. However, as Rābi'ah noted, the mystical practices of her time were based on fear of the Last Judgment or hope of Paradise. She rejected both. "If I worship You from fear of Hell, then burn me in Hell," she prayed, "and if I worship You from hope of Paradise, lock me out." For Rābi'ah, worship based on fear or hope was not worship at all. Even within worship based on love, she distinguished the "two loves"—the love that seeks its own ends and the love that seeks only the beloved (God) and his glory.

The earliest biography of Rābi'ah, other than a few short passages in mystical texts, was written by the Persian mystic Attār some 400 years after Rābi'ah's death. His account is thickly encrusted with myth. Rābi'ah was probably born in Basra around 717, the fourth (rābi'ah) daughter of a poor family. Orphaned soon after her birth, she and her sisters were separated during a time of famine and other hardships. Rābi'ah was sold into slavery. She fled her master after he tried to rape her.

As she ran, it is said, she fell and injured herself. Whether she had always been devout is not known, but that night, bowing in pain, she cried out, "O Lord I am a stranger, an orphan and a slave. My wrist is injured yet I am not grieved. I only wish to serve You. I would know if You are satisfied with me or not." Hearing what she understood to be God's approval, she returned to her master. He is said to have seen a halo around her head as she prayed. At dawn, he set her free.

Rābi'ah of Basra

A fragment from a 9th- or 10th-century edition of the Koran, the sacred text of Islam. Like Christianity and Judaism, Islam also has a tradition of mysticism, and Rābi'ah of Basra was one of its earliest practitioners.

BORN

About 717 C.E.
Basra, Iraq

DIED

About 801 C.E.
Basra, Iraq

TRADITION

Islam

ACCOMPLISHMENT

Early luminary of Islam's mystical Sufi movement

Rābi'ah went to the desert, built a small retreat hut, and devoted herself to prayer. She was not, however, a recluse. She apparently had friends, associated with other mystics, and refused more than one offer of marriage. She explained to her suitors that God was her heavenly bridegroom. Her love of God possessed her so completely, she said, that she had no capacity left for loving (or hating) anyone else. One of her best-known prayers, which she was said to recite at night from the roof of her home, exalts her position: "O Lord, the stars are shining and the eyes of men are closed and kings have shut their doors and every lover is alone with his beloved, and here am I alone with thee."

Rābi'ah lived a deliberately difficult life. It is said that she slept on an old woven mat and used a brick for a pillow. She refused to take any money to make her life easier. "God has concerned me with other things," she told friends who offered help. In one legend, Rābi'ah was said to have preferred to worship indoors in the dark rather than go outside to admire a beautiful spring day. "Contemplation of the maker has turned me aside from contemplating what He has made," she explained.

Rābi'ah looked on death as a chance to be united with her beloved. She died in 801 C.E. at about the age of 84 and was buried in Basra. Stories of miracles associated with Rābi'ah—that a camel she had taken on a pilgrimage died but was brought back to life so that she could go on, that light shining from her head replaced her need for a lamp—attest to her importance in Sufi tradition. Rābi'ah was the first Sufi to teach Pure Love, the love of God for his sake alone. "I have become one with God," she said, "I am altogether his."

FURTHER READING

Parrinder, Geoffrey. *Mysticism in the World's Religions*. New York: Oxford University Press, 1976.

Smith, Margaret. *Rabia the Mystic and Her Fellow-Saints in Islam*. Cambridge: Cambridge University Press, 1984.

Hildegard of Bingen

PICTURING GOD

L ike many other daughters of noble parents in Europe during the Middle Ages, Hildegard of Bingen was given to the Catholic Church at an early age. And like some other young women who received religious education, she experienced visions of God. Unlike the others, however, Hildegard of Bingen stepped out of the narrow role reserved for her sex. She became the first prominent woman theologian and preacher in Europe.

Hildegard was born in 1098 to a large German family. As a child, she was surrounded by nine siblings (two of whom also joined the church) and numerous servants. It may have been a relief for quiet, frail eight-year-old Hildegard to enter a hermitage, or monastery, with a single companion, her teacher Jutta.

Also a noblewoman, Jutta had rejected offers of marriage and chose instead to become an anchoress, or recluse. She taught Hildegard to read Latin and may have taught her music as well. Their hermitage was attached to a Benedictine monastery named for the 7th-century English saint Disibod. The Benedictines were distinguished for their achievements in medicine and music, particularly chanting. Hildegard would also distinguish herself in these areas.

Hildegard and Jutta's example of spirituality attracted other anchoresses. By 1113, when Hildegard entered her profession as a nun, the anchorage had become a small Benedictine convent. At Jutta's death, in 1136, Hildegard became its leader.

Five years later, she received a startling religious vision. Although she had experienced visions as a young child, they had confused her, and she had kept silent about them. At 42, as head of a convent, she viewed her visions differently. "A blinding light flowed through my entire brain," she wrote, "suddenly I understood the meaning of the...Old and New Testaments." Her vision commanded Hildegard to "say and write what you see and hear."

At first she felt unworthy and unsuitable, but she fell so ill that she became convinced that she had to obey the vision. At a time when women were considered weak and incapable of mental effort, Hildegard began writing about religion in Latin, the language of high culture. Rather than challenge the conventional wisdom, however, she claimed merely to be recording what God showed and told her.

Hildegard did take the precaution of getting theological advice on her writing, a step that enlarged her circle of readers. In 1148, Pope Eugenius III read a draft of Hildegard's first book—*Scivias* (*Know the Ways of the*

Hildegard created this illustration for her *Liber divinorum operum (Book of Divine Works)*. It depicts her idea that the body and health are influenced by cosmic forces such as the planets and constellations. Hildegard herself appears in the lower left-hand corner recording her vision.

Lord)—and sent her a letter of encouragement. The way was then clear for her to continue.

Although Hildegard took authority for her visions from God, she also had great personal authority. When the nunnery at Disibodenberg became crowded, she proposed to found a new community at Rupertsberg, near Bingen. Fearing that they would lose

An illustration of Hildegard's view of the celestial hierarchy appears to show a female figure, possibly Sapientia (Wisdom), at the top and scenes with attendant angels below. Hildegard saw God and creation as combining masculine and feminine elements. This illustration graced her original manuscript of the *Scivias* (*Know the Ways of the Lord*), Hildegard's first devotional work.

both income and status if she left, the monks forbade her to relocate. Hildegard took to her bed, refusing to speak or move until the monks changed their minds. In the end, the monks allowed her to leave.

In her first decade at Rupertsberg, Hildegard worked to forge an identity for her new community by writing poems, hymns, and music for the convent's religious services. She gathered some 77 poems she had written in the 1140s and set them to music for religious worship. This song cycle, known as the *Symphony of the Harmony of Celestial Revelations*, is still admired today. The poems are full of the startling imagery she used in recording her visions. The music, too, seems uniquely her own. Working with a small number of melodies, Hildegard wrote variation after variation on them. She also wrote a play in verse, *Ordo Virtutum*, that portrays a battle between the Devil and Virtue for a human soul. It, too, is based on variations of a very few melodic themes.

Hildegard's many interests also included natural history and medicine, and she wrote about both. She based her scientific books on her own careful observations of nature and on her study of the writings of Greek scientists and physicians. Her reputation as a healer and a wise counselor grew. Her correspondents included the German emperor Frederick Barbarossa; the English king Henry II and his wife,

Eleanor of Aquitaine; Pope Eugenius III; and many other clergy and lay followers.

At the age of 60, while working on her second book of theology, Hildegard made her first preaching tour through Germany. In doing so, she defied no less a Christian mentor than Saint Paul, who had discouraged women from teaching or preaching. But Hildegard was too popular to be stopped. Three more preaching journeys would call her out of the convent, the last when she was 72.

She established another convent across the Rhine from Bingen. Several miracles, said to have taken place as nuns traveled between the convents, were credited to Hildegard. At 65, called by a powerful new vision, she began her last theological work, the *Liber divinorum operum (Book of Divine Works)*.

Her religious writings, which were to influence Christian thought for several centuries, reflect a cosmic female presence often missing from conventional theology. In Hildegard's work, the figures of Sophia (wisdom), Scientia Dei (the knowledge of God), and Sapientia (divine wisdom in the church and the cosmos), are always female. Sometimes, they are even shown as the Bride of God, as ancient goddesses were. She consistently portrayed creation as balanced between male and female forces. In the illustrations, some of which she made

herself, clergy and worshipers are both male and female. Matter and spirit, things sacred and secular, are shown united, not separated.

Hildegard of Bingen died at 81. In her last year she became embroiled in a dispute over the local clergy's plan to disinter a man who had been excommunicated and buried in her churchyard. Convinced that the man had died repentant, Hildegard refused to have him exhumed and marshaled all her influence in the church to prevail.

In her books, Hildegard included a possible self-portrait, seated at her desk with books spread out before her. She looks up at the cosmos serenely, a confident student of its mysteries, one of the first women in the Western world to claim such a role.

FURTHER READING

Baird, Joseph L., and Radd K. Ehrman, eds. *The Letters of Hildegard of Bingen*. New York: Oxford University Press, 1994.

Flanagan, Sabina. *Hildegard of Bingen, 1098–1179*. New York: Routledge, 1989.

Hildegard of Bingen. *Hildegard of Bingen's Book of Divine Works with Letters and Songs*. Edited by Matthew Fox. Santa Fe, N.M.: Bear, 1987.

BELIEVERS

Hildegard of Bingen

BORN
1098
Bermersheim bei Alzey, Germany

DIED
September 17, 1179
Rubertsberg, near Bingen, Germany

TRADITION
Christianity (Roman Catholic)

ACCOMPLISHMENTS
Author of three books of theology, *Scivias (Know the Ways of the Lord*, 1151), *Liber vitae meritorum (Book of Life's Rewards*, 1163), and *Liber divinorum operum (Book of Divine Works*, 1170); two books on medicine and science, *Physica* or *Liber simplicis medicinae (Book of Simple Medicine*, about 1158) and *Causae et curae* or *Liber compositae medicinae (Book of Applied Medicine*, about 1158); one sacred play, *Ordo Virtutum* (1158); two volumes of a secret language, two biographies, sacred poems and music, and several volumes of correspondence

Moses Maimonides

PHILOSOPHER OF
JUDAISM

A much sought-after doctor, judge, and rabbi, Moses Maimonides was a giant of Jewish and early medieval philosophy. Descended from eight generations of rabbinical scholars, Moses ben Maimon, known as Maimonides, was born in Cordova, Spain. Cordova had been an intellectual center since its conquest by Muslims in 712. Jews, Christians, and Muslims lived together there until the Islamic Empire began to unravel in the 10th century. In 1148, Cordova fell to an Islamic sect that persecuted non-Muslims. The Maimon family fled.

After a decade of traveling through Spain and North Africa, they settled briefly in Fez, in present-day Morocco. With his younger brother David supporting the family as a jewel merchant, Maimonides was able to study and write, mostly in Arabic. His interests ranged from astronomy and physics to philosophy and Judaism. In Morocco he began writing on Jewish law. Jewish law consists of the written Torah, or first five books of the Hebrew Bible (what Christians call the Old Testament) and a body of commentary on the Torah that has been collected over time. This body of commentary is known as the Talmud.

Physician, philosopher, and teacher, Moses Maimonides sought to reconcile reason and faith in his influential writings on Jewish law.

Moses Maimonides

"When I find the road narrow, and can see no other way of teaching a well-established truth except by pleasing one intelligent man and displeasing ten thousand fools—I prefer to address myself to the one man."

—from *Guide for the Perplexed* (1190)

The first work that Maimonides wrote about the Talmud, completed when he was in his 30s, was his *Book of Light*, a commentary on the Mishnah, the earliest collection of Talmudic commentary, gathered in about 200 C.E. In *Book of Light,* he outlined his Thirteen Principles, or beliefs all practicing Jews are expected to have. These hold that God is eternal and has no body; that Jewish law, both written and oral, has a divine source; that worshiping idols is wrong; that a Messiah or savior is yet to appear on earth; and that God knows everything and rewards good and punishes evil.

Maimonides saw Jewish law not as a narrow code but as a great educational, intellectual, and ethical force. The *Book of Light,* like his other writings on Judaism, looks at his faith through the lens of Greek philosophy.

Both Islamic thinkers, such as Ibn Rushd (also known as Averroës), and earlier Jewish thinkers had begun to redefine their faiths in philosophical terms. They based their thinking on the Greek philosopher Aristotle. Like monotheists (who believe in a single God), Aristotle thought a single Being, or the One, was the unchanging source of all existence, the First or Prime Mover. He believed that this being could be understood through human reason.

Maimonides, too, wanted to find a rational basis for religious law and belief. A fool will believe anything, he argued, but an educated person will find the Bible full of problems. He thought that the Bible should be read not only on a literal level; readers should also be guided by reason to its deeper meaning and message.

Midway through his work on the *Book of Light,* Maimonides and his family moved again. His father had written a letter consoling Jews who had converted to Islam under pressure, assuring them that their conversions were invalid. Maimonides supported his father with such a well-argued essay that his views came to the attention of angry Islamic authorities. In 1165 the family left for Palestine (present-day Israel) and then for Alexandria, Egypt. Maimonides' father died soon afterward.

The family moved to Fostat, near Cairo, in 1160. For eight years, supported by his brother David, Maimonides devoted himself to his studies and to writing his greatest work on Jewish law (and his only work in Hebrew), the *Mishneh Torah (A Second Look at the Torah: The Laws of Judaism).*

Then, in 1168, David ben Maimon was lost in a shipwreck. A deeply grieving Maimonides undertook to support David's family and his own wife. Drawing on other skills and studies, he became a doctor. While his medical reputation grew, he continued to write. By this time, he was also recognized as the head of Fostat's Jewish community.

Maimonides completed the *Mishneh Torah* in 1180, although he continued to revise it throughout the rest of his life. Its 14 volumes comprise

BORN

March 30, 1135
Cordova, Spain

DIED

December 13, 1204
Cairo, Egypt

TRADITION

Judaism

ACCOMPLISHMENTS

Major philosophical interpreter of Judaism; major writings on Judaism include the *Book of Light* (1168), *Mishneh Torah* (1180), and *Guide for the Perplexed* (1190)

Pages from a 1399 edition of Maimonides' *Guide for the Perplexed*, which he wrote to guide Jews whose faith in a literal reading of the Bible had been challenged by philosophical questioning.

a masterful catalog of the written and oral traditions of Jewish law. Existing commentaries on Jewish law were both abundant and widely scattered when Maimonides determined to winnow and reorganize them. The resulting code was enormously influential.

A son, Abraham, was born to Maimonides in 1187. Abraham followed his father into medicine, religious writing, and leadership of the Egyptian Jewish community, a tradition that would last five generations.

Maimonides was in great demand as a legal and spiritual authority, and he was prized as well for his knowledge of Greek thought. But his primary interest remained religious philosophy. In 1190 he completed his most famous work, *Guide for the Perplexed*. His *Guide* is aimed at those believing Jews who have also studied philosophy and find themselves confused or perplexed by a literal reading of the Bible. Maimonides offered rational ways to understand and

interpret the Bible. He also offered philosophical proofs that God exists and that, despite God's superior knowledge, people have free will.

Although Jewish and Christian antirationalists, opposed to philosophical readings of the Bible, later condemned his work, Maimonides never elevated reason above faith. Reason is powerful, he said, but God is greater. The human mind can understand and interpret the Bible, but it cannot encompass God.

Maimonides exerted great influence on medieval Christian thinkers, such as Thomas Aquinas, and on philosophers of the 18th-century Enlightenment and more modern movements. His death in 1204 was officially mourned, and his tomb, in Tiberias, Israel, still attracts pilgrims.

FURTHER READING

Heschel, Abraham J. *Maimonides: A Biography of the Great Medieval Thinker*. Garden City, N.Y.: Doubleday, 1991.

Maimonides. *Book of Knowledge*. Translated by Moses Hyamson. Mishneh Torah series. Spring Valley, N.Y.: Philipp Feldheim, 1981.

———. *Guide for the Perplexed: A Fifteenth Century Spanish Translation by Pedro de Toledo*. Culver City, Calif.: Labyrinthos, 1989.

Marcus, Rebecca B. *Moses Maimonides: Rabbi, Philosopher, and Physician*. New York: Franklin Watts, 1969.

Seeskin, Kenneth. *Maimonides: A Guide for Today's Perplexed*. New York: Behrman House, 1991.

Twersky, Isadore. *Maimonides*. New York: Behrman House, n.d.

Francis of Assisi

IN PRAISE OF CREATION

rancis of Assisi was born in 1181 or 1182 as Giovanni Bernardone, the son of a wealthy Italian cloth merchant and his French wife, Pica. As a teenager, he changed his name to Francis to reflect his passion for French culture, particularly the songs and style of the lyric poets known as troubadours. Witty, good-natured, quick to break into song, he was a popular young man who dreamed of being a crusading knight. Instead, he

Saint Francis displays the stigmata—wounds identical to those suffered by Jesus on the cross. In Christian tradition, Francis is the first individual to develop the stigmata.

This illustration from a medieval psalter portrays Francis of Assisi preaching to the birds and animals of the fields, a well-known episode from his life. After his conversion, Francis's love for nature included not only living things, such as trees and flowers, but inanimate objects such as water and rocks. For Francis, all of creation reflected and revealed God's goodness.

> *"Praise to thee, my Lord, for all thy creatures,*
> *Above all Brother Sun*
> *Who brings us the day and lends us his light."*
>
> —from *Canticle of Brother Sun* (1225)

founded a new Catholic order and became one of the world's greatest celebrators of nature.

At 21, Francis became a soldier and fought for his city, Assisi, against neighboring Perugia. He was captured and spent two years in prison. When the two cities reached a truce, he was released after his father paid a ransom. Francis was still determined to be a soldier, but the next year he fell ill and became despondent.

At that low moment—sick, depressed, an ex-prisoner of war—Francis experienced a conversion. After reading Christ's command to "give without pay, to take no gold, nor silver, nor copper" (Matthew 10:7–14), Francis decided to dedicate his life to the Christian ideals of charity and neighborly love. He turned away from the worldly life, denying himself earthly pleasures.

Francis stole some of his father's cloth, sold it, and donated the money to a church in need of repair. To escape his father's wrath, Francis fled to a cave where he sometimes meditated. When the young man finally went home, his father beat him and

locked him in a dark room. (This was the standard treatment for insanity then and for a long time to follow.) When Francis was finally rescued by his mother, he agreed to a confrontation with his father before the bishop of Assisi. At that meeting, Francis stripped his clothes off to demonstrate his contempt for possessions. The breach with his father would never be healed.

Francis put on his oldest tunic, replaced his leather belt with rope, and began preaching. He even preached to the birds. His conversion experience had been so powerful that he saw the whole world and all its creatures as children of God. It is said that he stepped on stones with awe and greeted animals politely. Late in life, when his diseased eye had to be cauterized with a hot iron, he requested, "Brother Fire, be courteous."

Francis was not the only Christian of his time to turn to poverty, simplicity, and nature in imitation of Christ. For more than four centuries, Irish missionaries had spread a mystical, nature-based Christianity throughout Europe. Francis may have been exposed to their ideas through Italy's own group of Christians sworn to poverty, the Humble Men, who dominated the woolen industry.

Although Francis may have intended to act alone, his charming personality and enthusiasm for Christ and nature soon attracted followers. Under Francis, his followers would probably have remained a loose band. They would have traveled alone or in pairs, begging for their food, preaching, and helping people in need. But Francis's gift was for inspiration, not administration. Pope Innocent III appointed his nephew Ugolino to oversee the Franciscan order in 1215.

Two years later, Francis joined the Fifth Crusade. The Crusades were a series of Christian holy wars aimed at recapturing Palestine (present-day Israel) from the Muslims and halting Islamic conquests in southern Europe. Francis wanted to preach more than to fight, but he may also have wanted to martyr himself for his faith.

In Syria, a Muslim leader, Sultan al-Kamil, gave Francis a hearing in 1219. Francis tried to convert al-Kamil to Christianity, but the sultan resisted. Because he did not blaspheme the Islamic prophet Muhammad, however, the dirty, ragged Francis seems to have impressed the sultan, and Francis escaped with his life. Al-Kamil asked Francis to pray for him and returned him to the Christian camp.

Francis returned to Italy, where he found his order transformed by Ugolino and Brother Elias, a Franciscan monk. Although Francis had emphasized poverty, Ugolino and Elias had built up the order's property and wealth. Rather than challenge them, Francis left the order to live as a hermit. It was as a hermit that he became known as a miracle worker. Local people claimed that he cured the sick and raised the dead. He is also said to have developed the stigmata, wounds in exact imitation of those received by Christ during the Crucifixion.

Though seriously ill, Francis wrote his joyous *Canticle* [Song] *of Brother Sun* near the end of his life. He died at age 45. A year after his death, Ugolino was named pope, and Brother Elias, leader of the Franciscan order, built the first church named for Francis, in Assisi.

Francis was canonized, or officially named a saint, two years after his death. His example of poverty and simplicity left a lasting impression on Christianity. It contributed to the popular revulsion at the Catholic Church's opulence, an attitude that fed the Protestant Reformation three centuries later. In 1979, Pope John Paul II named Francis the church's patron saint of ecology.

"Francis was the summit of medieval civilization."

—from *Travels in Italy* (1914) by French historian Hippolyte Taine

FURTHER READING

Armstrong, Edward A. *Saint Francis: Nature Mystic*. Berkeley: University of California Press, 1973.

Erikson, Joan Mowat. *Saint Francis and His Four Ladies*. New York: Norton, 1970.

O'Dell, Scott. *The Road to Damietta*. New York: Fawcett, 1987.

Smith, John Holland. *Francis of Assisi*. New York: Scribners, 1972.

Francis of Assisi

BORN

1181 or 1182
Assisi, Italy

DIED

October 3, 1226
Assisi, Italy

TRADITION

Christianity (Roman Catholic)

ACCOMPLISHMENTS

Founder of Franciscan order; after his death, his followers collected his writings, letters, and prayers, the most famous of which is *Canticle of Brother Sun*

Joan of Arc

VIRGIN OF GOD

Early one summer, in the woods not far from her home, a 13-year-old French girl was astonished by a blaze of light and a heavenly voice. At first the voice, which identified itself as the archangel Michael, instructed her on moral behavior. Eventually, it was joined by two other voices, those of Saint Catherine of Alexandria and Saint Margaret of Antioch. They commanded her to lead French soldiers against the English and restore the French heir to his throne. Joan of Arc was called out of her peasant life into history.

For nearly a century, France and England had been fighting what came to be known as the Hundred Years' War. By the time of Joan's birth, in about 1412, the French king Charles VI was weak, probably insane, and unable to rule; the British king, Henry V, invaded France in 1415. Five years later, Henry married a French royal woman and claimed the French throne. When both Henry and Charles

Joan of Arc is both a French national hero and a saint of the Roman Catholic Church. Although Joan fell afoul of the church for revealing that she heard heavenly voices, in 1452 her admirers petitioned to have her case reopened. Four years later church authorities canceled her excommunication from the church. She was regarded popularly as a saint years before the Roman Catholic Church canonized her in 1920.

> *"I refer to God, who made me do everything I have done."*
>
> —from trial transcript (1431)

Joan of Arc

BORN

About 1412
Domrémy, France

DIED

May 30, 1431
Rouen, France

TRADITION

Christianity (Roman Catholic)

ACCOMPLISHMENTS

French martyr and military leader who was beatified by Pope Pius X (1909) and canonized by Pope Benedict XV (1920)

VI died in 1422, Henry's infant son was named king of France instead of Charles VII, known as the dauphin, which is the title given to the French king's eldest son. France appeared to be falling into English hands. The voices Joan heard urged her to enter the struggle and restore Charles VII to the French throne.

Very little is known about Joan of Arc. She was born Jeanne d'Arc—or Tarc, or Tart, or Dare, or Day—in the village of Domrémy in eastern France, one of five children of prosperous farmers. She never learned to read or write. Sewing, housework, and the rudiments of Catholicism, taught by her mother, formed the horizons of her early world. Periodically, marauding soldiers and military attacks disrupted her village, which was loyal to the dauphin.

Joan must have found her voices comforting, for she never confided her experience of them to anyone. She kept them to herself, addressing them in frequent prayers. In December 1428, after refusing a marriage her parents had arranged, she left home in obedience to the voices she heard. Identifying herself as the fulfillment of prophecies foretelling a virgin who would save France, Joan pleaded with Robert de Baudricourt, captain of the dauphin's forces in Vaucouleurs, a town near Domrémy, to be allowed to join the dauphin's struggle. Three times he rejected her offer, even suggesting that her father box her ears. Finally, he relented, but uncertain whether her powers came from God or the devil, Baudricourt had Joan exorcised, or cleansed of evil spirits, before sending her to the dauphin.

Joan adopted men's clothing and cut her hair short. Men's clothes were easier to move around in and helped her avoid being raped. For her, they probably also symbolized her transformation from peasant girl to national avenger. Dressed as a soldier, she appeared before a velvet- and ermine-clad Charles VII. Historians have usually portrayed the dauphin as indecisive and cowardly, plagued by rumors of his illegitimate birth. He was in fact also hampered by near-bankruptcy and may have preferred diplomacy and manipulation to outright battle.

Joan's supreme confidence in her mission swayed Charles. Before outfitting her as a knight, though, he sent her to Poitiers to establish that she was a virgin rather than a witch. Like the ancient Greeks and Romans, medieval Christians attributed special moral, spiritual, and physical strengths to virgins.

By early 1429, the English had attacked and nearly surrounded Orléans, in the Loire valley of France. A British victory over the city would have fatally weakened the French cause. That April, Joan led a company of soldiers against the British at Orléans. During battle, she received an arrow wound to the neck. After resting briefly, she remounted her horse and urged on the French forces. All the British officers and some 1,400 soldiers

A soldier ties Joan of Arc to the stake. She was burned for heresy in Rouen, France, in 1431, after asserting that she had heard the voices of the Archangel Michael and Saints Catherine and Margaret.

were killed. It was a turning point in the war. Volunteers flooded Joan's army and popular opinion began shifting to the dauphin's favor.

Joan was not the first medieval woman to participate in combat, but she was the first to take a leadership role. Throughout her military career, Joan took guidance from her voices but never expected God to win her battles. She demanded discipline of her soldiers and inspired them by her own courage. Joan routed the English from a series of cities in the Loire Valley. At the battle of Patay, in June 1429, a disheveled English army lost more than 2,000 men. France lost only 3.

Joan pushed on to Reims, north of Paris, to proclaim the dauphin as king. In July, Charles was ritually anointed with

holy oil, a tradition dating back 1,000 years to Clovis, France's first Christian king. Holding her banner high, Joan stood at the dauphin's side. Less than a year later, she would be captured and her glorious career would end.

Joan's impulse was to take action; she wanted to march on Paris. The king, with a strong distaste for blood, favored diplomacy instead. In September, Joan led a failed attack on Paris and was injured. Rejoining the king in the Loire Valley, she directed some small skirmishes there before returning north. On May 23, 1430, against the king's wishes, Joan tried to take Compiègne, a town situated north of Paris. The attack went badly, and the forces allied with England captured her.

The English viewed Joan as a witch. Although a prisoner of war and available for trade or ransom, she was tried—by French clerics in Rouen who supported the English cause—as a heretic, a dissenter from church doctrine. Her claim that she had direct inspiration from God (and therefore her refusal to accept church hierarchy) invited this heresy charge against her. That was ironic because although Joan's views were not strictly orthodox, she condemned heretics herself.

Among many irregularities in her trial, her chief prosecutor, Bishop Pierre Cauchon of Beauvais, was allowed to try Joan outside his own district. Although she had a church trial, Joan was not jailed in a church prison, where her guards would have been women. She was held in a criminal's cell, subject to the brutality of her male guards. Attempting escape, she jumped from her 60-foot-high tower and fell unharmed. Her jailers moved her to a tower in Rouen and kept a tighter watch.

In the opening session of her trial, Joan swore to answer all questions about her faith but none about the voices. Nevertheless, the trial focused on those voices and on her wearing of men's clothing, which at that time was regarded as sinful. Joan was blunt and impatient in her replies. She warned Cauchon to "consider well what you do for in truth I am sent by God and you put yourself in great peril." Despite her agility in dodging the snares her inquisitors set, Joan finally broke down and described the voices she heard.

On April 12, 1431, after days of testimony and questioning, Joan was accused of 12 counts of heresy, lying, dressing like a man, and attempted suicide (her escape effort). She was allowed no reply. Several churchmen from the University of Paris reviewed her case. Some openly questioned her guilt; others said the case should go to a church court in Rome. Cauchon suppressed their views. He pressed Joan to recant and deny that she heard voices. On May 24, after threats of torture, she did. Her sentence was reduced to life in prison, where she was ordered to wear women's clothing.

Four days later, she was in men's clothes again, either because she feared rape or had been tricked by the guards into dressing in men's clothes. She withdrew her recantation, declaring that she would rather die than endure further imprisonment and that her voices rebuked her for recanting. "A fatal answer," the court reporter jotted alongside his record.

Cauchon visited her a final time. "Bishop, I die through you," she told him. More than 80 English soldiers led her to the executioner's cart. A pointed hat, like a bishop's miter, with the words "heretic, relapsed, apostate, liar" was placed on Joan's head. Her final prayers were said to have reduced many, including Cauchon, to tears. She stepped onto a platform piled with wood, and the executioner tied her to a stake to be burned. Joan cried out to Saint Michael as the executioner lit the wood surrounding the stake. As she burned to death, her last words were, "Jesus, Jesus!" Joan's admirers carefully gathered her ashes and cast them into the River Seine.

Charles VII, who had had little to do with Joan after his coronation in Reims in 1429, went on to strengthen his power. Twenty-two years after Joan's death, France at last defeated England in battle. Worried that he owed his crown to a convicted heretic, Charles ordered Joan's case reopened. In 1456 her conviction was overturned. In 1920, Joan was canonized as a saint, although the church had never acknowledged her right to interpret the voices she heard. Today, Joan of Arc remains a powerful symbol of French identity and an inspiration for self-determination among people everywhere.

FURTHER READING

Banfield, Susan. *Joan of Arc*. New York: Chelsea House, 1988.

Brooks, Polly Schoyer. *Beyond the Myth: The Story of Joan of Arc*. New York: Lippincott, 1990.

Gies, Frances. *Joan of Arc: The Legend and the Reality*. New York: Harper & Row, 1981.

Smith, Dorothy. *Saint Joan: The Girl in Armor*. Mahwah, N.J.: Paulist Press, 1990.

Smith, Holland. *Joan of Arc*. New York: Scribners, 1973.

Trask, Willard. *Joan of Arc: Self Portrait*. New York: Stackpole, 1936. [This is a transcript of the trial.]

Guru Nānak

WORSHIPING THE NAME OF GOD

Guru Nānak, the founder of Sikhism, was born in 1469 near Lahore, in present-day Pakistan. His father worked as a bookkeeper and farmer. His family was Hindu, although the dreamy young Nānak was educated by a Muslim schoolteacher. The part of India in which Nānak was raised (before Pakistan separated from India in 1947) had long been a meeting place for Muslim and Hindu cultures, since Islamic soldiers and merchants had entered northwest India in the 11th century.

A marriage was arranged for Nānak when he was 12, and when he was 19, his wife came to live with him. Together they had two sons, and Nānak worked as a cowherd and tradesman. He was not very good at either, however, so he left his wife and children with his parents and traveled to the capital of his district, Sultanpur, where he had better luck working as a store manager. In Sultanpur Nānak made friends with a Muslim musician, Mardana. Both men were drawn to religion and met often to talk and sing hymns. A group of other religious seekers gathered around them.

The story of Nānak's religious awakening is drawn from the *janam-sakhis*, or later stories told about him. Bathing in the river one morning in his 30th year, Nānak experienced something extraordinary. What he took to be the hand of God offered him a sweet drink, and what he heard as the voice of God promised him that "I will save whoever follows you" and commanded Nānak to teach others how to pray and do God's work in the world.

Nānak responded with a jubilant prayer, now used as the Sikh morning prayer, which begins, "There is one God. He is the supreme truth."

Nānak became so absorbed in his experience that his friends concluded he had drowned and reported him dead. Four days later, Nānak appeared, gave away all his possessions except a loincloth, and with Mardana joined a band of beggars. "There is no Hindu or Muslim," he declared when he began preaching the next day. Religion, he taught, should not separate people from one another.

Nānak had been troubled by the struggles between Hindus and Muslims. When he traveled, preaching and singing to Mardana's musical accompaniment, he wore a deliberately silly outfit, combining clothing from both Hindu and Muslim traditional dress. His costume announced his message that there was a higher truth, beyond Hinduism or Islam. The students, or followers, who gathered around Nānak became known as Sikhs; the word *sikh*, from the Sanskrit *sishya*, means "disciple."

"*Make mercy your mosque and devotion your prayer mat, righteousness your Koran.*"

—from *Ādi Granth*

Guru Nānak (right) explains his belief that grace begins with service to God. He also taught his followers—called Sikhs, from a Sanskrit word meaning "disciple"—to approach God with help from a teacher, or guru.

Nānak's teachings were later gathered in a book known as the *Ādi Granth*. His central idea was that "God [is] the True Name." God is above the separate names that different religions invent for him, Nānak taught. Meditating on this True Name of God was a kind of worship. Nānak also taught that a Sikh should approach God in the company of a guru, or teacher, who

Guru Nānak

BORN
April 15, 1469
Near Lahore, Pakistan

DIED
1539
Kartārpur, Pakistan

TRADITION
Sikh

ACCOMPLISHMENTS
Founder of Sikhism; teachings collected in the *Ādi Granth*, compiled by the fifth guru, Arjun, in the early 17th century

would help him reach God through prayer and meditation.

Nānak's worship of God's name has parallels in the Hindu tradition of *bhakti,* or devotion to a divine being, but in other ways Nānak broke with Hinduism. Because he believed that God was present in everyone and that all people were equal before God, he rejected the caste system by which Hindus inherited their social status from their parents. Because he believed that God was revealed in the natural world as well as the human soul, he rejected both Hindu and Muslim ceremonies as meaningless and unnecessary; he also rejected their ascetic, or self- and pleasure-denying, traditions.

During the last 15 years of his life, Nānak returned to live as a guru, or teacher, in his native village of Kartārpur. Although he had not formally organized his followers or established a missionary movement, before he died he did name a successor guru to lead the Sikhs after him. Nine gurus eventually succeeded Nānak. In their hands, the Sikh religion was transformed from Nānak's original meditative discipline to one with more active, and ultimately armed, members.

The first gurus made modest changes. The third guru, Amar Dās, introduced a common meal as a central Sikh ritual (later Sikh common meals would include as many as a thousand diners). The fourth guru, Rām Dās, began building the Sikh's Golden Temple at Amritsar, India. His son, Arjun, served as the fifth guru. Arjun completed the temple and began the Sikh tradition of ritual bathing. In his lifetime, Sikhs came under attack from northwest India's Muslim rulers, and Arjun was totured to death in prison. Under his son, earlier Sikh emphasis on physical fitness became battle-readiness and skill in guerrilla warfare. The 10th and last guru, Gobind Singh (1666–1708), transformed the Sikhs into a formal fighting force. He invited men of all backgrounds to join his Khālsā, or Community of the Pure. They would be distinguished by their uncut beards and hair, their knee-length *kach* (khaki) pants, and the knives or daggers that they carried.

Gobind also ended the tradition of gurus, declaring that the *Ādi Granth* itself would serve as the Sikhs' guru. Today, the *Ādi Granth* is the central component of Sikh worship. In addition to Nānak's teachings, it also contains the teachings of other religious figures, notably among them the writings of Kabir (1440–1518), a Muslim poet whose ideas about one God and the importance of meditation seemed to have influenced Nānak.

Today, the Sikhs number about 9 or 10 million. Their political difficulties persist: the partition of India into mostly Hindu India and mostly Muslim Pakistan bisected the Sikhs' homeland. Fighting broke out among Sikhs, Muslims, and Hindus. Tensions, particularly between Sikhs and Hindus, continue to erupt into fighting.

FURTHER READING

McLeod, W. H. *The Sikhs.* New York: Columbia University Press, 1989.

Singh, Harbans. *The Heritage of the Sikhs.* New Delhi: Manohar Publications, 1983.

Thomas More

SCHOLAR, LAWYER, SAINT

I n his 56th year, the brilliant English lawyer, diplomat, and writer Thomas More laid his head on the king's execution block. His lifelong habit of meeting trouble with wit compelled him to quip, "I trust *this* hath not offended the king," as he pushed his long beard out of harm's way.

In 12 years, More had gone from being King Henry VIII's most trusted adviser to a convicted traitor. Thomas More was a deeply religious man who also achieved considerable worldly success. He lost his life when his religion came into conflict with politics.

As a boy, More served as a page, or aide, to John Cardinal Morton, the Archbishop of Canterbury, England's highest religious authority. In 1492, More entered Oxford University. There he distinguished himself as a first-rate classical scholar and began his lifelong friendship with the Dutch student Desiderius Erasmus.

Both More and Erasmus championed what was known as the New Learning. In the 14th century, European artists

As a lawyer and prominent politician in 16th-century England, Sir Thomas More was an extremely worldly figure, but he steadfastly maintained that no earthly king could presume a power greater than Christ's.

A woodcut illustration of Utopia from the third edition (1518) of More's *Utopia*. The name he chose for this imaginary island, the model of a perfect social state, literally means "nowhere"; the river Anydrus, which flows near the edges, means "no water."

and thinkers had rediscovered ancient Greek, Hebrew, and Latin languages and literature, after centuries of neglect. Together with the recently invented printing press, this New Learning transformed European culture. A new respect for human dignity emerged, the result of combining two ideas from the ancients—the Greek notion of man as "the measure of all things" and the Hebrew image of people as children of God. This focus on human dignity was called Humanism. Humanism also promised that the Catholic Church could be reformed by its lay, or non-priestly, members.

Erasmus became a notable Humanist scholar. Aside from publishing his own, widely popular writings, Erasmus translated the works of many of the Catholic Church's early founders and published the Greek New Testament, giving scholars a new perspective on the Latin Bible.

Two years into his Oxford experience, More was called back to London. His father, a successful lawyer, wanted Thomas to join him in that profession. More lived in a London monastery while he pursued his legal training. He thought seriously of joining the priesthood, and agonized over the decision.

On the advice of his mentor, the Humanist John Colet, and after listening to his own heart, More finally decided against the religious life, though he continued the humbling monastic practice of wearing an uncomfortable hair shirt for the rest of his life.

More married Jane Colt and was elected to Parliament, the English legislature, in 1504. Five years later, he was appointed undersheriff of London. His wife died the next year, shortly after the birth of their fourth child. More then married Alice Middleton, a widow with several children of her own. He took an active interest in his children's education, particularly in educating the girls, which was uncommon in his day. All his children studied classical languages, and More wrote to them in Latin. He was particularly close to his oldest child, Margaret. Her husband, William Roper, became More's first biographer.

More's skills as a lawyer quickly won him many clients. A diplomatic career grew out of his legal one, for he began to represent English trade guilds, or associations of craftsmen, in England and abroad. King Henry VIII,

crowned in 1509, called on the brilliant young lawyer to represent England in trade negotiations six years later. More's diplomatic tours brought him in greater contact with his close friend Erasmus and other Humanists. It was during one such tour that More wrote his most famous work, *Utopia*.

More coined the word *utopia* from two Greek words meaning "no place." His *Utopia* was an imaginary island society that enjoyed perfect social, legal, and political health without the benefit of religion. On Utopia, there was no money, no private property, or fashion. Everyone dressed in the same simple clothing, and only serfs wore jewelry. Food was free and large communal meals were encouraged. Everyone worked, but for only six hours a day. Some people have read *Utopia* as a witty, tongue-in-cheek critique of English politics and religion; others have seen in it a blueprint for the perfect society.

More accepted the post of royal adviser in 1517, after much deliberation. (In Book I of *Utopia*, the hero, Raphael Hythloday, speaks eloquently on the folly of royal service; More waited a year before he told Erasmus of his decision to accept the king's appointment.)

More moved his family to a large farm in what was then a suburb of London. For the next 12 years, his public life centered on the law and the king's court. His honesty and diplomacy made him the one man both King Henry VIII and the new archbishop of Canterbury, Cardinal Wolsey, trusted. More continued to represent England overseas, and in 1520 negotiated a peace with the king of France that would last 14 years. Other honors followed: he was knighted, named undertreasurer of the nation, elected speaker of the House of Commons, and finally replaced Wolsey as lord chancellor, the king's highest adviser.

Thomas More

BORN

February 7, 1478
London, England

DIED

May 19, 1535
London, England

FORMAL EDUCATION

Attended Oxford University; legal training at Lincoln's Inn of the Court, London

TRADITION

Christianity (Roman Catholic)

ACCOMPLISHMENTS

Author of *Life of John Picus* (1510), *History of Richard III* (1543), *Utopia* (1516), *Dialogue Concerning Heresies* (1528), *Apologye* (1533), *Dialogue of Comfort Against Tribulation* (1535), and *Treatise on the Passion of Christ* (1535); undersheriff of London (1510); British envoy to Flanders (1516); privy councillor (1518); speaker of the House of Commons (1523); high steward, Oxford University (1524); high steward, Cambridge University (1525); lord chancellor of England (1529–31)

> *"A man may lose his head and have no harm."*
>
> —from More's letter to his daughter Margaret (1534)

More also enlisted in the struggle against Martin Luther and the emerging Protestant movement. Humanism had already pointed to the need to reform such medieval institutions as the Roman Catholic Church. In the hands of the German priest Martin Luther, Humanist ideas became revolutionary.

Both More and Henry VIII abhorred Luther. Henry's defense of Roman Catholicism written by More, *An Assertion of the Seven Sacraments* (1523), earned high praise from Pope Leo X. More's *Dialogue Concerning Heresies* (1528) attacked both Luther and William Tyndale, who first translated the New Testament from Greek into English in 1526. From the legal bench, More vigorously prosecuted heretics, or dissenters. As lord chancellor, he oversaw the executions of six men accused of expressing or holding Protestant views.

To England's rising religious tension between Protestants and Catholics, Henry VIII added the issue of a royal divorce. Because his wife, Catherine of Aragon, was unable to provide him with a male heir, Henry wanted to end his marriage. He planned to marry Anne Boleyn, the sister of his mistress. According to Catholic doctrine at that time, remarriage after divorce was utterly forbidden. More advised the king that he could not support him and asked to be excused from future discussions of "the great matter" of Henry's divorce.

More resigned as chancellor and happily returned to his writing. In 1533, Henry did marry Anne Boleyn, and the new pope, Paul III, excommunicated the English king from the Roman Catholic Church. More declined an invitation to Queen Anne's coronation. His writings from that period show that he knew the danger he courted.

In September 1533, Anne Boleyn gave birth to a daughter, Elizabeth. Henry pushed Parliament to rule his earlier marriage to Catherine invalid. Then he proceeded, through a series of Royal Acts, to sever England from papal control, to give the English king the power to select bishops, and to name himself head of the English church. This church came to be known as the Church of England, or Anglican Church.

These changes appalled More. He refused to support them, despite efforts by his family and friends to persuade him to do so. Henry charged More with treason and imprisoned him in the Tower of London. In July 1535, More stood trial. He argued that no earthly government could presume a spiritual power greater than Christ and the church. The court found him guilty of "traitorously and maliciously" attempting to deprive the king of his role as head of the Church of England.

It condemned More to death. More replied that all the councils of Christendom supported him.

On the way back to the tower, he told his daughter Margaret, "Tomorrow long I to go to God, it were a day very meet and convenient for me." At the execution block, he called himself "the king's good servant, but God's first."

Henry buried More's body in the Tower of London but posted his head on London Bridge. Admirers across Europe mourned More's death. In 1886 the Catholic Church beatified More, marking him as especially holy, and in 1935 named him a saint. His popular image today owes much to Robert Bolt's play, *A Man for All Seasons* (1961). For many, More remains the quintessential man of courage, willing to sacrifice his life for his principles.

FURTHER READING

Kenny, Anthony. *Thomas More.* New York: Oxford University Press, 1983.

Marius, Richard. *Thomas More: A Biography.* New York: Knopf, 1984.

Sargent, Daniel. *Thomas More.* New York: Sheed & Ward, 1933.

Smith, Dorothy. *Thomas More: The King's Good Servant.* Mahwah, N.J.: Paulist Press, 1990.

Martin Luther

"FAITH ALONE"

ometime around the year 1515, a young German monk and professor named Martin Luther found himself in despair. Luther often examined his conscience—his sense of right and wrong—and it always troubled him. He felt in great need of redemption, of freedom from his human weaknesses, but the God to whom he prayed for such redemption seemed distant and critical, far from Luther's reach.

Sometimes anxiety caused Luther to break into a sweat and feel that the devil had taken hold of him. His path to God seemed blocked. The Roman Catholic Church, of which Luther was a member, provided little guidance that he felt could help him. A trip to Rome five years earlier had convinced him of the church's shortcomings—its concern with wealth and fine buildings. The church, for instance,

As a leader of the Protestant Reformation, Martin Luther challenged several beliefs and practices of the Roman Catholic Church. In defiance of a church ban, for example, he translated the Bible into German, making it available to the general public.

In this satirical 16th-century Swiss engraving, Martin Luther (far left) inscribes his 95 theses on the door of the church at Wittenberg with a huge pen. Although Luther never actually nailed his theses to the door, his pointed questioning of the Roman Catholic Church ushered in one of the most tumultuous periods of religious, political, and social upheaval in European history.

addressed bad consciences by selling indulgences, or pardons, to people who believed they had sinned, or wronged God. Indulgences were no solution to the scrupulous young monk.

In 1515, Luther was preparing to lecture on the Psalms, a book in the Hebrew Bible, or Christian Old Testament, at the University of Wittenberg. He was also studying the writings of Saint Paul, the early Christian evangelist. One day, Luther later wrote, "the door of paradise opened." He suddenly felt he understood Paul's letter to the Romans, included in the Christian New Testament, that says "the just shall be saved by faith."

Luther's question of how to please God, how to awaken from the nightmare of damnation, dissolved. Redemption was in God's hands. It was a

matter, Luther now began to believe, of God's grace—a freely given, unearned mercy. Luther's role, as he saw it, was simply to have faith, to turn away from his preoccupation with his own shortcomings and put his trust in God. That trust, or faith, would be Luther's bedrock, the one certainty in his life.

Luther had grown up in a strict, thrifty household. Beatings were not uncommon: once, his mother struck Martin in the face, drawing blood, for taking a nut. His father was the son of a peasant but was himself a successful miner. He wanted Martin to study law and join the emerging business class in Germany.

Martin hated school. Classes were in Latin, and students were punished for speaking German. Still, he earned his bachelor's and master's degrees and began studying law in 1505. His father selected a wife for him.

That summer, however, Martin found himself unable to obey his father. Returning to the university after a visit home, he was caught in a thunderstorm. A brilliant bolt of lightning struck near him, and he dropped to the ground in fear. "Help me, Saint Anne," he pleaded, "I will become a monk." (Saint Anne was the patron saint of miners; Martin was not yet free of his father's influence.) He survived the storm and that fall entered an order of monks based on the teachings of Saint Augustine. His parents did not approve.

In the monastery, Luther found a mentor. The vicar Johann von Staupitz listened to the young man and encouraged him to earn a higher degree. Luther's doctoral studies, completed in 1512, centered on two thinkers: Saint Augustine, the towering Roman Catholic theorist of the 4th century, and Aristotle, the pre-Christian Greek philosopher. Luther admired Augustine but came to detest Aristotle and even the idea of human reason, which he called "a dark chaos."

Like Augustine, Luther considered sin, or the inclination to do wrong, as part of the human condition. People cannot make things right, he argued, either through knowledge or good actions. Only the grace of God, which people experience through faith, can free them from sin.

This view put Luther in conflict with the Roman Catholic Church's custom of allowing people to erase their sins by buying pardons or indulgences. In October 1517, angered by yet another church campaign to raise money, Luther proposed to debate whether the church should sell indulgences. In a famous scene, he is said to have nailed his Ninety-five Theses, or debating points, to a church door. This story was invented; Luther actually sent them to the Archbishop of Mainz, who sent them to Rome in December 1517. The pope dismissed them.

Luther gave his Ninety-five Theses to a printer and ignited a revolution. Movable type, the precursor to the printing press, had been invented by Johannes Gutenberg in the previous century, and for the first time in history, writing could be copied mechanically rather than by hand. This new technology enabled Luther's ideas to spread widely and rapidly.

After Luther's first clash with Catholicism over indulgences, his conflicts with the church grew, perhaps faster than he had intended. He had not meant to break completely with the church, and for a time, reconciliation seemed possible. He wrote Pope Leo X, "If I have deserved death I will not refuse to die," but he avoided visiting Rome.

Although Luther had promised to stay silent, he agreed to debate Johann Eck, a Catholic critic of his Theses. That brilliant theologian cornered Luther into stating heretical views—views the Church regarded as false and dangerous. In a letter to a friend early the next year, in 1520, Luther affirmed his own views. "I will not reconcile myself to them [the church] in all eternity," he wrote.

Luther produced three important, defiant pamphlets that year: *The Address to the Christian Nobility of the German Nation, Concerning the Babylonian Captivity of the Church,* and *The Freedom of a Christian.* In these he argued that all Christians, lay members and priests, were equal. Together they formed a "priesthood of all believers." He called for eliminating all the Christian sacraments, or ritual observances, except three: baptism, the Eucharist (Lord's Supper), and penance (atonement for sins).

Pope Leo X charged Luther with heresy, or holding false beliefs, and

Martin Luther

BORN
November 10, 1483
Eisleben, Germany

DIED
February 18, 1546
Eisleben, Germany

FORMAL EDUCATION
Attended University of Erfurt; baccalaureus biblicus, doctorate, University of Wittenberg

TRADITION
Christianity (Protestant)

ACCOMPLISHMENTS
Leader of the Protestant Reformation; his collected works run to 55 volumes in English translation; among his major works are *The Freedom of a Christian* (1520), a translation of the Bible (1534), *The Address to the Christian Nobility of the German Nation* (1520), and *Concerning the Babylonian Captivity of the Church* (1520); composed numerous religious hymns and songs

gave him 60 days to recant, or take back, his statements. Luther burned the charges in a public ceremony. The pope threatened to expel Luther from the Catholic Church but gave him one final chance to defend himself.

In 1521, before a formal church meeting in Worms, Germany, Luther apologized for speaking violently but recanted nothing.

Now an outlaw, his work formally forbidden, Luther disguised himself as a knight and escaped to a castle in Wartburg. There, alone for the first time in his life, he produced his masterwork, a translation of the New Testament into German.

In 1080, the church had banned translations of the Bible into modern languages. Those who were not priests were forbidden to read the entire Bible. In an act of defiance, Luther put the Bible into the hands of all German-speaking people.

In 1525, "to spite the pope and the devil," as he put it, Luther married Katharina von Bora, a former nun. Moving into a converted monastery, the former ascetic embraced life. He populated his household with six children and presided over a steady stream of food, drink, and visitors.

If Luther's life settled into a happy domesticity, the larger world remained far from peaceful. Tensions between wealthy Germans and the peasants, small landowners and laborers, had simmered for years and finally erupted into war in 1525. Although the young Luther had written passionately about democracy, and the peasants had borrowed liberally from his writings, the middle-aged Luther was firmly conservative. "No insurrection is ever right," he wrote, comparing the hostile peasantry to a mad dog. In all, some 130,000 peasants died in the Peasants' War.

Others who took Luther's words and, in his view, distorted them, were his immediate followers in the move-ment that came to be known as Protestantism, or the Protestant Reformation. In Switzerland, the reformers Huldrych Zwingli and John Calvin broke even more sharply with the Catholic Church than Luther had. Whereas Luther had been willing to keep some of the Catholic sacraments, or rituals, intact, Zwingli and Calvin created a far more Bible-centered Protestantism. Both men, for instance, rejected transubstantiation, which in Catholic belief is the miraculous change of the bread and wine of the Eucharist into the body and blood of Christ while they maintain the appearance of food and drink. Rejection of such a ritual incensed Luther.

Luther was unable to reconcile with the church or to accept the radical direction that his followers were taking. His last book betrays his unsettled state. He titled it *Against the Anabaptists, Against the Jews, Against the Papacy at Rome, Founded by the Devil*. Toward the end of his life, he was often ill; he died in 1546 on a family business trip to the town of his birth.

Luther was not the first person to question the Catholic Church's preoccupation with wealth and power. Earlier reformers had paid for their outspokenness with their lives, however. Jan Hus was burned at the stake in 1415 and Girolamo Savonarola was hanged and then burned in 1498 for saying what Martin Luther now boldly said.

How did Luther survive criticizing the Catholic Church and its leaders? In part, the intellectual climate had changed. Individual conscience was becoming an accepted moral compass. In addition, the church was preoccupied with an emerging Turkish threat on the eastern edge of its empire. Finally, and perhaps most important, Luther used the new technology of his day, the printing press, to remarkable purpose. Trained in the old, oral tradition, he was the first master of the new, printed one.

> *"The law says, 'Do this!' and it is never done. Grace says, 'Believe in this one!' and forthwith everything is done."*
>
> —from *Theses for Heidelberg Disputation* (1518)

FURTHER READING

Fehlauer, Adolph. *The Life and Faith of Martin Luther*. Milwaukee, Wis.: Northwest Publications, 1981.

Grimm, Harold John. *The Reformation Era, 1500–1650*. New York: Macmillan, 1965.

Hillerbrand, Hans Joachim. *The World of the Reformation*. New York: Scribners, 1973.

Nohl, Frederick. *Martin Luther: Hero of Faith*. St. Louis, Mo.: Concordia, 1962.

Schwiebert, Ernest G. *Luther and His Times: The Reformation from a New Perspective*. St. Louis, Mo.: Concordia, 1950.

Spitz, Lewis William. *The Protestant Reformation, 1517–1559*. New York: Harper & Row, 1985.

Stepanek, Sally. *Martin Luther*. New York: Chelsea House, 1986.

Ignatius of Loyola

THE SOCIETY OF JESUS

Sometimes illness or accident disrupts a person's life enough to alter its course completely. Such was the case with Ignatius of Loyola. Born at the end of the 15th century, his greatest desire was to be a perfect knight and distinguish himself in battle. Instead, he devoted his life to the poor and founded the Roman Catholic religious order known as the Society of Jesus, or the Jesuits.

Ignatius was born Iñigo de Oñaz y Loyola, the 13th and youngest child of a Basque nobleman in northern Spain. As a teenager, Iñigo (he took the name Ignatius in his 30s) was adopted as a page by a wealthy and powerful nobleman. Court behavior and weaponry formed the poles of his education. His enthusiastic reading of popular tales of chivalry further shaped his ambition to be a knight.

As a young man, Iñigo distinguished himself at gambling, dueling, and romance, clashing with legal authorities more than once. With the death of his patron in 1517, he joined the service of a duke as a courtier. Three years later, defending the Spanish city of Pamplona against a French attack, Iñigo was struck by a cannonball, which wounded

Frustrated in his desire to become a knight, Ignatius of Loyola instead founded the religious order known as the Society of Jesus, or Jesuits.

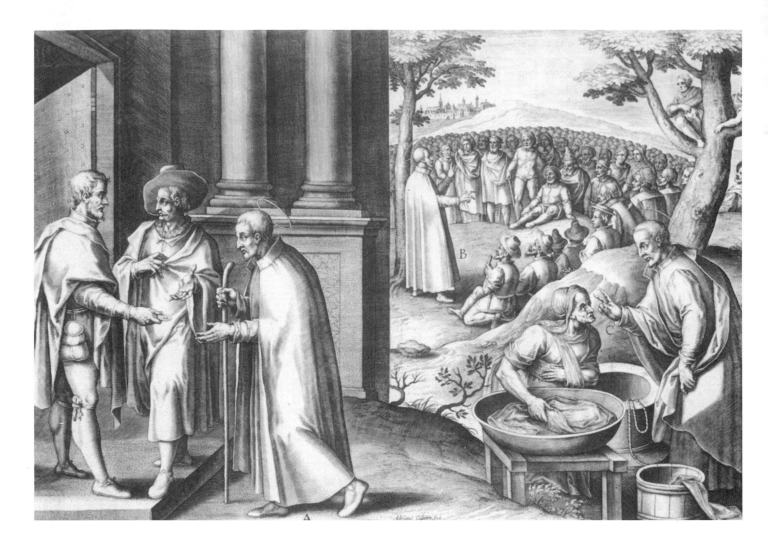

This medieval engraving depicts three scenes in the life of Ignatius Loyola—returning as a beggar to his homeland (left), preaching (center), and healing a woman (right). Throughout their history, the Jesuits have been famed for their learning, their missionary zeal, and their extreme devotion to the pope.

both legs. His initial treatment left him crippled, with one leg shorter than the other. But Iñigo still dreamed of being a knight, and he wanted to impress a certain woman, too. He endured excruciating surgical repair of his legs without the benefit of painkillers.

Iñigo was restricted to bed during his recovery. Unable to find any of the courtly novels he enjoyed, he began reading two books of mystical Christianity: Ludolph of Saxony's *Life of Our Lord Jesus Christ* and Jacobus de Voragine's *Golden Legend*. These inspiring stories of Christian life moved him deeply. Turning abruptly from his former life, he found himself, he said, "filled with desire to do great things in the service of God." At 23, he left his armor at an altar to the Blessed Virgin Mary, mother of Christ.

He gave away his clothes, his mule, and his weapons, and he set forth for Jerusalem. He adopted the begging bowl and rough sackcloth of a pilgrim. An outbreak of the plague prevented him from completing his travels, however, and he stopped for 10 months at a monastic retreat in Manresa, Spain. There, he subjected himself to a regime of fasting, penance, prayer, and study, immersing himself in the devotional handbook by Thomas à Kempis called *The Imitation of Christ*. Resolved to record any of his religious experiences that would be useful to others, he began writing his *Spiritual Exercises*.

The *Spiritual Exercises* are Loyola's account of and guide to what he called the "spiritual way." Based on visions that appeared to him when he decided to live for God, the exercises describe four stages, or weeks, of mystical development. They begin with a recognition of sin, move through an appreciation of Jesus' life and death, and end in meditations on Christ's resurrection. A final "Contemplation to Obtain Love" encourages the believer to dedicate his or her life to God. Completed some 16 years later, in 1541, the *Spiritual Exercises* were quickly recognized as original and valuable, earning the first of many papal commendations in 1548.

Loyola finally reached Jerusalem in 1523 but was forbidden by the pope to stay: bandits often kidnapped religious pilgrims and held them for ransom. Returning to Spain, Loyola furthered his studies in Barcelona, Alcalá, and Salamanca and taught his *Spiritual Exercises*. He rapidly drew followers—and earned the distrust of the Spanish Inquisition. This was a particularly harsh branch of the Roman Catholic Inquisition founded in the 13th century to root out heretical, or deviant and false, teachings. Loyola's ideas were new enough for the Spanish Inquisition to imprison him twice before he finally left Spain to study philosophy at the University of Paris.

In Paris, Loyola began attracting religiously minded men whom he persuaded to join him in doing works of Christian charity. Among the first was Francis Xavier, who would eventually carry Loyola's ideas to India and Japan.

By August 1534, Loyola and six other men had pledged their lives to help others and to journey to Jerusa-lem. War made their trip to Jerusalem impossible. The following year, Loyola and his men travelled to Venice, Italy, and were ordained as priests. There, after long discussion with his fellow priests, Loyola resolved to organize their small group on a permanent basis. A vision convinced him to name his brotherhood the Society of Jesus.

In Rome, Loyola and his fellows opened a shelter and bread line for the poor. Eventually, they helped some 3,000 homeless Romans, almost one-tenth of the population.

Although Loyola had no thought of founding a formal Catholic religious order when he gathered his society, in 1539 he laid plans for a new order before the pope. In keeping with the stricter requirements of an order, he and his followers swore to observe poverty, perpetual chastity, obedience to God, and allegiance to the pope. A year later, the Society of Jesus was formally instated. His peers elected Loyola leader, or general, of the order, and he began writing its constitution. New members of the order were tested at length before they were allowed to join. Men unfit for work were quickly dismissed.

Members of the Society of Jesus, popularly known as the Jesuits, traveled in pairs, initially in Italy, at first to preach but later to teach as well. They founded orphanages, helped the poor, and eventually established schools, opening the first in Sicily in 1548. The Society of Jesus would have its greatest impact through education,

Ignatius of Loyola

BORN

1491
Loyola, Spain

DIED

July 31, 1556
Rome, Italy

FORMAL EDUCATION

M.A., University of Paris

TRADITION

Christianity (Roman Catholic)

ACCOMPLISHMENTS

Founder of Society of Jesus and author of its constitution; author of *Confessions* (1522) and *Spiritual Exercises* (1541)

"What would happen if I acted as St. Francis and St. Dominic did?"

—from *Confessions* (1522)

bringing discipline and uniformity to what became an international effort.

By the time of Loyola's death in 1556, his followers numbered more than a thousand. Although Loyola originally intended to serve the poor, his educational efforts earned the Jesuits adherents among the wealthy and powerful as well. Loyola's men were granted freedoms forbidden to others, notably the right to perform religious plays. Their influence extended to European stagecraft as well as education. Their greatest successes came, however, through missionary work. Within a century of Loyola's death, Jesuits had founded missions from China and Southeast Asia to the Americas.

Loyola was canonized, or made a saint, in 1622. He was a contemporary of Martin Luther and John Calvin, whose criticisms of Roman Catholicism prompted the breakaway religious movement known as Protestantism. Loyola's inspired leadership helped revitalize the Catholic Church in the face of Protestant rejection. His *Spiritual Exercises* continue to appeal to students and religious seekers.

FURTHER READING

Brodrick, James. *The Origin of the Jesuits.* Chicago: Loyola University Press, 1986.

Mottola, Anthony. *The Spiritual Exercises of St. Ignatius.* New York: Image Books, 1964.

O'Malley, John. *The First Jesuits.* Cambridge: Harvard University Press, 1993.

Rahner, Hugo. *The Spirituality of St. Ignatius Loyola.* Chicago: Loyola University Press, 1953.

Van Dyke, Paul. *Ignatius Loyola: The Founder of the Jesuits.* Port Washington, N.Y.: Kennikat Press, 1926.

John Calvin

RELIGION AND THE NATION

John Calvin was a reserved, self-effacing man, but his ideas have shaped Western, and particularly American, culture as those of few thinkers have. Raised as a Roman Catholic, he converted to the new Protestant religion and left the stamp of his powerful mind on Protestantism forever.

John Calvin grew up in a small town in France. His mother died when he was young. John's father, wanting his son to enter the priesthood, sent him to study in Paris. There he studied logic and the works of Aristotle, until his father decided that John should study law. The elder Calvin may have thought the law offered a better career, or he may himself have already run afoul of the Roman Catholic Church.

In law school at Orléans, France, Calvin befriended a group of young men who were secretly sympathetic to the changes sweeping through the church. These changes had begun with the Renaissance movement known as Humanism. Humanism, or the New Learning, encouraged study of the classics of ancient Greece and Rome. Beginning in the mid-14th century, European scholars began to study and teach the works of classical philosophers, artists, historians, and writers. They believed that these works could be used to instruct modern Christians in ethics and train them in reasoning.

A pen-and-ink drawing of John Calvin by a student who attended one of his lectures. Through public lectures and several important books, Calvin helped shape the Protestant Reformation. His ideals of democracy, simplicity, and hard work were especially influential in northern Europe and the United States.

"If we ask why God takes pity on some, and why he lets go of the others, there is no other answer but that it pleases Him to do so."

—from *Institutes of the Christian Religion* (1538)

The great Humanist thinker Erasmus of Rotterdam had published his *Enchiridion (The Handbook of a Christian Soldier)* in 1503. In this work he argued that lay, or non-priestly, members could reform the Catholic Church. *Enchiridion* went through 26 editions, making Erasmus the Western Hemisphere's best-selling author of his time. The German priest Martin Luther, educated as a Humanist, openly challenged the Roman Catholic Church and sparked the Protestant Reformation.

Calvin began his career as a Humanist. Leaving Orléans for Paris, he earned his law degree shortly before his father's death in 1531. The next year he published his first book, at his own expense. Reflecting his interest in Humanism, it was a commentary on the Roman philosopher Seneca. Although it showcased his learning, it found few readers.

Sometime after this, Calvin experienced a religious conversion, or spiritual change. He compared his conversion to a horse that is finally tamed by its rider. Calvin was the horse; God was the rider. Calvin felt he had been lifted up from his worthless condition to do God's work.

For the next few years, Calvin was increasingly involved with the church reform movement—and sometimes in

John Calvin examines a religious text in his study in Geneva. The concept of predestination—that some people are destined from birth to be saved while others are damned—was Calvin's most original contribution to Protestant theology.

trouble as a consequence. Finally, in 1534 he was forced to flee France. Protestant rebels had plastered the major French cities with anti-Catholic posters. Authorities made hundreds of arrests and executed some 35 Protestants, including Calvin's brother.

Calvin escaped to Basel, Switzerland. There he began writing his *Institutes of the Christian Religion*. Initially intended to defend Protestantism to the king of France, the *Institutes* are the core of Calvin's ideas about both God and government.

Taking advantage of a rule allowing religious exiles to return if they disavowed their views within six months, Calvin went back to France. He planned to go to Strassburg, an imperial German city, when circumstances forced him to Geneva, Switzerland, instead. There God "thrust me into the fray," as he later said. Geneva had recently converted to Protestantism at the urging of Guillaume (William) Farel, a religious reformer. Farel persuaded Calvin to stay in Geneva to help build the "city of God," the New Jerusalem that Augustine of Hippo had written about more than a thousand years before.

Farel and Calvin designed a religious society spelled out in a constitution and enforced by threats of excommunication. Calvin also produced a summary of beliefs, the "Confession of Faith," which he and Farel asked the Genevans to swear to. Only those who swore to the Confession would be allowed to remain part of the church and the city. But within two years the citizens of Geneva rebelled: they elected a new government and exiled Calvin and Farel.

This time, Calvin reached Strassburg. Remaining there three years, he served as pastor of a Reform church of French refugees and gave public lectures on Christianity. He revised his *Institutes* and wrote two other books, a commentary on the Epistle to the Romans (a book in the Bible) and *A Short Treatise on the Lord's Supper*.

The Lord's Supper, called the Eucharist by Catholics, was one of the issues then dividing Protestants. From the Greek word for "thanksgiving," the Eucharist is a Christian ritual of sharing bread and wine in commemoration of Jesus' last meal. In Catholic belief, formally adopted in 1215, the bread and wine changed during the eucharistic ritual into the actual body and blood of Christ, although it still appeared to be bread and wine. Believers understood that because of this change, known as transubstantiation, the Eucharist reenacted Christ's suffering on the cross.

Protestants and Catholics viewed the role of sacred ritual differently, however. Whereas Protestants saw the Bible as the supreme source of God's wisdom, Roman Catholics saw both the Bible and Catholic ritual as equally important paths to God. The German reformer Martin Luther agreed with the Catholic Church on the issue of transubstantiation, but other Protestant reformers believed the bread and wine merely symbolized the body and blood of Christ.

Calvin took a middle position. He believed that Christ was present during the Eucharist meal but not in the bread and wine itself. Similarly, he argued that in Christ both man and God were present, yet distinct.

Calvin believed that God "bent down," as he put it, to become human. God speaks to humans only in ways that they can understand, he said, much as a parent uses simple language with a child. In this way, Calvin tried to free Christian belief from a literal reading of the Bible. He still believed that the Bible was the way to God, but he did not say it was the word of God.

Calvin also saw nature, including human nature, as an avenue to God, in that God has made himself visible in the world. This view of the world permitted, and even encouraged, scientific exploration in a way that earlier Christian dogma had not.

The human tragedy, in Calvin's view, was Adam's Fall. The Christian notion of original sin comes from the Bible. Genesis 3 describes how the first people, Adam and Eve, disobeyed God and ate the fruit from the Tree of Knowledge. For this, they—and all humankind—were banished from the idyllic Garden of Eden. "We have not been deprived of will," Calvin wrote,

BELIEVERS

John Calvin

BORN

July 10, 1509
Noyon, France

DIED

May 27, 1564
Geneva, Switzerland

FORMAL EDUCATION

M.A., University of Paris

TRADITION

Christianity (Protestant)

ACCOMPLISHMENTS

Major interpreter of Protestantism; his works include *Institutes of the Christian Religion* (1538), *Commentary on Romans* (1541), *A Short Treatise on the Lord's Supper* (1541), and *Farewell Address* (1564)

> *"Man stumbles, then, even as God ordained that he should, but he stumbles on account of his depravity."*
>
> —from *Institutes of the Christian Religion* (1538)

"but of healthy will." He believed that all humankind had been stained by original sin.

Like Luther and Augustine before him, Calvin believed that God's grace, or freely given mercy, provides the only way out of this fallen state. But Calvin added another element: predestination. He believed that people are so fully in God's hands that some are destined from birth to be saved and others are destined to be damned. Although Calvin recognized that people are capable of great goodness, he saw such goodness not as a way to earn God's grace but rather as a result of God's grace. God's chosen, Calvin thought, were marked by their righteous actions.

After returning to Geneva in 1541, Calvin spent the rest of his life there. Permanently denied Genevan citizenship and barred from voting or running for office, Calvin nevertheless transformed his adopted city. In the name of building an ideal Christian society, he improved the schools, founded the University of Geneva, and promoted a universal moral (and dress) code. Under his influence, Geneva became a model Protestant city and a center of Protestant missionary activity.

Calvin reformed church government, too. Traditional Catholic churches followed the pope's leadership. Calvin introduced democracy: his church leaders were elected by local church members. Calvin's Protestantism expanded because local churches could survive independently of a central church authority. Under Calvin, Protestantism grew into an international movement.

New forms of economic activity expanded along with Protestantism. Calvin played a role in what is known today as the market economy by taking steps to reverse the medieval Catholic ban on charging interest. This meant that people could in good conscience earn interest on money they lent out. Money itself—also known as capital, hence *capitalism*—could become a way to generate more wealth, in the way that land or labor was a source of wealth.

Many of Calvin's writings have political as well as religious importance. He defended taking action against tyrannical rulers and helped break down the system of so-called divine right, which claimed that kings and queens receive their right to rule from God. Calvin's nonliteral understanding of the Bible encouraged science and technology.

Calvin's ideas spread rapidly among the French Protestants, known as Huguenots, and also found a ready audience in Great Britain. In 1559 the Scottish Protestant reformer John Knox introduced Calvinism to Scotland, and the whole country converted. Five years later, very ill, Calvin detailed his suffering in his *Farewell Address* and died in Geneva.

In England, Calvin's philosophical heirs included the British general and statesman Oliver Cromwell, who, as ruler of England from 1653 to 1658, favored a national religion with Calvinist overtones. Ultimately disappointed by the Church of England's efforts to "purify" British Protestantism, England's Puritans would take Calvin's ideas to the New World. The Calvinist values of thrift, hard work, and sobriety were ideally suited to meet the challenges of the vigorous new country.

In the 19th century, Calvin's notion of predestination underlay such ideas as America's "manifest destiny" to expand across the continent and the "gospel of wealth," the idea that wealth was a sign of divine favor. The Presbyterian and Reformed Presbyterian churches grew out of Calvin's Protestantism.

FURTHER READING

McGrath, Alister E. *A Life of John Calvin: A Study in the Shaping of Western Culture*. London: Basil Blackwell, 1990.

Parker, T. H. L. *John Calvin: A Biography*. Philadelphia: Westminster Press, 1975.

Spitz, Lewis W. *The Protestant Reformation: 1517–1559*. New York: Harper & Row, 1985.

Stepanek, Sally. *John Calvin*. New York: Chelsea House, 1987.

Isaac Luria

REGATHERING THE SPARKS

orn in Jerusalem in 1534 and raised in Egypt, the businessman Isaac ben Solomon Luria emigrated at age 35 to Safed, in Palestine's Galilee, to be near the center of Jewish mystical study. In the two years of life remaining to him, he transformed Jewish mysticism.

As a young man in Egypt, Luria had built a reputation both as an outstanding student of Jewish law and as a minor poet. Sometime in his 20s, however, he secluded himself on an island in Egypt's Nile River and began to study Jewish mysticism.

Mysticism, from the Greek word meaning "[the eyes and mouth] closed," appears in all religions. It refers to the effort to reach direct, immediate communion or union with God or ultimate reality. This effort, often made through meditation, fasting, prayer, or other physical activities, such as dancing, is sometimes contrasted with Rationalism.

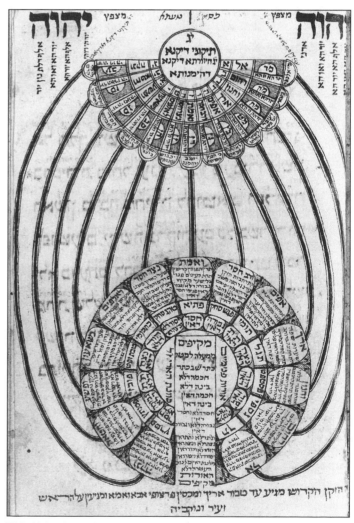

This Kabbalistic diagram depicts various aspects of God's mercy, such as sympathy, kindness, and forgiveness. These attributes are described in the 13 sections in the bottom circle.

A view of the city of Jerusalem from a Haggadah published in Amsterdam in 1712. Jews who had been exiled from or harassed in their native lands found comfort in Isaac Luria's teachings, which held that each Jew was still morally bound to God and to other Jews.

Rationalists approach God or ultimate reality through analysis and discussion. Rationalists try to understand reality by thinking, which depends on language; but a mystical experience characteristically escapes the attempt to describe or explain it.

A mystical tradition has existed in Judaism since its origins. It flowered during the Middle Ages, after the religiously tolerant Islamic Empire was defeated by Christians, and anti-Semitism began to threaten Jewish life.

The medieval Jewish study known as Kabbalah (tradition) arose in Europe in 11th-century France. Like Rationalists, Jewish mystics read the Bible both as a literal and a symbolic story. But while Rationalists analyze and try to interpret the symbols using logic, Kabbalistic mystics interpret them

using more mystical means, such as Gematria— interchanging words whose letters have the same numerical value when added.

Many mystical traditions stop short of defining God or ultimate reality. The Kabbalists described God simply as *En Sof* (without limit). The source of all existence, En Sof is approachable through 10 *sefiroth*, or levels, of divine reality. Kabbalists often depict the *sefiroth* as limbs of a tree, the Tree of Life. Each limb corresponds to one of God's divine qualities, such as *Hokhmah* (wisdom) or *Hesed* (mercy). All existence springs from these branches; they also represent the stages a mystic goes through on the path to divine understanding.

During its early days, the study of Kabbalah was restricted to an elite of married men over the age of 40. But beginning in 1421, Jews were expelled from most major European cities; in 1492 Spanish authorities gave Jews the option of converting to Christianity or leaving Spain entirely. In the face of this persecution, the inward-looking spirituality of mysticism attracted many Jews.

A number of Jewish exiles, among them the parents of Isaac Luria, settled in Palestine. The city of Safed in particular drew students of the Kabbalah. In 1570 Isaac Luria settled in Safed and quickly attracted a circle of followers. Although Luria never recorded his ideas, he created a revolutionary new model of Kabbalah.

Traditional religious philosophers had described the creation of the universe as an expansion of divine power. Luria taught instead that in the beginning, God contracted, or shrank, to make room for creation. In the space opened by this *tzimtzum*, or contraction, God created a set of sacred vessels or containers to hold the divine light of creation. Some vessels were too weak to contain the divine light; they broke, scattering the light. These scattered sparks constituted the material out of which God created the universe. The human task became *tikkun*, to regather the scattered sparks—to discover, kindle, and preserve the fragments of divine wisdom scattered through creation.

Luria's story transformed Jewish mysticism and thought. Every Jewish act could now be understood to have universal importance. Jewish law honors deeds that contribute to *tikkun*; unlawful deeds continue to disturb creation. At a time when Jews were being dispersed throughout Europe, Luria's story told Jews that they were still part of a cosmic community: each Jew's actions could help save or harm the universe.

Luria's 30 or more followers in Safed regarded him as a saintly man.

Like the Christian mystic Saint Francis, he was said to understand the language of the birds. His followers said that he could diagnose the spiritual condition of each soul he met and suggest specific spiritual remedies. Luria claimed to be able to find the unmarked graves of Galilean holy men and to have conversed with their spirits. (Pilgrims still visit these sites.)

Luria's interpretation of the meaning of Jewish life was preserved by his student Chaim Vital and others. His ideas spread rapidly throughout Europe and gave Jews hope that sustained them through times of severe religious persecution. Later forms of Jewish mysticism—including the heretical movement that developed around Sabbatai Zevi, a self-proclaimed messiah of the 17th century, and the Hasidic movement, centered around the Polish prophet Baal Shem Tov in the mid-18th century—grew out of Luria's teachings.

FURTHER READING

Ashlag, Yehuda. *An Entrance to the Tree of Life*. Edited by Philip S. Berg. Kew Gardens, N.Y.: Research Center of Kabalah, 1977.

Epstein, Perle. *Kabbalah: The Way of the Jewish Mystic*. Boston: Shambhala, 1988.

Fielding, Charles. *The Practical Qabalah*. York Beach, Maine: Samuel Weiser, 1989.

Jacobs, Louis. *Hasidic Thought*. New York: Behrman House, n.d.

Pick, Bernhard. *The Cabala: Its Influence on Judaism and Christianity*. Rising Sun, Md.: Sun Publications, 1993.

Wineman, Aryeh. *Beyond Appearances*. Philadelphia: Jewish Publication Society, 1988.

BELIEVERS

Isaac Luria

BORN

1534
Jerusalem, Palestine, Ottoman Empire

DIED

1572
Safed, Palestine, Syria (now Zefat, Israel)

TRADITION

Judaism

ACCOMPLISHMENTS

Chief interpreter and definer of Jewish mysticism and Kabbalistic studies; none of his writings survive, although his students memorized and later recorded his teachings

Anne Hutchinson

THE COVENANT OF GRACE

One of the first people to challenge New England's fledgling government was a middle-aged English woman named Anne Hutchinson. The Massachusetts Bay Colony was less than 20 years old when Hutchinson caused such an uproar that she was exiled from Massachusetts and excommunicated, or cast out, from the Church of England.

Anne Hutchinson grew up in the last days of the reign of Queen Elizabeth I. Her father, Francis Marbury, was an outspoken minister often in trouble with the Church of England (Anglican) leaders. Marbury openly criticized weak ministers; Anne Hutchinson would, too. Marbury taught Anne to read and reason. In 1605, when she was 14, her father moved the family from their rural village to London.

England's cities were ablaze with religious questions. Queen Elizabeth's father, Henry VIII, had rejected Catholicism and founded the Anglican Church in 1534. That year, the French theologian John Calvin had begun writing his influential *Institutes of the Christian Religion*. Calvin's radical Protestantism swept through the Church of England. The Calvinists, known as Puritans, wanted to strip their church of all its Roman Catholic elements, such as elaborate dress and ritual. Francis Marbury was deeply involved in this "purifying" movement. The family dinner table was the scene of intense religious and political discussions among Marbury and his colleagues. Anne listened in.

From her mother, Bridget Dryden Marbury, Anne learned medicine, midwifery, and the practical arts of sewing, cooking, and gardening. One of 13 children, she helped to deliver and raise the youngest ones. Anne married William Hutchinson, a wealthy merchant and friend from her childhood, a year after her father died in 1611.

Anne and William Hutchinson returned to their native village and began rearing the first of their 14 children. William's business flourished, while Anne managed the large household and offered medical care to her neighbors. She also continued to think about the religious discussions she had heard in London.

Lincolnshire, where the Hutchinsons lived, was a center of Nonconformist—that is, pro-Puritan—activity. Because their village had no preacher, the Hutchinsons regularly traveled 25 miles to Boston, England, to hear the Reverend John Cotton, a dynamic Nonconformist minister.

Six years after her marriage and return to Lincolnshire, Anne seems to have had some kind of spiritual crisis. Weathering her doubts and conflicts through fasting and prayer—she named the child born during that time Faith—

Anne Hutchinson was the first important female religious leader in the history of North America. This bronze statue of her and her daughter, in which Hutchinson holds a Bible, stands on the grounds of the Massachusetts State House in Boston.

she emerged with a unique spiritual gift. She could tell, she said, which ministers, such as Cotton, preached the gospel of Christ and which preached only the outer trappings of Christianity.

Hutchinson began holding meetings in her home to discuss Cotton's sermons and the Bible. She quickly gained followers of her own. She was not alone in this; other women preached in her part of England.

So might matters have remained had a different ruler sat on the English throne. But Charles I, crowned in 1625, was an incompetent economist and a religious tyrant. Under his rule, England's economy worsened, and leaders of the Church of England tried to silence Nonconformist thinkers, among them Puritan John Cotton. Some Puritans had left England even before Charles reached the throne; one group went to Holland in 1608 and another reached the American colonies in 1620. Reverend Cotton slipped out of the country, bound for Massachusetts, in 1633.

A model of the Augustus Saint-Gaudens statue entitled *The Puritan,* which stands in Springfield, Massachusetts. Anne Hutchinson broke with the Puritan religious authorities of her adopted homeland over the issues of predestination and direct inspiration from God.

"Better to be cast out of the Church than deny Christ."

—from court testimony (1637)

Anne Hutchinson persuaded her husband that they should follow Cotton to Boston, a settlement in the Massachusetts Bay Colony. She was 43, with a newborn baby.

Including its surrounding villages, Boston in 1634 was home to fewer than 4,000 people. Life there was much harsher than it had been in England, but the Hutchinsons settled in rapidly. As in England, William's business thrived; Anne managed a household in the center of town and practiced midwifery and the healing arts.

The Massachusetts Bay Colony operated as a theocracy; that is, its rulers were its religious leaders as well. Religion provided almost the sole focus for life in English Massachusetts. This would have been ideal for Anne, who was passionately interested in religion, except that her ideas differed from those of the authorities.

Anne Hutchinson believed in direct inspiration, the idea that God still spoke personally to men and women. Most Puritans considered direct inspiration a heresy, an unacceptable, false belief. They believed that only the Bible contained the word of God and that God did not speak directly to individuals any longer.

Anne's conflicts with Puritan views did not emerge immediately, however. A skilled healer, she attracted many people and began offering spiritual as well as medical care. Breaking with the Puritan idea, taken from John Calvin, that God chose, or "elected," only certain people for eternal salvation, she comforted all her friends and patients. "God is love and you are His dear child," she told them.

Eventually, as in England, Hutchinson began holding prayer meetings in her home. Initially offered to colonial women, who were forbidden to speak during official prayer meetings, they soon attracted men as well. Hutchinson's meetings were so well attended that overflow crowds gathered at her windows. Within two years of her arrival, she was intensely popular, more sought out "for counsell and advice than any minister," a minister noted.

The colony's governor, John Winthrop, complained that as a result of Hutchinson's meetings, "many families were neglected and much time lost." More to the point, by offering her own religious interpretations, Hutchinson was dividing the colony.

Hutchinson felt that many preachers were falling short of the colony's religious ideals. She preached a "covenant of grace," claiming that salvation was achieved through faith alone; much of the Massachusetts clergy, she claimed, had become too concerned with appearances, or "good works." She urged devout citizens to reject the false teachings of such preachers and seek direct communication with God.

All Massachusetts became caught up in the controversy. The theocracy became ensnared in theology. Hutchinson declared that only two preachers in the entire colony preached "grace, not works." She scandalized authorities by walking out on a sermon by a preacher who displeased her. And she further upset the colony's leaders and threatened the established order by holding meetings in her home in which she assumed the role of a preacher.

Church leaders labeled Hutchinson an antinomian, which means "anti-law," and treated her as a heretic. They called the first synod, or assembly, of Congregational churches in America solely to address the question of what to do about Anne Hutchinson. In a debate from which she, as a woman, was excluded, Hutchinson was declared "disorderly."

Her courtroom trial took place in November 1637 in Newtowne (now Cambridge), Massachusetts, across the river from her supporters in Boston. She had no lawyer. Repeatedly, she asked to know what charges had been brought against her. Governor Winthrop scolded her: "We do not mean to talk with one of your sex about this.... We are your judges, and not you ours." The court voted to banish her from the colony but allowed her to pass the winter in Roxbury, Massachusetts, near Boston, because her health by then was poor.

Fearful of riots on Hutchinson's behalf, the authorities confiscated all guns in the colony that winter. Anne Hutchinson had no visitors except clergymen intent on convincing her of her errors. They collected some 30 more of her theological errors and tried her again.

No pictures of Anne Hutchinson survive, but the few verbal portraits of her invariably mention both her fluent tongue and her haughty bearing. Hutchinson had alienated the colony's ministers and leaders at the very time her own political support was weakening. Her friend Harry Vane, the former governor, had returned to England after losing the election to John Winthrop. John Cotton would support her only so far; at her second trial he was asked to criticize her publicly and he did. Pressed to recant, or take back, her errors, Hutchinson complied at first, then balked. She was not only banished from the colony but excommunicated—cast out from the Puritan church.

The Reverend Hugh Peters summed up the colony's complaint: "You have stept out of your place. You have rather been a husband than a wife; and a preacher than a hearer; and a magistrate than a subject." Only Mary Dyer, who would later be hanged for her Quaker beliefs, offered the shaken Hutchinson an arm as she left the courtroom.

William Hutchinson moved the family to Rhode Island, then a haven for Massachusetts dissidents. But Boston's religious controversy raged on even in Anne Hutchinson's absence. A committee from Boston sought William out, insisting that he renounce his wife's views. He refused, saying, "I am more nearly tied to my wife than to the church and I look upon her as a dear saint and servant of God." Anne threw the committee out. In Boston, rumors surfaced that she was a witch.

When William died in 1642, Anne left Rhode Island, to be farther away from Massachusetts. With her children, other relatives, and friends, she settled in New York, then under religiously tolerant Dutch rule. Soon after, she and her youngest children were slain at home by Native Americans, casualties of a war between the Dutch and the Indians over land.

The first open dissenter to question the Massachusetts theocracy, Anne Hutchinson foreshadowed later American religious movements, such as Transcendentalism, whose members believed in personal avenues to the divine, and such social movements as feminism. In her day, she was the most powerful woman in the New World.

FURTHER READING

Crawford, Deborah. *Four Women in a Violent Time*. New York: Crown, 1970.

Delbanco, Andrew. *The Puritan Ordeal*. Cambridge: Harvard University Press, 1989.

Fradin, Dennis B. *Anne Hutchinson: Fighter for Religious Freedom*. Hillside, N.J.: Enslow, 1990.

IlgenFritz, Elizabeth. *Anne Hutchinson*. New York: Chelsea House, 1991.

Miller, Perry, and Thomas H. Johnson. *The Puritans*. Rev. ed. New York: Harper & Row, 1963.

Rugg, Winifred King. *Unafraid: A Life of Anne Hutchinson*. Cambridge, Mass.: Riverside Press, 1930.

Anne Hutchinson

BORN

July 17, 1591
Alford, Lincolnshire, England

DIED

1643
Pelham Bay, New York

TRADITION

Christianity (Protestant)

ACCOMPLISHMENTS

Challenged the Puritan orthodoxy in early America

William Penn

PACIFISM AND POLITICS

The Quaker leader William Penn was born in London, the son of an ambitious naval officer and his status-conscious wife. His early childhood took place against the dramatically changing English political scene. In 1649, when William was five years old, Oliver Cromwell's Puritan army overthrew and beheaded the English king Charles I. Although the Puritan era lasted less than a decade, the reserved and stern style of the Puritans—who favored a Christianity "purified" of costume and ritual—would color Penn's life.

William's father had every expectation that his son would follow him into the military. But the boy was pulled in a different direction. At age 11, William had a religious experience that showed him what he called "external glory." This episode convinced him that God was real and that men and women could commune with him. At this time, William also befriended a family of Quakers, a pacifist, mystical Christian sect. Their daughter, Guli Springett, would one day be his wife.

Some years later, William had another glimpse of Quakerism. Cromwell, who ruled England under the title of Lord Protector of the Realm, had given William Penn, Sr., land in Ireland. The family moved there after Penn suffered a military defeat. In Ireland, William heard the compelling Irish Quaker Thomas Loe preach. Loe's message that people could commune directly with God corresponded to William's own mystical experience of "external glory." He did not, however, join the Society of Friends, as the Quakers called themselves, for some years.

The Penns returned to London. England was once again ruled by a king—Charles II, the son of Charles I. For his efforts to restore the monarchy, William Penn, Sr., was knighted. He also won a seat in the House of Commons. Like other well-born young men of his time, William, Jr., went off to study at Oxford University.

Although he had not yet converted to Quakerism, William may have known that Quakers were often subjected to beatings at Oxford. Other religious conflicts were also played out at the university. The Royalists, loyal to the king and Church of England and its ceremonial, formal aspects, were on one side; the Puritans, who wanted a "pure" church and state, stripped of colorful, distracting, Catholic-inspired rituals and styles, were on the other. Neither cared for the Quakers. William would dress like a colorful Royalist, behave like a sober Puritan, but think like a mystical Quaker.

William's most influential teacher at Oxford was Dr. John Owen, whose unconventional writings on religion and

William Penn (center) meets with the Native American inhabitants of Pennsylvania in 1681 in order to sign a treaty of mutual coexistence. The Quakers were known for their tolerance.

science prompted university authorities to fire him. Owen's replacement, the more pliable Dr. Fell, made students attend church. William rebelled. He refused to worship in the Church of England and instead attended evening meetings at Dr. Owen's house. In 1661, Oxford authorities expelled William for attending these meetings.

Penn's father was furious but thought that he might bring William into line by sending him to France. William quickly adapted to French court life but did not play the stylish role completely. Late one night, a Frenchman who imagined William had insulted him challenged him to a duel. William overpowered him but refused, at the end, to take the Frenchman's life.

Equally important was William's meeting with Moise Amyraut, a distinguished French Protestant

theologian. Like the Quakers, Amyraut taught that the aim of religion was not obedience to, but communion with, God. William lived and studied with Amyraut until the older man died in 1664.

Penn returned to England and studied law; his father thought that legal studies would add polish to his intelligent, serious son. But his father pulled William out of school before he finished so that they could fight together in the British navy against the Dutch. Their earlier differences dissolved in the glory of William's father's victory over the Dutch.

A year later, managing his father's estate in Ireland, William tasted battle again. He even considered a military career, but it was not to be. A chance encounter led him to a Quaker meeting where Thomas Loe was speaking. Loe

"Force may make hypocrites but it can never make converts."

—from *No Cross, No Crown* (1669)

preached the Quaker message that God was love, not fear. For William, that was all he needed to hear. When Irish authorities came to round up Quakers, he named himself a Quaker, too, and was imprisoned with them.

The Quakers received their name because an English judge thought they "quaked" before the Lord. They preferred to call themselves the Society of Friends. The Friends were one of several new religions that arose during Oliver Cromwell's rule, when hard times coincided with a brief period of religious tolerance.

The founder of Quakerism, George Fox, was an uneducated weaver's son. Fox's personal experience of God led him to preach, or "publish," his gospel aloud. He taught that God's relationship to people was private and that churches were unnecessary: "God who made the world did not dwell in temples made with hands." Fox believed that humans have an "inner voice" or "inner light" that connects them to God and that all people are equal before him.

When Penn returned to London, he again fought with his father and moved in with a Quaker family. He began writing, and for the next 12 years devoted himself to organizing and popularizing the Quaker movement. George Fox and his wife, Margaret Askew Fell Fox, became his good friends. Along with the Foxes, Penn favored a central Quaker authority and defended the movement against those who wanted to break it into small groups. Penn's writings on tolerance influenced many other Christians struggling for religious freedom.

Penn's first book, *The Sandy Foundation Shaken* (1668), attacked such conventional Christian ideas as the Trinity—the three persons, or manifestations, of God (Father, Son, and Holy Ghost)—asserting that they conflicted with a more fundamental tenet of Christianity, monotheism, or

belief in one God. He also condemned the idea—known as Atonement—that Christ was sacrificed in order to achieve a reconciliation between God and humans. The bishop of London imprisoned Penn in the Tower of London for publishing the book. There, Penn wrote *No Cross, No Crown* (1669), which placed the authority of individual conscience above that of both religion and the state.

The bishop freed Penn in 1669, but a year later, the mayor of London jailed him and other Quakers for preaching in public. Serving as the group's lawyer, Penn persuaded the jury of the Quakers' right to preach. The mayor responded to the verdict by throwing the Quakers *and* the jurors into jail. Penn was freed only six days before his father's death.

Penn inherited his father's considerable wealth and traveled through northern Europe, meeting others who shared his liberal politics and mystical religion. In 1672 he returned to England and married Gulielma (Guli) Springett, his childhood friend.

Both to rid England of its outspoken Quaker and to repay a debt owed to Admiral Penn, Charles II gave William Penn land in the American colonies. Pennsylvania (the "forests of Penn"), as Charles called it, made Penn the largest private landowner in the world. Rather than exploit his land for personal gain, Penn embarked on what he called a "holy experiment." Quakers were under attack in both England and the American Colonies, and Penn offered his land to them to create a model democracy.

The new state would have no army. It would guarantee religious freedom, freedom of association, and free enterprise. Only two crimes would carry the death penalty: murder and treason. Penn willingly limited his own power in the community and wrote the world's first constitution that contained provisions for amendment. (Although individual Quakers denounced slavery, Penn himself owned slaves and the

The seal of the state of Pennsylvania, which was formed from lands granted to William Penn by King Charles II of England. Penn decided to use this land to conduct a "holy experiment" in which Quakers would come together to form a model democracy.

Society of Friends did not officially condemn slavery until 1758, half a century after Penn's death.)

Penn arrived in Pennsylvania in 1682 and began to work. He laid out Philadelphia, the first planned city in the colonies, and designed a home for his family, from which he supervised the organization of his new society. Pennsylvania differed from other parts of the colonies because it had no army at first and because women played a more active role than they did in the Puritan colonies such as Massachusetts. Under Penn's leadership, Pennsylvanians also agreed, uniquely among European settlers, to live with the Delaware Indians "in love as long as the sun [gives] light."

A border dispute with Lord Baltimore, owner of land south of Pennsylvania, erupted in 1684. Penn returned to England to press his border claim with the new king, James II, who was secretly sympathetic to Catholicism. For his friendship with the king and for advocating religious tolerance, Penn was labelled a Catholic himself. When the Glorious Revolution (1688–89) put James's daughter Mary and her husband, William, on the British throne, Penn narrowly escaped arrest as a traitor.

"It is a reproach to religion and government to suffer so much poverty and excess."

—from *Some Fruits of Solitude* (1693)

For two years he remained in hiding, probably in London, and he began writing again. In one of his books, *An Essay Toward the Present and Future Peace of Europe* (1693), Penn proposed a permanent international organization to resolve international differences, anticipating the United Nations by more than two centuries.

Penn's troubles began to mount. His assistant, Philip Ford, made fraudulent claims to Penn's money and his American land. Penn's wife died in February 1694, without ever reaching America. Penn married Hannah Callowhill that spring, but a month later his eldest son, Springett, died.

Penn returned to Pennsylvania with Hannah and their young children. He established one of the first public schools (for boys only) in North America. Under his guidance, Quakers—who were innovators in creating humane approaches to social problems, such as prison reform—also made many advances in medicine and the care for the mentally ill.

A second threat to Penn's lands forced him back to England in 1701. He left America a poor man and would never see Pennsylvania again. His son William had run through his money, and a malicious lawsuit against Penn by his former assistant Philip Ford, and later Ford's widow, eventually pushed Penn into debtors' prison.

Penn left jail in 1713 and settled his accounts with the Fords. While making arrangements to leave Pennsylvania to the British Crown and prepare what was left of his estate for his heirs,

he suffered a stroke. Unable to speak or write clearly, he lived for five more years while Hannah managed his affairs. William Penn died on July 30, 1718.

In Penn's day, there were two major beliefs in the Christian tradition about how human beings could find God. Catholics believed in a path to God through sacramental rites, such as Communion. Protestants believed that people could approach God through faith in his word as revealed in the Bible. William Penn offered a third way, open to everyone, through the Quaker teachings: an individual can receive understanding of divine truth through the "inner light" that God has placed in all humans to guide them peacefully into good works.

FURTHER READING

Bronner, Edwin B. *William Penn's Holy Experiment: The Founding of Pennsylvania, 1681–1701.* 1962. Reprint. Westport, Conn.: Greenwood Press, 1978.

Dolson, Hildegarde. *William Penn, Quaker Hero.* New York: Random House, 1961.

Fantel, Hans. *William Penn: Apostle of Dissent.* New York: Morrow, 1974.

Foster, Genevieve. *The World of William Penn.* New York: Scribners, 1973.

Hull, William Isaac. *William Penn: A Topical Biography.* New York: Oxford University Press, 1937.

Peare, Catherine Owens. *William Penn.* Ann Arbor: University of Michigan Press, 1956.

Penn, William. *No Cross, No Crown.* Revised, abridged, and edited by Ronald Selleck. Richmond, Ind.: Friends Unite, 1982.

Vining, Elizabeth G. *Penn.* Philadelphia: Philadelphia Yearly Meeting, Religious Society of Friends, 1986.

Wildes, Harry Emerson. *William Penn.* New York: Macmillan, 1974.

William Penn

BORN

October 14, 1644
London, England

DIED

July 30, 1718
Ruscombe, England

FORMAL EDUCATION

Attended Oxford University

TRADITION

Christianity (Quaker)

ACCOMPLISHMENTS

Founder of Pennsylvania; author of numerous works, including *The Sandy Foundation Shaken* (1668), *No Cross, No Crown* (1669), and *An Essay Toward the Present and Future Peace of Europe* (1693)

Cotton Mather

OF ANGELS AND WITCHES

Whatever his own talents and interests, Cotton Mather was born to be a minister. Religion was his family's business. One grandfather, Richard Mather, was a Puritan preacher who left England for the American colonies in 1635. (He later played a role in condemning the Puritan dissenter Anne Hutchinson.) His other grandfather, John Cotton, led Anne Hutchinson and other English Puritans to the New World. Cotton Mather's father, Increase Mather, was the outstanding American preacher of his time. He led Boston's North Church for more than 60 years; Cotton preached alongside him for 43 of those years.

Although Cotton Mather expressed interest in being a doctor, in his day the sons of strong-willed ministers did not stray from the paths their fathers had charted for them. An extremely gifted child, Cotton entered Harvard College, then a training ground for ministers, at age 12. Three years later, in 1678, he earned his bachelor's degree in theology and was ordained a minister in his father's church in 1685.

A participant in the Salem witch trials as well as a supporter of such scientific breakthroughs as the smallpox vaccine, Cotton Mather was a complex and powerful man in colonial Massachusetts.

But becoming a man of God was not easy for Cotton Mather. Struggling in the shadow of his prominent father, he developed a bad stutter and was plagued by religious doubts. Even as a child, he had prayed often, on the floor, with his "mouth in the dust," as he put it, for signs that God existed. As a teenager, he did feel "divine glory," but his certainty about God came and went.

Mather's longing for some experience of the invisible, spiritual world, coupled with his eagerness to please people in authority, drew him into one of early America's most dramatic events: the Salem witchcraft trials.

Witches or sorcerers, people who seem to have magical powers, have been thought to exist in all cultures throughout history. Witches often attract attention, particularly in times of trouble or upheaval, because their apparent powers can be blamed for outbreaks of disease, untimely deaths, mental illness, or crop failure, among other disasters.

In Europe between the years 1450 and 1700, some 100,000 people accused of being witches, mostly poor and older women, were killed. They were likely the scapegoats for a society disrupted by new ways of communicating, worshiping, and doing business. The outbreak of witchcraft accusations in Salem Village (present-day Danvers, Massachusetts) in 1692 was minor in comparison—only 20 accused witches died.

For Cotton Mather, as for many other men of his time, witches were real and fearsome. The world was populated, it was commonly believed, not only by the things and beings we can see and touch but also by invisible beings, such as angels and demons. Angels, he thought, were in God's service; demons tempted people to do evil; and the devil was evil itself. A demon in "possession" of a human could cause that person to become a witch. Mather was deeply curious about these invisible beings and devoted his first two books to them: *Memorable Providences* (1689) and *Wonders of the Invisible World* (1693).

Mather feared that the dawning of the new century in 1700 would provide an opening for the devil to do more damage. As a sometime authority on witches—he had earlier helped free a young Boston girl of demonic possession —Mather was drawn into the Salem witchcraft trials and was then dragged down by them. A man of naturally cautious and scientific outlook, he at first urged the Salem fathers to proceed slowly, so that innocent people would not suffer. But as the witch hysteria gripped Salem and spread rapidly through the village, Mather seems to have panicked, too. Relinquishing caution and the urge to protect the innocent, Mather pushed Salem officials to prosecute the witches quickly and bring the matter to a hasty close. This stance damaged Mather's reputation, allowing his enemies to paint him as an impulsive, superstitious, and even unscrupulous man.

Not long after the witch trials were concluded, Mather lost a son who had been born badly deformed, which seemed to be further proof of the devil's work, and Mather began to pray to angels. For the rest of his life, he would pray to angels during difficult times. Sometimes, he believed, angels visited him.

In his quest to understand invisible beings—which may strike people today as an unusual preoccupation—Mather was a man of his time. In other respects, however, he was one of the most advanced thinkers on the continent. The author of more than 300 books and pamphlets, he wrote about science, medicine, history, music, anthropology, and religion.

In 1713, Mather was made a Fellow of England's Royal Society for his

Cotton Mather

BORN

February 12, 1663
Boston, Massachusetts

DIED

February 13, 1728
Boston, Massachusetts

FORMAL EDUCATION

A.B., M.A., Harvard College

TRADITION

Christianity (Protestant)

ACCOMPLISHMENTS

Author of some 380 books on religious, historical, scientific, and moral subjects, including *Wonders of the Invisible World* (1693), *Magnalia Christi Americana* (1702), and *Curiosa America* (1712–24); contributor to scientific journals and early advocate of inoculation

FAIR DEALING
between Debtor *and* Creditor.

A very brief ESSAY
ᴜᴘᴏɴ
The CAUTION to be uſed,
about **coming** in to

DEBT,

And **getting** out of it.
Offered at BOSTON-Lecture;
5. d. XI. m. 17$\frac{15}{16}$.

By Cotton Mather, D.D.& F.R.S.

Stultus eſt Debitor, qui gaudens Pecunias acci-
pit, et Tempus quo reddere debeat, non attendit.
Gregor. in Moral.

BOSTON:
Printed by B. Green, for Samuel Gerriſh,
at his Shop over againſt the North ſide of
the Town-Houſe. 1716.

The title page of one of the more than 300 published books and pamphlets Cotton Mather wrote in his lifetime. The D.D. abbreviation that appears after his name refers to the doctor of divinity degree awarded to him by the University of Glasgow in 1710; F.R.S. indicates that he was a Fellow of the Royal Society.

contributions to science. A diligent observer of American natural history, he was also a scientific innovator. When a smallpox epidemic erupted in Boston in 1721, Mather was one of the few people to champion inoculation, which prevents an infectious disease in a person by giving him a mild dose of it, causing the body to develop resistance.

Mather wrote the first medical text in America, *The Angels of Bethesda,* in 1726, although it was not published until the 20th century. In it, he proposed that illnesses have psychological causes and that diseases are spread by germs. He also suggested that a vital essence was the basis of health. Neither spirit nor matter, this essence was, Mather believed, the connection between body and soul. A number of 19th-century medical treatments were based on the belief in such an essence.

Mather also wrote the first history of Christian New England, *Magnalia Christi Americana* (1702). In his *India Christiana* (1721), a history of Christian missionary efforts among Native Americans, Mather was one of the first to suggest that Indians had crossed to North America over a land bridge from Asia.

Mather published his sermons in such collections as *Words of Understanding* (1724). In *Religion of the Everlasting Maxims* (1715), he spelled out what he saw as the core beliefs of Protestantism: the Trinity (the Father, the Son, and the Holy Spirit), salvation through Christ alone, and the need to love one's neighbors out of love for Christ. He sought to promote union among Protestant churches and to oppose what he thought to be the growing heresy that God was only a Unity, not a Trinity. (The Unitarian Church would result from that split.)

The book that Mather intended to be his greatest contribution to religion, his *Biblia Americana,* was a colossal attempt to understand all history and

"When we are wading thro' some grievous and some tedious Trouble, we are prone to flatter our selves, Well, this is the last! If I were once to get well out of this Trouble, all would be well. 'Tis a great mistake. There will soon come another Trouble in the room of that which is gone. Men are Fools, if they think, their mirth can last any longer, than Sparks, or than the Cracking of thorns under a Pot."

—from *Words of Understanding* (1724)

the Bible. It never found a publisher. There were other disappointments in his life. Mather's first wife, Abigail, died in 1713 after a long illness. In the same two-week period, he watched his newborn twins, his young son, and a maidservant also die.

Mather survived his second wife as well. His third wife, a wealthy widow and more flamboyant than his other wives, fought noisily with Mather and once even left him. She also brought debts, for which Mather was held liable, into the marriage. Mather was twice passed over for the presidency of Harvard, a position that his father had held for 16 years. In 1724, he suffered an enormous loss: his beloved son Increase died at sea. Only 2 of Mather's 15 children survived to adulthood.

In his last years, perhaps recognizing that Puritanism was fading in influence on American life, Mather extended friendship to other Protestant groups, such as the Quakers. He also relaxed some rules of his own church to permit more people to join. By opening American Protestantism to new ideas, Mather contributed to the flowering of a 1730s religious movement known as the Great Awakening.

Toward the end of his life, Cotton Mather became convinced that the world was ending. A series of earthquakes, the most severe ever experienced in New England, began in October 1727, confirming his beliefs. He died that winter, five years to the day after his father's death.

Cotton Mather was a complicated man. Although he wrote and preached earnestly about the need to do good, he quarreled often and publicly with other men. His enormous gifts never quite brought him the acclaim for which he strove. He died nearly impoverished, feeling unappreciated and abused.

FURTHER READING

Beall, Ortho T., and Richard H. Shyrock. *Cotton Mather.* Baltimore, Md.: Johns Hopkins University Press, 1954.

Levin, David. *Cotton Mather: The Young Life of the Lord's Remembrancer.* Cambridge: Harvard University Press, 1978.

Shapiro, Laura. "The Lesson of Salem." *Newsweek,* August 31, 1992, 64-68.

Silverman, Kenneth. *The Life and Times of Cotton Mather.* New York: Harper & Row, 1984.

Wendell, Barrett. *Cotton Mather.* New York: Chelsea House, 1981.

Junípero Serra

SAINT PAUL OF THE NEW WORLD

Father Junípero Serra, a Spanish Franciscan monk, arrived in Mexico City in 1749. To get there, he had crossed three seas and had walked 250 miles inland from the coast. This was only the first of many journeys that he would undertake to convert the people of the New World to Catholicism.

While the largely Protestant communities of North America's Atlantic seaboard were declaring their independence from England, Spain was still actively colonizing the continent's western coast. Serra was only one of some 4,000 Catholic missionaries, but his name is forever linked to the history of California.

The son of farmers and occasional quarry workers, Miguel Serra (he took the name Junípero when he became a priest) grew up in tiny Petra, on the island of Majorca. He was drawn into religious life by his own high intelligence; entering the clergy was the best way for a bright boy to get an education. Serra joined the Franciscan order, founded by the 12th-century monk Saint Francis. He was ordained a priest in 1738.

Serra earned a doctorate in theology and taught philosophy for a number of years, rising in the hierarchy of the Roman Catholic Church. He also gained a reputation as a brilliant speaker. In his 30s, he became caught up in a revival of Franciscan missionary activity, and he asked to serve in Spain's colonial empire. When word came that he was being posted to Mexico, Serra quickly boarded a ship. Fearing that his parents and younger sister Juanita would beg him to stay, he notified them by letter of his plans only after he had left.

In 1749, two centuries after its initial conquest by Spain, Mexico stretched from what is now Guatemala to Santa Fe, in present-day New Mexico. It was home to some 6 million people, most of them Native Americans and *mestizos*, people of mixed European and Native American ancestry. By Serra's day, Mexico was divided into nine provinces. He would add a tenth: present-day California.

Quoting the biblical prophet Isaiah—"Here am I! Send me."—Serra first volunteered to work among the Pame Indians of present-day Sierra Gorda, Mexico. His biographer, a fellow monk and friend named Francisco Palou, wrote that Serra made a point of learning the Pame language and taught Christianity and its prayers in that tongue. Taking advantage of Catholicism's theatrical possibilities, Serra involved the entire Pame community in the drama of Easter Week. At other times, he paraded an illuminated statue of Saint Mary through the village at night. Serra also introduced farming, the care and raising of animals, building crafts, and business skills

Father Junípero Serra believed that serving as a missionary was the highest service a person could render to God.

Now president of the five Sierra Gorda missions, Serra made a name for himself at age 45 as a dramatic public preacher in Mexico City. To make vivid Jesus' suffering on the cross, he struck his chest with a stone while preaching, beat himself with chains, and sometimes burned his flesh.

Serra preached throughout Mexico, logging some 5,000 miles over the next eight years. Then, in the late 1760s, two circumstances propelled him north to California. First, the Spanish government asked Franciscan missionaries to replace the Jesuits, whose growing influence in the countries of Europe made them less obedient to Spanish rule. Second, Russian explorers threatened to claim Upper California before Spanish explorers could.

Serra was named head of the Franciscan order sent to Upper California. The expedition's military leader, Don José de Galvez, divided the party into overland and seagoing parties. Despite a leg injury dating from his first walk to Mexico City 20 years earlier, the 56-year-old Serra went overland. Palou wrote that the first Spanish party astonished the Native Americans who saw them: because the Spaniards had no women among them, the California Indians concluded that they had been born of horses.

Serra established his first mission at San Diego in July 1769. From there he surveyed the rest of the territory, devising a network of missions, ports, and *presidios* (military bases) for the region. One of his first tasks was to establish laws for the new colony. Serra's *Reglamento Echeveste,* completed in July 1773, became the basis of future California law. Another key task was to establish a supply network to bring goods, people, and animals to and from California. Serra achieved this by the close of 1773.

Serra himself settled at a mission in present-day Carmel, California. Conflicts with his military counterpart, General Fages, arose almost immedi-

to his new parishioners. The fact that he labored alongside the Pame was also noted—a priest who worked with his hands must have been unusual.

Nine years after arriving among the Pame, Serra was recalled to Mexico City for larger tasks. As he left them, he smuggled out their statue of Cachum, Mother of the Sun, whom they had worshiped before Jesus.

A typical Spanish mission in California. Serra himself founded nine such missions along the California coast, from San Diego to Monterey.

ately. Fages saw in Serra a dreamer whose best use was to say mass; Serra saw in Fages a greedy thug and rapist. Serra finally sailed back to Mexico City to speak with the Spanish viceroy, or governor, about Fages.

Serra had a powerful organizational mind and made his case clearly before the viceroy: mistreatment of the Indians, fraud, and rape would destroy the missions. The viceroy relieved Fages of his post and offered Serra an administrative job. Serra refused the job, preferring to return to his Carmel mission. In what may have been the high point of his experience in Upper California, Serra returned to find abundant food and optimism at the mission.

Serra recognized, however, that his Native American converts, now numbering in the hundreds, were primarily attracted by the offer of food and clothing. "Love God, Father!" they would call to him. "Hail Jesus! Do you have any tobacco?" Nevertheless, Serra continued to build his network of

missions along the coast, with a distance of three days' travel between them.

Indians to the south, grasping that the missionaries meant to replace their native religion with Christianity, attacked the San Diego mission and the military compound. Several Franciscans were killed and the buildings left in ruins. "Now the land has been watered," Serra said when he heard: the New World had its first martyrs for Christ. But he counseled mercy for the Indian attackers: "When the missionary is alive, let the soldiers...watch over him, like the pupils of God's very eyes.... But after the missionary has been killed, what can be gained by campaign?... As to the murderer, let him live, in order that he should be saved."

Serra required that his Indian converts accept Christianity voluntarily, and that, once converted, they live at the mission. Indians who returned to their traditional homes were sought out and punished. Like the monks at the monastery, the Indians lived by the sequence of bells marking the prayer and activity periods of the day.

Serra's mission system was perhaps America's most thorough theocracy, or government by religious leadership. But it was short-lived. The viceroy decided that Upper California should be settled not only by Franciscan brothers, but by Spanish laymen, women, and children. The first such town was present-day San Jose, founded in 1777. Four years later, Los Angeles was also founded as a civil settlement.

The shift away from the missions to towns signaled the decline of Serra's power. Increasingly challenged by the civil governor, Serra blessed his last mission, San Buenaventura, in 1782. That same year General Fages, who had plagued Serra as a military leader, assumed leadership of Upper and Lower California. Two years later, Serra died while touring his missions.

Under Serra's leadership, thousands of Indians converted to Christianity.

"The day came [the founding of the mission at Carmel]… we all made our way to a gigantic cross which was all in readiness and lying on the ground. With everyone lending a hand we set it in an upright position. I sang the prayers for its blessing…and thus, after raising aloft the standard of the King of Heaven, we unfurled the flag of our Catholic Monarch likewise. As we raised each one of them, we shouted at the top of our voices: 'Long live the Faith! Long live the King!' All the time the bells were ringing and our rifles were being fired, and from the boat came the thunder of big guns."

—from Serra's journal (about 1771)

Junípero Serra

BORN

November 24, 1713
Petra, Majorca, Spain

DIED

August 28, 1784
San Carlos Mission, California

FORMAL EDUCATION

Doctorate, the Royal and Pontifical University of Palma, Spain

TRADITION

Christianity (Roman Catholic)

ACCOMPLISHMENTS

Founded nine missions in California; beatified by Pope John Paul II in 1988

Although his monastic republic may have provided the native Californians with a kind of stability, it came at a high price: Indian labor, usually forced, maintained the missions. As the local leader of the Roman Catholic Church, Serra oversaw harsh punishments for those natives who broke Christian rules. Finally, infectious diseases and crowded living quarters created fatal conditions; huge numbers of Indians died under mission rule.

In 1988, when Pope John Paul II beatified Junípero Serra, identifying him as worthy of special honor, the Cahuilla tribe of Native Americans protested vehemently. They argued that Serra was among those who had enslaved Native Americans in California.

California remained part of the Spanish Empire until 1850, when it joined the United States. Earthquakes had destroyed most of Serra's mission buildings earlier, in 1812. Today, in recognition of their historical and architectural interest, many missions have been restored.

FURTHER READING

Dolan, Sean. *Junípero Serra*. New York: Chelsea House, 1991.

Englebert, Omer. *The Last of the Conquistadors: Junípero Serra, 1713–1784*. Westport, Conn.: Greenwood, 1974.

Engstrand, Iris H. *Serra's San Diego: Father Junípero Serra and California's Beginnings*. San Diego, Calif.: San Diego Historical Society, 1982.

Helen, Mary. *Wait for Me: The Life of Junípero Serra*. Boston: St. Paul Books, 1988.

Martin, Teri. *Junípero Serra: God's Pioneer*. Mahwah, N.J.: Paulist Press, 1990.

Serra, Junípero. *Writings*. Edited by Antonine Tibesar. Washington, D.C.: Academy of American Franciscan History, 1955.

Weber, Francis J. *The Life and Times of Fray Junípero Serra*. San Luis Obispo, Calif.: EZ Nature, 1989.

Wise, Winifred E. *Fray Junípero Serra and the California Conquest*. New York: Scribners, 1967.

Ann Lee

"A WOMAN CLOTHED WITH THE SUN"

Since the 1st century C.E., Christians have awaited the return, or Second Coming, of Christ. In the late 18th century, a small band of believers in England became convinced that Christ had returned to earth in their time—as a woman.

The "female Christ," as she was called, was a short, stout woman with fair skin, light chestnut hair, and penetrating blue eyes. Ann Lee crossed the Atlantic with a small company of believers and planted the Shaker religion in the American wilderness. Her followers willingly adopted her regimen of hard work, ecstatic worship, and abstinence from sex.

Ann was the second of eight children born to John Lees, a blacksmith, and his wife in the grimy industrial city of Manchester, England. Remembered by others as a serious child, Ann claimed to have experienced visions of God or supernatural beings at an early age.

Family life was crushingly close, with the bathroom and bedroom more public than private rooms. Like many Manchester children of her time, Ann worked in a textile factory for six days a week, 12 hours a day. She never learned to read or write. Her mother died when Ann was still young, and she then helped raise her brothers and sisters.

Ann Lees found relief from the pressures of everyday life in religion. Although baptized as an Anglican (a member of the Church of England), she began attending meetings led by a Quaker prophet, Jane Wardley, and her tailor husband, James. "Mother Jane," as Wardley was known, preached in the streets because women were forbidden in the pulpits. She proclaimed the imminent end of the world and Christ's return as a woman. Her services included public confession of sins and religious dancing, so her followers were called Shaking Quakers. Ann began to unburden her soul in open confession and became a Wardley disciple.

When Ann Lees was 26 years old, her father arranged for her to marry Abraham Stanley, a blacksmith, in an Anglican church. Ann does not appear to have wanted the marriage, and she kept her own name, shortening it to Lee. In rapid order, Lee and Stanley had four children. Three died at birth; the fourth died at the age of six.

These losses caused Lee immeasurable grief. Convinced that her children's deaths resulted from her own sins, Lee wept, fasted, and prayed to God to be delivered from sin. According to a history of the Shakers written in 1823, Ann shook the bed so fiercely at times that Stanley was "glad to leave it." Mother Jane advised Lee: "James and I lodge together but we do not touch each other any more than two babes. You may return and do likewise."

From that point on, the Shaker history recounts, Lee avoided Stanley's bed "as if it had been made of embers." He fought her over this, even asking the local ministers to help restore his wife to him. Their arguments left Lee unmoved, however. Her sexual life was over. Stanley soon became a Shaker, Ann's first convert.

Soon after, Lee converted her father, brother, and other relatives to Shakerism. Local authorities began to find her public preaching a nuisance and chased her from the streets. They disrupted Shaker meetings in her home and imprisoned her and other Shakers.

While in jail in 1770, at the age of 34, Lee experienced a vision of Adam and Eve's disobedience in the Garden of Eden and their banishment from it. Sex, she resolved, was the basis of

human evil. She returned to preaching with renewed force, even disrupting services in established churches, for which she was jailed again.

Three years later, imprisoned in an insane asylum, Lee had another important vision. "A light shone on her," a follower later wrote, "and the Lord Jesus stood before her in the cell and became one with her in form and spirit." Ann Lee, the former mill worker, became "Ann the Word." Her followers saw her as "the woman clothed with the sun," promised in Revelation, the final book of the Christian New Testament. The Wardleys passed the leadership of the Shaking Quakers to the new Mother, Ann Lee.

But not everyone in Manchester warmed to Ann Lee and the Shakers.

Meetings of the Quaker sect called Shakers were known for the vigorous dancing that was part of their religious worship. Although men and women were often separated within a Shaker village, they regarded each other as equals and shared decision-making power.

Mother Ann Lee is buried in the present-day town of Watervliet, New York, six miles north of Albany. After establishing her Shaker community there, Ann Lee spread her ideas throughout New England and attracted many converts with her powerful public preaching.

Many were angered when their families broke up after a member joined the Shakers. Manchester authorities judged Lee to be a dangerous nuisance, and a mob attacked her and four other Shakers with stones. Inspired by the promise of religious freedom in America and guided by a vision, Ann Lee decided to emigrate.

Within the year, Ann Lee and eight Shakers—including Lee's husband, her brother William, and businessman John Hocknell—left England for the American colonies. Without her leadership, the English Shaker movement withered.

Hocknell booked cheap passage for the Shakers on a dilapidated ship. During the crossing a plank worked itself loose and water flooded the boat. "The captain turned pale as a corpse," wrote a Shaker chronicler, but Mother Ann reassured him: "Be of good cheer. There shall not a hair of our heads perish.... I just now saw two bright angels of God standing by the mast." Mother Ann and the Shakers worked alongside the crew to plug the leak, and a large wave smacked the loose plank back into position.

The little band arrived in New York City on August 6, 1774. They walked the quiet town, in those days so green and unlike Manchester. Mother Ann encountered a woman seated outside a house and told her, "I am commissioned of the Almighty God to preach the everlasting gospel to America, and an Angel commanded me to come to this house, and to make a home for me and my people." The woman took them in. Lee worked as her maid, and Stanley worked in her husband's smithy. The other Shakers found jobs and lodgings nearby.

Abraham Stanley fell ill that winter, and Ann quit work to nurse him. When he recovered, he decided that he had had enough of the Shakers. He left Ann and her followers for a more conventional life. Lee spent the rest of the winter impoverished and alone.

Meanwhile, John Hocknell had found land near Albany, New York, for a Shaker community. In the spring of 1776 the Shakers left New York City for Niskeyuna ("where the water flows"), as the native Mahicans called the valley that Hocknell purchased. The Indians taught the Shakers how to store seeds, dry herbs, and make baskets—arts at which they would later excel. Along with faith in God, Lee preached industry and economy.

Mother Ann directed her group to stock up on food because she antici- pated great numbers of American converts. Apart from one neighbor, though, the Shakers gained no converts until 1779. That summer, a large, quarrelsome Baptist revival meeting took place in nearby New Lebanon, New York, and two disillusioned Baptists happened upon the Shakers at Niskeyuna.

Traditional Christians believe that at the end of the world, all humankind will be judged, and at this Last Judgment, some people will be saved for eternal life. Ann Lee believed salvation was more immediate. By openly confessing their sins, she taught, men and women were personally saved and spiritually resurrected. That was how the "world"—that is, "worldliness," or being attached to material things and pleasures—would end. Moved by Mother Ann's preaching, the two Baptists brought a pastor, Joseph Meacham, into the Shaker community with them. Lee converted all three and later named Meacham her successor as the leader of the Shakers.

On May 10, 1780, Mother Ann conducted her first public preaching in the United States. An eclipse of the sun that day enhanced her powers in local reports. By summer's end, so many people filled Niskeyuna that Lee and the English Shakers often slept on the floor.

Although Lee's public testimony was riveting, her most effective method of converting others seems to have been personal contact. One woman reported, "As I sat by [her] side, one of her hands, while in motion, frequently touched my arm; and at every touch of her hand, I instantly felt the power of God run through my whole body."

Besides preaching, Shaker worship included plentiful and strenuous dancing. An account of early Shaker worship describes the dancers "springing from the house floor...moving about as thick as they can crowd [men and women in separate rooms].... They sometimes clap hands and leap so as to strike the joists above their heads." Shakers usually worshiped in this way every night.

As Lee's reputation grew, so did attention from civic authorities. Mistaken for British spies, several Shakers, including Lee, were arrested and jailed in the summer of 1780. Complicating matters, they refused on religious grounds to swear allegiance to the United States. Finally, a Shaker elder prevailed upon the governor of New York to free them.

Invited to spread her teachings through New England, Lee, her brother William, and a handful of Shakers set out on a missionary trip. In 1781, they established a foothold in Harvard, Massachusetts. The next year, traveling through Connecticut, Rhode Island, and Massachusetts, they spread their message and laid the foundation for later Shaker communities in New England.

Ann Lee's message represented salvation or threat, depending on the listener. To the established order, she stood as rebuker. Rejecting the traditional trappings of Christian religion—clergy, liturgy, and sacraments—she stripped religion to its core of belief. For her, that core was faith in God and freedom from worldliness. In consequence, Lee condemned marriage, sex, government, and war.

In place of government and traditional Christianity, Lee offered radical alternatives: communal ownership of property, celibacy, and equality of the sexes, including equal access to preaching. Teaching that God is both male and female, Lee railed against the idea that women were inferior to men.

Although men and women had distinct and separate jobs in Shaker villages, women conducted worship services and had an equal voice in village decisions.

The Shakers were often attacked during their mission to New England. Once, a crowd of men dragged Mother Ann away in a wagon, tearing her clothes off to discover if she were a man or a woman. In September 1783, the Shakers were driven back to Niskeyuna.

A year later, physically weakened and mourning the death of her brother William, Mother Ann Lee died. Through the efforts of her disciples, Shaker communities spread as far as Indiana and Florida. While maintaining Lee's strictures to be "in the world but not of the world," they successfully adapted to life in the United States. Shakers made a name for themselves as farmers, artisans, businesspeople, and inventors. At its height, the Shaker movement numbered some 6,000 members. Lee's ideas, however, reached beyond this community. Her stance on pacifism later attracted the attention of the Russian author Leo Tolstoy, who in turn inspired Mohandas Gandhi and others. With eight members, the last surviving Shaker community is located in New Gloucester, Maine.

FURTHER READING

Campion, Nardi Reeder. *Mother Ann Lee: Morning Star of the Shakers*. Hanover, N.H.: University Press of New England, 1990.

Morse, Flo. *The Shakers and the World's People*. Hanover, N.H.: University Press of New England, 1987.

Stein, Stephen J. *The Shaker Experience in America: A History of the United Society of Believers*. New Haven: Yale University Press, 1992.

Yolen, Jane. *Simple Gifts: The Story of the Shakers*. New York: Viking, 1976.

BELIEVERS

Ann Lee

BORN

February 29, 1736
Manchester, England

DIED

September 8, 1784
Watervliet, New York

TRADITION

Christianity (Protestant)

ACCOMPLISHMENT

Founder of the Shaker religion in America

Richard Allen

"TO BUILD EACH OTHER UP"

One Sunday in November 1787, a young African-American preacher and two of his friends eagerly took seats in the new addition to St. George's Methodist Episcopal Church in Philadelphia. Almost instantly, a church trustee pulled them from their pews and ordered them to leave. Although black church members had contributed to the new addition, they were expected to continue to stand in a section of the old building, segregated from the whites. The resulting uproar disrupted the church service and propelled that preacher, Richard Allen, into the forefront of African-American religious life.

Born a slave in Philadelphia in 1760, Allen was sold with his family to a farmer in Delaware when he was seven years old. Ten years later, his master sold Allen's mother and two siblings. Allen would never see them again. Soon after, he attended a secret, outlawed meeting of black Methodists, where he experienced a religious conversion so powerful that

In 1799, Richard Allen became the first African American ordained as a Methodist minister.

> *"If you love your children, if you love your country…clear your hands from slaves; burden not your children or your country with them."*

—from *An Address to Those Who Keep Slaves and Approve the Practice* (1795)

Richard Allen

BORN

February 14, 1760
Philadelphia, Pennsylvania

DIED

March 26, 1831
Philadelphia, Pennsylvania

TRADITION

Christianity (Protestant)

ACCOMPLISHMENTS

First black ordained as a Methodist minister (1799); founder of the African Methodist Episcopal Church and served as its bishop (1816–31)

he was moved to convert his brother and a sister to Methodism as well.

Allen's master gave his slaves time off for worship, and later, he also opened his house to traveling preachers known as circuit riders. One of these circuit riders, Freeborn Garrettson, was a former slave trader. Garrettson preached so persuasively against slavery that Allen's master offered to let Allen and his siblings purchase their freedom.

In three years Allen was a free man. Feeling that he had been "called," he said, he began preaching. He was extremely popular, and officials at America's premier Methodist church, St. George's in Philadelphia, invited him to preach there. As Allen later wrote, "My labor was much blessed." He attracted great numbers of blacks to St. George's. But the white leaders of the church, reflecting the prejudices of the time, separated blacks from whites during services.

The founder of Methodism, John Wesley, had been an outspoken antislavery advocate. He preached that all men and women, whatever their color, stood in need of God's grace. Blacks and whites worshiped together in early American Methodist meetings, but as the religion spread through America, it became more conservative and lost its earlier racial openness.

Even before his scuffle in St. George's new addition, Allen and other African Americans had proposed to form a separate black Methodist church. To do this, they needed the approval of St. George's elder, or church official, who had the authority over all the Methodist churches in Philadelphia. When both the elder and his successor rejected the idea of a black church, Allen helped found the Free African Society. This was a charitable organization devoted to helping the poor and sick. It was not a formal church, though it did host weddings.

As it grew, the Free African Society began to drift toward Quakerism, which offered an informal, personal style of worship that did away with the need for ministers. Allen did not favor that trend; he still believed in Methodism. In addition to faith, repentance, and the need for salvation, John Wesley's religion—called Methodism because of its strict discipline—stressed education, hard work, and clean living. Allen found these ideas valuable, particularly for former slaves. He also found Methodism's ecstatic, demonstrative form of worship more congenial than that of any other Christian denomination. In 1793, he offered land of his own as a building site for a black Methodist church.

Construction of Allen's church was delayed, however, by a devastating outbreak of yellow fever (a mosquito-borne infection) in Philadelphia. Allen and a fellow minister, Absalom Jones, the first black Episcopal (Church of England) priest in the United States, devoted themselves to containing the

"This plain and simple gospel [Methodism] suits best for any people; the unlearned can understand, and the learned are sure to understand, and the reason that the Methodists [are] so successful [in] the awakening and conversion of the colored people, [is their] plain doctrine and good discipline."

—from *The Life Experience and Gospel Labors of the Right Reverend Richard Allen*

disease and caring for its victims. Allen's heroism may have impressed St. George's elders because they finally approved his church.

The first black church in the United States was a converted blacksmith's shop that the congregation moved onto Allen's land. The Bethel African Methodist Episcopal (AME) Church, as Allen's church was formally named, held its first service on July 29, 1794. It had 20 members, all of whom were black. The goal of the church, wrote Allen, was "to build each other up." Within two years, the church grew to 120 members.

Allen began to write pamphlets expressing his views about the important issues of the day. His *Address to Those Who Keep Slaves and Approve the Practice* traced the destructive course of slavery. He admonished white Americans to "clear your hands from slaves; burden not your children or your country with them." Another pamphlet, *To the People of Color*, commanded more fortunate blacks to help those in need. Allen believed that free blacks had special debts to other blacks and to society at large. A third Allen pamphlet, *A Short Address to the Friends of Him Who Hath No Helper*, thanked those white Americans, such as Philadelphia physician Benjamin Rush, who had aided black Americans.

In 1799 Allen was ordained a Methodist minister, another first for a black American. The next year he married a free black woman and former slave. The first of their six children was born the following year. Allen was also a successful businessman. He ran a prosperous chimney-sweep business and later expanded into shoemaking as well.

Allen's domestic and professional standing did not protect him completely from the abuses experienced by most free blacks. In 1804, a slave trader seized him at home and dragged him to jail as a runaway. Only his public

reputation as a man of good works saved him. His anger at the slave system aroused, Allen began sheltering runaway slaves and urged his congregation to do so as well.

Periodically, Allen had to deal with attempts by the leaders of St. George's Church, who were made uneasy by an independent black church, to undermine or take over his Bethel Church. Bethel was not finally free of St. George's influence until 1816, when Allen rescued it from the auction block for more than $10,000. That spring, the African Methodist Episcopal Church held its first organizational conference, to institute a separate branch of Methodism, and named Allen its first bishop.

But racial problems, never far away, loomed again the next year. A group of whites organized the African Colonization Society (ACS) with the aim of sending free American blacks to Africa. Such prestigious leaders as Kentucky senator Henry Clay, President James Madison, and future President Andrew Jackson belonged to the ACS. Even former President Thomas Jefferson proposed that "the ocean divide the white man from the man of color." Allen devoted the rest of his life to fighting the ACS.

Richard Allen and the AME leadership considered the ACS an effort to exile black leaders from the United States. It was an outrage, he charged, and removed the hope of freedom from enslaved blacks by taking free black men and women out of America. Blacks were among the first settlers of America, Allen noted; the country belonged to them, too. He swore to defy any effort to exile him and in January 1817 organized a meeting to oppose the ACS. Three thousand people attended.

The African Methodist Episcopal Church formed the backbone of the anti-ACS movement. The AME expanded throughout the United

In 1845, the congregation of the Bethel Church in Baltimore gathers for the presentation of a gold snuffbox to the white pastor of another church. Richard Allen's efforts to establish the African Methodist Episcopal Church helped spur the development of other black churches throughout the United States.

States, particularly in New York, Ohio, and the New England states. In 1823, at the request of the Haitian government, the AME began sending missionaries to Haiti, an island nation in the Caribbean with a predominantly black population.

In 1827, invoking an old law, Ohio began requiring its black citizens, many of them AME members, to post bonds of $500 per person as guarantees of good behavior. That was more money than most people, black or white, could afford in 1827. Many blacks fled to Canada. To defend black rights and help those blacks moving to Canada, Richard Allen organized the first national black convention, the American Society of Free Persons of Color. The society elected him president in April 1830. Allen declared July 4 a day of fasting and prayer for American blacks. Later that year, Allen organized the Free Produce Society to boycott goods sold by slave owners.

Richard Allen died the following spring, leaving his family wealthy, even by white standards of the day. He also left the black community some of its earliest, and still enduring, institutions. His opposition to the ACS contributed to its eventual failure, although slavery was not abolished in the United States until 1865. With nearly 6,000 churches in the United States, the AME church today counts more than 1.5 million members.

FURTHER READING

Klots, Steve. *Richard Allen: Religious Leader and Social Activist.* New York: Chelsea House, 1991.

Lincoln, C. Eric. *The Black Church in the African American Experience.* Durham, N.C.: Duke University Press, 1990.

Smith, Charles Spencer. *A History of the African Methodist Episcopal Church.* Philadelphia: Book Concern of the AME Church, 1922.

Elizabeth Ann Seton

AMERICA'S FIRST SAINT

The first American-born Roman Catholic saint had her beginnings in New York City's prosperous merchant class. Elizabeth Ann Bayley Seton was the second daughter of the prominent physician Richard Bayley and his first wife, Catherine Charlton. In 1777, when Elizabeth was three, her mother died, and her father soon remarried. By all accounts a headstrong, though contemplative, girl, Elizabeth never developed a close relationship with her stepmother.

When she was 14, Elizabeth was left with relatives in the country north of New York while her parents went to England on business. She spent three years there and another two on Staten Island. She never lived with her father and stepmother again.

In the country Elizabeth seems to have experienced her first religious longings. She wished, she wrote a friend, that she could stay in a convent, "where people could be shut up from the world and pray and be good always." Less profoundly, she also expressed a wish to be a Quaker because "they wore such pretty, plain hats."

When she was 19, Elizabeth married a young banker named William Magee Seton. The couple moved to New York City's Wall Street and began rearing their children, eventually five of them. Elizabeth became involved in charitable works, founding with Isabella Graham a society to help impoverished widowed mothers. She also found time to follow the intellectual currents of her time, reading the works of the French philosopher Jean-Jacques Rousseau and the American writer Thomas Paine (though she would later call them heretics).

In 1798, when Elizabeth was 24, her father-in-law, William Seton, Sr., died, and the slow decline of the Seton family finances began. Two years later, Elizabeth's own father died. She turned for consolation to her church, New York's Trinity Episcopal, and was befriended by its minister, John Henry Hobart.

Then William Seton fell very ill. Taking their oldest child, Anna Marie, with them, the Setons traveled to Italy in hopes of restoring his health. But the family was quarantined, or put into isolation, at the Italian border. William, suffering from tuberculosis, was too sick to enter the country beyond the coastal city of Leghorn, where they landed.

For months, Elizabeth cared for her husband in a small, unheated room. She pulled herself out of despair only by reflecting that "I was offending my only Friend [God] and resource in misery." Despite her efforts, William died on December 27, 1803.

Elizabeth Ann Seton

BORN

August 28, 1774
New York, New York

DIED

January 4, 1821
Emmitsburg, Maryland

TRADITION

Christian (Roman Catholic)

ACCOMPLISHMENTS

Founder of Sisters of Charity (1809), first American sisterhood; first Catholic saint born in the United States

Mother Seton, as she is often called by Catholics, founded the Sisters of Charity in the United States. She was the first native-born American to be canonized by the Roman Catholic Church.

Her Italian friends, chief among them her husband's friend Philip Filicchi, urged Seton to visit Italy before returning to the United States. Elizabeth and Anna toured Florence and the surrounding country, visiting churches and art galleries. When their return boat was delayed, they stayed on with the Filicchi family. Elizabeth attended mass with them and was deeply moved by the idea that God was present at the altar.

Seton's encounter with Catholicism seems to have had a strong impact on her. On the way back to the United States, she compared the human soul to coral that turns pink when lifted from the ocean; that is, the soul, usually submerged in an ocean of worldliness, is transformed when God raises it up.

Seton returned to New York in 1804, undecided about whether to convert to Catholicism. Praying and fasting often, she struggled with the question over the next year. Hobart and Seton's Protestant friends and relations urged Seton to remain a Protestant; the Filicchis and New York's Catholic clergy urged her to convert.

On New Year's Day 1805, still undecided, Seton took down a book of sermons and read at random. Somehow, the words, "Where is He who is born king of the Jews?" convinced her

"So the wheel goes round. Peace and love, my soul's darling. Look up at the blue heaven and love Him, He is so good to us."

—from a letter to her daughter Kit (July 2, 1820)

to convert to Catholicism. On Ash Wednesday of that year, she began attending St. Peter's Catholic Church and spoke of an "unloosing" after a kind of bondage. A disappointed Reverend Hobart cautioned her friends against absorbing her beliefs, which, in his view, were misguided.

With her religious quandary settled, Seton turned to her very serious financial situation. The decline in the family's wealth that had begun during William's lifetime was now complete. She and the children moved into her sister's house with plans to open a school, but news of Seton's conversion to Catholicism turned away potential students. She moved to a house of her own and took in boarders to pay the bills.

Seton's conversion seemed to warm her relationship with her stepmother, but it alienated parts of William's family. When William's sister Cecilia, a close friend of Elizabeth's, also converted to Catholicism, the Seton family threatened to burn Elizabeth's house. Although eventually reconciled with the Setons, Elizabeth still felt unsettled in New York. When she was approached by a Catholic group from Baltimore, where a Catholic community flourished, Elizabeth agreed to open a Catholic girls' school there.

After a year of teaching and guiding a small community of religious women, the first in the United States, Seton was convinced of the rightness of her path. She moved her school to nearby Emmitsburg, Maryland. Seton was helped financially in this move by a Baltimore man whom she surely would have married under other circumstances. Of Samuel Cooper she wrote, "If we had not devoted ourselves to the heavenly spouse before we met I do not know how the attraction would have terminated."

The success of Seton's Emmitsburg school enabled her to provide free schooling for needy girls. Because of these efforts, she was later known as the founder of the parochial (church-run) school system in the United States. Seton's growing convent joined the Catholic religious order of the Daughters of Charity of Saint Vincent de Paul, a 17th-century French saint. In addition to their work as teachers, the convent members cared for the sick, the poor, and orphans. As superior of her community, Elizabeth became known as Mother Seton.

The Emmitsburg community typically had 50 students and 18 sisters, or nuns. An observer wrote, "Mrs. Seton would take the whole country [in] if she could." Under Seton's firm hand, the American Sisters of Charity expanded to Philadelphia in 1814, to New York in 1817, and to Baltimore in 1821. Many members of the order served as teachers and school administrators.

Though her community grew, Seton's family became smaller. In 1809 she lost her two sisters-in-law, Harriet and Cecilia, and in 1812, her first child, Anna Marie. Four years later her youngest child, Rebecca, died. Seton's own health declined following Rebecca's death, but she tried to maintain a cheerful attitude. She wrote a friend, "Death grins broader in the pot every morning and I grin at him." On January 24, 1821, she died from tuberculosis, as had William and Anna Marie. The Catholic Church proclaimed Elizabeth Seton a saint in 1975.

FURTHER READING

Daughters of St. Paul. *Mother Seton.* Boston: St. Paul Books, 1975.

Feeney, Leonard. *Mother Seton: Saint Elizabeth of New York.* Cambridge, Mass.: Ravengate Press, 1991.

Melville, Annabelle M. *Elizabeth Bayley Seton: 1774–1821.* 1951. Reprint. New York: Scribners, 1976.

Stone, Elaine M. *Elizabeth Bayley Seton: An American Saint.* Mahwah, N.J.: Paulist Press, 1993.

Handsome Lake

IROQUOIS SAVIOR

Born at the height of his people's power, in the early 18th century, the Seneca prophet Handsome Lake lived through the near-collapse of his tribe and became an important agent of their rebirth.

The Seneca were the mightiest tribe of the Iroquois Confederacy, an alliance that united the Onondaga, Oneida, Mohawk, Cayuga, and Seneca tribes. The territory of the Iroquois Confederacy, which was also known as the Five Nations, stretched from the Hudson River to Lake Erie. The confederacy was nearly 300 years old when Handsome Lake was born in 1735 in the Seneca village of Conawagas, near present-day Avon, New York.

The Iroquois way of life, centered around farming, was even older. With the men absent for long periods of time hunting, trading, or making war, women managed daily life. They were responsible for the houses, the garden plots, and the tools, and they distributed the tribe's food. Clan matrons (elder women) also chose the local chiefs. When a man married, he joined his wife's people, and children inherited property through the mother's family. The important social link was between mother and daughter. The Iroquois year was punctuated by festivals of gratitude, from Thanks to the Maple in the spring to the fall Harvest Thanksgiving.

Holding a wampum belt, the Iroquois prophet Handsome Lake preaches to his followers. He offered to his people a religion in which they could maintain traditional beliefs while adapting to white customs.

The flag of the Six Nations Temperance Society, the first temperance league in the United States. In a vision, Handsome Lake encountered the Great Spirit, who denounced the Indians for drunkenness and other failings. The eagle at the center of this flag is the symbol of the Six Nations; it is dropping to its doom a monstrous figure that represents the destructive power of the "firewater" introduced to the Six Nations by whites.

"Now this is the way ordained by the Creator: Talk slowly and kindly to children and never punish them unjustly."

—from *The Code of Handsome Lake* (1850)

For the Iroquois, as for many other Native American peoples, the spiritual power of the universe took two forms. It could take the form of a "high god," vast and impersonal, the source of all life— the Great Spirit or Great Mystery—but it could also take human form. In this form, the power could be capricious and even dangerous. Among the Iroquois, this dangerous power was represented by witches, magical beings who could harm or kill people. For protection, the Iroquois turned to the Society of Faces, a group of healers who assumed spiritual powers by wearing false faces—comic, strange, or hideous masks.

The Iroquois supported the British during the American Revolution, although some, including Handsome Lake, argued for neutrality. When the British lost, so did the Iroquois. None of the peace agreements between the Americans and the British even mentioned the interests of Native Americans.

Within 10 years, the population of the Iroquois had dropped drastically and much of their land had been sold or taken outright by whites. Most Iroquois moved to reservations established by the U.S. government. Handsome Lake went to Cornplanter, a Seneca village in northern Pennsylvania named for his half brother, who had arranged for

Seneca people to move there. About 350 Senecas lived in Cornplanter.

Quaker missionaries—members of the pacifist Society of Friends—soon moved onto the Seneca reservations. They taught the Indians how to adapt to white ways and encouraged them to adopt white methods of farming, building houses, making useful objects, and selling their goods. They scolded the Seneca for drinking and insisted that men do the farming, traditionally the work of Iroquois women. The Friends agreed not to try to convert the Indians to Christianity, but their presence helped further destroy traditional Seneca life.

It was during this period of Iroquois decline that Handsome Lake reached a turning point. He returned from a hunting trip so drunk that his family thought he was dead. They even prepared his burial robes. But the next morning he awoke from the first of several visions that would reverse his people's course.

Handsome Lake's first vision, which occurred in June 1799, revealed that the Great Spirit was very angry. The Great Spirit denounced the Iroquois for drunkenness, lying, and stealing. The Christian figure Jesus instructed Handsome Lake, too: "Tell your people that they will become lost

"The Creator has given different people knowledge of different things, and it is the Creator's desire that men employ their knowledge to help one another."

—from *The Code of Handsome Lake* (1850)

Handsome Lake

BORN

1735
Near Avon, New York

DIED

August 10, 1815
Onondaga, New York

TRADITION

Native American

ACCOMPLISHMENT

Seneca religious prophet who founded the *gai'wiio*, an alternative to Christianity that incorporated Native American traditions

when they follow the ways of the white man."

Handsome Lake's later visions foretold the end of the world, explained sin, and described how to be saved. He did not, however, turn his back on the old Iroquois ways. He did not alter the ritual calendar of thanksgiving or his people's relationship with nature and spirit forces. Handsome Lake called for public repentance, an end to drinking, and personal and social reform.

Not everyone followed Handsome Lake's call. His acceptance of Quaker ways, which elevated the husband-wife relationship above the traditional mother-daughter one, angered some Senecas. Others were probably angered by his witch hunting, which resulted in at least one death. For a time, Handsome Lake had to leave Cornplanter for his own safety.

By 1803, however, Handsome Lake and his disciples were preaching his new *gai'wiio* ("good word") throughout what remained of the Iroquois nation. Because he offered the Iroquois a way to adapt to modern civilization and interact with white American society without sacrificing all their traditional beliefs, his religion quickly attracted followers.

As a representative of the Seneca, Handsome Lake traveled to Washing-ton, D.C., and arranged with President Thomas Jefferson for the return of some Seneca land. Although he was never able to amass much power of his own, Handsome Lake was a very successful preacher. During the last decade and a half of his life, he lived to see Iroquois culture revived, inspired by his visions.

A generation after his death, his followers gathered his sayings into the *Gai'wiio*, translated as *The Code of Handsome Lake*. In northern New York and southern Canada, Iroquois still gather at thanksgiving festivals to celebrate and retell the Way of Handsome Lake.

FURTHER READING

Hirshfelder, Arlene, and Paulette Molin. *The Encyclopedia of Native American Religions*. New York: Facts on File, 1992.

Wallace, Anthony F. C. *The Death and Rebirth of the Seneca*. New York: Knopf, 1970.

Joseph Smith

MORMON VISIONARY

The founder of Mormonism was born into a Massachusetts family of restless Christians. They had moved on to Vermont by 1805, when Joseph Smith was born. Eleven years later, the family moved farther west to Palmyra, New York, a part of the country called the "burnt-over district" because it had been the site of so many fiery religious revivals.

Smith's mother and brothers were reluctant Presbyterians. His father was known to have religious visions. The Smiths were unmoved, but probably not untouched, by the many religious sects and experimental communities that flourished on what was then America's frontier.

Joseph Smith was a handsome, lively, likable young man who entertained his friends with magic tricks and tall tales. He worked as a laborer and farmer but made a colorful name for himself as a treasure seeker. In much the same way that people use dowsing sticks to search for water, Smith used a "finding stone" to divine, or intuit, the location of buried wealth. He was seldom successful.

On a treasure-divining trip to northern Pennsylvania, Smith fell in love with his host's daughter, Emma Hall. Smith found no treasure, however, and he was arrested for disorderly conduct. Emma's father denounced Smith as a "cheap impostor."

Smith gave up treasure seeking, though he kept his finding stone, and persuaded Emma Hall to elope. They returned to his parents' land in New York State. It was there, first in 1820 and again in 1823, that Smith had dramatic encounters with a being he understood to be an angel, a messenger from God. The angel, who called himself Moroni, said God had called Smith to restore the Christian church to the world. In 1827 Moroni led Smith to unearth a set of Golden Plates. These plates contained, Smith believed, ancient religious texts that identified Native Americans as a lost tribe of biblical Israelites. Smith's family was deeply moved. "At last," his mother later wrote, "we had something upon which we could stay our minds."

Smith translated the plates with the angel's help. At Moroni's insistence, he showed them to no one else. Many people, particularly journalists, dismissed Smith's work as a fraud. Others, however, found something vital in Smith's preaching about the plates and the visions that he had received. His first convert was his father. Another early convert, Oliver Cowdery, wrote late in life that Joseph Smith had a "mysterious power, which even now I fail to fathom." Smith was never ordained by a religious authority. In 1829, a being whom Smith and Cowdery

"You don't know me; you never knew my heart. No man knows my history. I cannot tell it; I shall never undertake it. I don't blame anyone for not believing my history. If I had not experienced what I have, I could not have believed it myself."

—from an 1844 sermon

Though it draws on older Christian traditions, the Church of Jesus Christ of Latter-Day Saints developed by Joseph Smith is one of the few true American-born religions.

understood to be an angel conferred priesthood on the two men.

By the time *The Book of Mormon* was completed later that year, Smith identified himself as "Seer, a Translator, a Prophet, and Apostle of Jesus Christ and Elder of the Church." His Church of Christ was formally established on April 6, 1830. Within a month it had 40 members, but Smith had been arrested again for disorderly conduct. Many people openly disliked him. His hometown of Palmyra refused to let him use the town hall for church meetings.

Supported solely by his followers, Smith sent missionaries west to convert Native Americans. On one such mission, Oliver Cowdery also converted Sidney Rigdon, an wellspoken Ohio preacher who had just left the Disciples of Christ, a breakaway Presbyterian movement. Most of Rigdon's congregation, in Kirtland, Ohio, converted with him.

Following another revelation, Smith decided to build a Mormon colony in Kirtland and changed the name of his church to the Church of Jesus Christ of Latter-Day Saints.

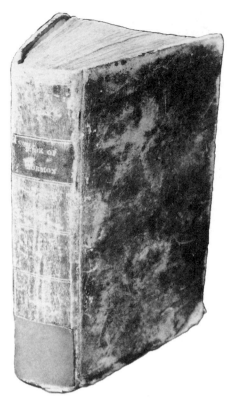

An original copy of *The Book of Mormon*, first published in Palmyra, New York, in 1830. *The Book of Mormon* is a history of early North America which suggests that some ancient Hebrews left Israel and emigrated to North America, where they split into two groups—the Lamanites (Native Americans) and the Nephites. According to *The Book of Mormon*, Jesus Christ appeared to the Nephites and left them his wisdom (recorded on golden plates) before they were destroyed by the Lamanites.

Emma, who had buried the couple's first child in New York and was now pregnant again, moved west with Smith and more than 150 followers.

Smith had come from a part of the country where revivalism—an emotional call to religious ideals—was common, but he was not himself a revivalist, appealing more to people's reason than emotion. Other idealist movements popular in America at his time did influence Smith, however. For example, communalism—the idea that people should share their property and govern themselves in small groups—was an early cornerstone of his church, dating to his first days in Ohio.

But Smith's time in Ohio was hard. Emma gave birth to twins, both of whom died. Smith, who had apparently worked a few miracles—curing a paralyzed arm, predicting an earthquake—found his powers failed him before a sizable crowd when he tried to revive a dead child. Two donors who had promised to give the church land withdrew their offer. A further revelation pointed Joseph Smith to Missouri.

Traveling by foot to Independence, Missouri, Smith showed his followers where to build the temple that would gather all church members together. At Sidney Rigdon's insistence, however, Smith returned east to manage both the Ohio and Missouri enterprises from Kirtland, Ohio.

The two communities pooled their earnings, and for a time both flourished. By 1832, the Missouri community had 300 converts and was growing. That same year, Joseph Smith, Jr., was born, and Brigham Young, a fellow Vermont-born religious seeker who would lead the church after Smith's death, joined the Mormons.

Smith's revelations continued, with increasing specificity. He received the design for a temple in Kirtland and the layout for an entire city of 12 temples for Zion, Missouri. Though the city was not built in Smith's lifetime, Brigham Young later followed Smith's layout in devising Salt Lake City in Utah.

The Mormons' religious enthusiasm, their industry, their sympathy for blacks and Native Americans, and especially their practice of sharing all their property under church leadership brought them into conflict with their more conventional Missouri neighbors. The first outside support for Smith's church came as the result of popular revulsion at the brutality of Missouri mob attacks on Mormon settlers. Still, Smith ended the Mormons' communal property requirement as the result of public pressure, and he returned to Ohio.

Ohio was then a center of the national temperance, or nondrinking, movement. Bowing to the times, Smith's 1833 book, *The Word of Wisdom*, advocated partial vegetarianism and total avoidance of tobacco, alcohol, coffee, and tea—practices later Mormons would continue to uphold. Smith also began translating some Egyptian hieroglyphics brought to him by Michael Chandler, an Egyptologist. Presenting his translation as a quasi-biblical text, *The Book of Abraham* was published in 1842. In it, Smith drew on his study of biblical Hebrew to suggest that many gods had "organized" the earth, for in Genesis, the first book of the Hebrew Bible, the name given for the creator God has a plural ending. In 1861, however, scholars established that Smith's translations were invented (the hieroglyphics were ordinary funeral documents).

The Kirtland temple was dedicated in 1836, during an extraordinary economic boom. Smith and the Mormon Church became deeply involved in banking and financial speculation, forming their own (never legalized) bank and issuing notes that could be exchanged for hard currency. When an economic crash occurred in 1837, and people panicked and tried to cash their notes, the Mormons' debt approached $150,000. The Ohio church disintegrated as the result of lawsuits and accusations, and Smith fled to Missouri.

There, he found 1,500 Mormons living in modest prosperity. Smith began expanding Mormon holdings beyond the single county originally granted to them by the Missouri legislature, and 600 Ohio congregants moved to Missouri. Remembering the earlier anti-Mormon violence in Missouri and aware that his church's mild antislavery stance could still incite local hostility, Smith agreed to the formation of a small armed militia, known as the Danites.

Trouble broke out in July 1838 when Smith ended a public speech with a promise to seek vengeance on his Missouri adversaries. Anti-Mormon feelings surged: millers refused to grind Mormon grain, and foraging Mormons were savagely beaten. Selling their property and houses for a fraction of their worth, the Mormons retreated to a corner of their land known as the Far West. When Missouri's governor called for the extermination of Mormons, Smith and his fellows armed themselves for battle.

In October, mobs attacked a Mormon flour mill a few miles from the Far West, killing or injuring all but 6 of the 38 men and boys defending the mill. Drastically outnumbered, Smith surrendered on behalf of the Mormons. The Missouri militia jailed Smith and many of the Mormon leaders, then overran the Far West. Smith spent four months in jail before Missouri public opinion, now inflamed over the mistreatment of the Mormons, turned in his favor. He and the other Mormons were freed.

Brigham Young, who had escaped capture, had meanwhile led the Mormons out of Missouri to Illinois. When Smith left jail, early in 1839, he joined Young and the others in a town that Smith named Nauvoo, after the Hebrew word meaning "beautiful plantation."

Within a year of Smith's arrival, Nauvoo had more than 250 houses, laid out according to the instructions he received in his visions. Mormon missionaries were extremely active, and Nauvoo grew. By 1844 it was the largest city in Illinois, with about 11,000 citizens.

As his community prospered, Smith petitioned the U.S. government to create a "sovereign Mormon state," as he put it. Fifty of his highest officers crowned him king of the Kingdom of God. The Mormon leader ran unsuccessfully for President in 1844 on a Theodemocratic platform that included forgiveness for debts, penal reform, and free trade.

Smith's ideal government was a theocracy, a religious state, governed by a prophet. His theology celebrated the glory of learning and the eternal progress of humanity. In Nauvoo, Smith developed his theology more fully. He began teaching that "God himself was once as we are now, and is an exalted man." Ever an optimist, Smith preached that the human horizon was boundless, that practicing Mormons could become godlike. Borrowing from the Freemasons, a secret fraternal organization, Smith adopted a set of temple ceremonies for his inner circle. These included ritual washing, the wearing of ritual clothing, and staged enactments of the expulsion of Adam and Eve from the Garden of Eden.

There was no Masonic precedent for another Mormon invention, however: Joseph Smith and other Mormon leaders took "spiritual," or additional, wives. This practice undermined the congregation's faith in their leaders.

Joseph Smith

BORN

December 23, 1805
Sharon, Vermont

DIED

June 27, 1844
Carthage, Illinois

TRADITION

Christianity (Mormon)

ACCOMPLISHMENTS

Founder of the Church of Jesus Christ of Latter-Day Saints; his writings include *The Book of Mormon* (1830), *Doctrine and Covenants* (1835), and *The Book of Abraham* (1842)

> *"Man is that he might have joy."*
>
> —from *The Book of Mormon* (1830)

There had always been Mormon dissenters. Oliver Cowdery, one of Smith's first followers, had been excommunicated, or expelled from the church, for accusing Smith of adultery. Others quit on their own, unable to accept all of Smith's ideas, which included baptism for the dead and the preexistence of souls.

William Law, one of Smith's defectors, set up a rival Mormon church with himself as head. Law founded a paper, the *Nauvoo Expositor*, to address Smith's shortcomings. Under Smith's orders, his protection squad, known as the Legion, wrecked Law's press. Anti-Mormon feelings in Illinois raged out of control.

Smith named his brother, Hyrum, his successor, told his followers to scatter, and he and Hyrum tried to escape from Illinois. Captured, they were returned to Nauvoo to stand trial for destroying Law's press. While Smith and his brother were in jail awaiting trial, a mob stormed their cell. Hyrum Smith was killed instantly. Joseph Smith was killed as he tried to escape through a window.

Martyrdom cast Joseph Smith's life story in a new light. It became the story that bound the Mormon people together. Brigham Young took over the church and led the Mormons west to Utah to carry out Smith's work.

Joseph Smith remains one of America's most successful religious leaders. His theology, with its multiple gods and multiple wives, was a radical departure from conventional Protestantism. But his message of hard work, education, and material success, was well suited to a frontier land. From its base in Utah, his church today claims nearly 9 million members worldwide. As a result of its strong missionary activity, Mormonism is expanding rapidly among converts overseas.

FURTHER READING

Bernotas, Bob. *Brigham Young*. New York: Chelsea House, 1993.

Brodie, Fawn. *No Man Knows My History: The Life of Joseph Smith, the Mormon Prophet*. New York: Knopf, 1971.

Featherstone, Vaughn J. *The Aaronic Priesthood and You*. Salt Lake City: Deseret Books, 1987.

Fischer, Norma J. *Portrait of a Prophet's Wife: Emma Hale Smith*. Murray, Utah: Aspen Books, 1992.

Jackson, Ron. *The Seer: Joseph Smith*. Salt Lake City, Utah: Hawkes, 1977.

Leone, Mark P. *Roots of Modern Mormonism*. Cambridge: Harvard University Press, 1979.

Madseon, Susan A. *The Lord Needed a Prophet*. Salt Lake City, Utah: Deseret Books, 1987.

McCloud, Susan E. *Joseph Smith: A Photobiography*. Murray, Utah: Aspen Books, 1992.

Tanes, Ernest H. *Trouble Enough: Joseph Smith and the Book of Mormon*. Buffalo, N.Y.: Prometheus, 1984.

Isaac Mayer Wise

REFORMING JUDAISM IN AMERICA

The founder of American Reform Judaism, Isaac Mayer Wise, was born in Bohemia (present-day Czech Republic). His father was a poor schoolteacher who died during Wise's childhood. As a young man, Wise studied Judaism in Prague and Vienna before returning to Bohemia in 1843 to serve as a rabbi. In 1846, he concluded that his future, both as an individual and as a Jew, was not promising in Bohemia. With his wife and young son, he left for the United States.

Wise had no reputation or formal religious credentials (he may not have been an ordained rabbi) when he arrived in the United States. The first people he spoke with in New York advised him to take up peddling.

Instead, Wise opened an English-language school for Jewish immigrants and then secured a position as a rabbi to a congregation in Albany, New York. There he began to make himself into an American. He perfected his English,

Isaac Mayer Wise was the driving force behind the growth of Reform Judaism in the United States. With Wise as president, Hebrew Union College opened in Cincinnati in 1875; it was the first U.S. institution to train Reform rabbis.

"American Judaism [will be] free, progressive, enlightened, united, and respected."

—from *Reminiscences* (1874)

Temple B'nai Jeshurun in Cincinnati, Ohio, known as the Plum Street Temple, became the headquarters for Wise's Reform movement. Almost 40 percent of American Jews follow the Reform tradition.

extended his education with hours of library study in philosophy, history, and comparative religion, and befriended politicians and Christian clergymen.

Wise had so much faith in his adopted country that he believed Judaism would become its national religion. In the United States, he felt, people could express their ideas freely and convince others of the truth of those ideas. Many of Wise's own ideas came from the "Science of Judaism." This German movement was reexamining Jewish history and literature with an

eye to modernizing Judaism. Wise probably first encountered these ideas in Prague and Vienna.

With the support of many in his Albany congregation, Wise initiated a range of reforms in traditional Jewish practice. He introduced a Jewish day school, a mixed choir and seating (traditional Judaism separated men and women during worship), organ music, and English-language hymns. Although many praised him, he was not universally liked or appreciated. He antagonized some congregation members for condemning gambling and others for denying belief in a messiah, or savior, in the form of a person.

The congregation's anti-Wise faction had him dismissed, but Wise nevertheless proceeded to conduct Yom Kippur services, the holiest in the Jewish calendar. In the middle of the service, the congregation president physically attacked Wise. The county sheriff finally had to quell the brawl, which had emptied into the street. Wise and his followers began a new temple, where he continued his reforms.

Eight years after he arrived in Albany, Wise left to serve as rabbi of a reform-friendly congregation in bustling Cincinnati, Ohio, where he found an apt setting for his pioneer spirit. With his Albany experience fresh in mind, Wise introduced his reforms more slowly. Within three years, his congregation was the second largest in the country. In 1856, he published his revolutionary *Minhag America (American Ritual)*, which describes Jewish custom as it had evolved in America.

In his 1874 autobiography, *Reminiscences*, Wise described his early years as dampened by feelings of depression, unworthiness, and despair. Part of his self-transformation had been to convert these feelings into creative action. Possessed of a sense of divine mission (he compared himself to the biblical Isaiah), he had turned his attention to national Jewish concerns. His weekly newspaper, *The American Israelite*, founded in 1854, soon rivaled Jewish papers in the East. In its pages he began calling for a national conference of American Jews.

Although he became caught up in disputes about the nature of Reform Judaism, Wise's larger goal was always to promote Jewish unity. He scheduled a meeting of both traditional and radical Jews for October 1855, in Cleveland, Ohio. Despite a heated atmosphere, Wise and the conference attendants agreed to work toward unity; develop a common liturgy, or religious service; and reorganize Jewish education. Wise compromised his own beliefs to draft a conference document affirming the divine origin of the Bible. Full of hope, he announced that a unified American Judaism—one that was "free, progressive, enlightened, united, respected"—was at hand.

He was wrong. Beyond religious issues, American Jews were divided on social issues, particularly slavery. Trying to appease the conservative, pro-slavery faction, Wise permanently alienated the radical, antislavery one. Conflicts with eastern radicals, led by the German-born intellectual David Einhorn, eventually weakened Wise as a national organizer of American Judaism. On his conservative flank, he watched a new Jewish movement assert itself in reaction to Reform Judaism. Calling itself Orthodox, this movement was dedicated to resisting the changes in Jewish education, dress, conduct, and worship the Reform movement had introduced. In time, a third, Conservative movement emerged, opposing extreme changes but permitting some.

Wise's educational efforts, however, bore fruit. He nurtured America's first rabbinical seminary into existence, along with a basic curriculum and a union of congregations to support it. Hebrew Union College opened in Cincinnati in 1875, with Isaac Mayer Wise as its president; the United States now had a training ground for its own Reform rabbis. Fourteen years later, with some of those newly ordained rabbis at his side, Wise founded the Central Conference of American Rabbis. He presided over it until his death in 1900. Wise's son, Jonah Bondi Wise, ordained a rabbi by Hebrew Union College, also served as a leader of American Reform Judaism.

FURTHER READING

Borowitz, Eugene, and Naomi Patz. *Explaining Reform Judaism.* New York: Behrman House, 1985.

Heller, James Gutheim. *Isaac M. Wise: His Life, Work, and Thought.* New York: Union of American Hebrew Congregations, 1965.

Knox, Israel. *Rabbi in America: The Story of Isaac Mayer Wise.* Boston: Little, Brown, 1957.

Meyer, Michael A. *Response to Modernity: A History of the Reform Movement in Judaism.* New York: Oxford University Press, 1988.

Temkin, Sefton D. *Isaac Mayer Wise: Shaping American Judaism.* Washington, D.C.: B'nai B'rith Books, 1992.

Wise, Isaac Mayer. *Reminiscences.* Edited by David Philipson. 1901. Reprint. Manchester, N.H.: Ayer, 1969.

———. *Selected Writings of Isaac Mayer Wise.* Edited by David Philipson and Louis Grossman. 1900. Reprint. Salem, N.H.: Ayer, 1969.

BELIEVERS

Isaac Mayer Wise

BORN

March 29, 1819
Steingrub, Bohemia (now Cheb, Czech Republic)

DIED

March 26, 1900
Cincinnati, Ohio

FORMAL EDUCATION

Attended University of Prague and possibly University of Vienna

TRADITION

Judaism

ACCOMPLISHMENTS

Author of several novels and histories of ancient Israel, including *History of the Israelitish Nation from Abraham to the Present Time* (1854), the autobiography *Reminiscences* (1874), and *The Cosmic God* (1876); founder of *The American Israelite*, Jewish weekly newspaper (1854); founder of Union of American Hebrew Congregations (1873); founder of Hebrew Union College (1875); founder of Central Conference of American Rabbis (1889)

Mary Baker Eddy

ILLNESS AND THE MIND OF GOD

hen Mary Morse Baker dreamed of writing a book when she grew up, neither she nor her adoring family had any idea that she would write the text of a new religion. Bright and beautiful but often ill, Mary was cherished as the youngest child of a large family in Bow, New Hampshire. Her family belonged to the Protestant Congregationalist tradition, an English movement that grew out of Puritan calls for the separation of church and state. Her father, a stern, God-fearing farmer, "kept the family in the tightest harness I have ever known," she later told a biographer.

The first sign that Mary Baker might follow an unconventional path was her childhood rejection of predestination. This is the idea, promoted by the Protestant theologian John Calvin, that God has chosen beforehand which people will be eternally blessed and which will be damned. A God of eternal punishment "will find me a hard case,"

Her sickly childhood and later experiences of death and loss convinced Mary Baker Eddy that illness was an illusion resulting from "a denial of God."

Mary told her mother. She argued with her family, chiefly her father, over Calvin's doctrine. After one dispute, she fell ill and on her mother's advice, prayed for divine guidance. When the fever broke, she said, so too did the hold predestination had on her.

Mary's faith in God never wavered, but it did take a unique form. As a result of her struggle with illness, Mary would later develop her own system of religious healing; as a result of her struggle to find her place in the world, she would eventually lead a vast religious organization. Both her system of healing and her religious institution are known as Christian Science.

At the age of 12, Mary began writing poetry. Although she was a good student, illness disrupted her schooling. She was an attractive young woman and much admired, and in December 1843, at age 22, she married George Washington Glover, a friend of her brother's. Glover had a construction business in South Carolina, where Mary joined him.

At this point, her life began to unravel. Glover's building supplies were destroyed in a fire, and in June 1844 he died of yellow fever. Mary bore her only child, George Washington Glover II, in New Hampshire that fall. Too weak to attend to him, she had to hire a wet nurse. In 1849, her new fiancé, the lawyer John Bartlett, died, and so did her mother. Her father remarried, and Mary left home to live with her sister Abigail, but Abigail could not accommodate George.

In 1853, Mary married Daniel Patterson, a dentist. Circumstances still did not permit her to bring her son to live with her; she was weak and her husband's business was shaky. Three years later, the family raising George left for the American West, taking the boy with them. Mary fell ill again. She was bedridden, her husband was away looking for work, her young son was far from her. She might have given up in despair.

Instead, she turned to alternative medical cures, such as a diet of coarse bread and vegetables, the "water cure" of bathing and fresh air, and homeopathy. Homeopathy involves treating an illness with small doses of medicines that would, in large doses, produce the symptoms of that illness. The use of placebos was especially impressive to Mary. A placebo is a preparation containing no medicine that cures a patient because he believes in it. Mary began exploring the mind's role in health.

The Pattersons were still struggling when the Civil War broke out in 1861. The year before, the couple had lost their house and Patterson's business was now failing. Daniel Patterson went on a war-related mission for the Union army and was captured by Confederate soldiers. Mary continued to be ill. She decided to visit Dr. Phineas P. Quimby, who practiced a "mind cure" in Portland, Maine.

Quimby was a former clock maker who had become an enthusiast of mesmerism. Named for the Viennese physician Franz Mesmer, mesmerism was the idea that health and illness are subject to the movements of an invisible, magnetic fluid in the body. This fluid could be influenced by a mesmerist's "animal magnetism." Today, we understand the Mesmer treatment to be hypnosis. Quimby used both hypnosis and counseling, which we would today call psychotherapy, with his patients.

Quimby's treatment worked with Mary. He "heals as never man healed since Christ," she wrote to a Portland, Maine, newspaper. When her husband escaped from his southern prison cell and returned north in 1862, Mary began studying with Quimby. Then she and Patterson settled in Lynn, Massachusetts. Mary became active in

"The prayer that reforms the sinner and heals the sick is an absolute faith that all things are possible to God."

—from *Science and Health*

From its beginning in parlors where Mary Baker Eddy conducted prayer-based healings, Christian Science has become a large international organization, with 2,000 churches in the United States alone. At center foreground is the domed First Church of Christ, Scientist in Boston, Massachusetts, known as the Mother Church, the organization's international headquarters.

the temperance movement, the crusade to ban alcoholic beverages. Hard times still followed her. Her father died, leaving his estate to his widow. And Quimby died of cancer.

In February 1866, a few weeks after Quimby's death, Mary was walking to a temperance meeting when she slipped on the ice. Knocked unconscious, she was carried to a nearby house and treated by doctors. Her friends feared that she might die. For three days she drifted in and out of consciousness. Awakening at one point, she read an account of one of Jesus' healings in the New Testament (Matthew 9:2) and felt herself healed.

Mary was unable to explain the exact nature of her cure; she said only that it came from feeling the presence of God. She began praying with other sufferers and found that she had healing powers, too. This ability was not universally appreciated. It alienated her family and possibly Patterson, who deserted her. For the next nine years, Mary moved from boardinghouse to boardinghouse. She began teaching her healing method, which she called "Christian science." It was based on prayer, a close reading of the Bible, and an openness to spiritual experience. When some of her students opened healing practices, Mary began to attract attention.

Inspired by her continued reading of the Bible, she began writing. Her book *Science and Health* was published in October 1875, the same year that Mary finally bought herself a house. Initial reviews of *Science and Health* were caustic: "This book is indeed wholly original, but it will never be read," wrote an early critic. In fact, *Science and Health* went through more than 400 printings in Mary's own lifetime.

The basis of her teachings is that God, the source of all life, is wholly good. Whatever is not good—sin, disease, and death—result from a denial

of God and are not ultimately real. Disease is an illusion. God, whom she also referred to as Life, Truth, and Love, destroys illusions. Healing, in her view, grows out of openness to God.

On July 4, 1876, Mary formed the Christian Scientists' Association, an informal school and fellowship center, to continue working with her students. But her personal life was seldom calm. In January 1877, she married one of her students, a former sewing machine salesman named Asa Gilbert Eddy. Two of her other students became outraged. One sued her for unpaid services; another, Daniel Spofford, accused her of letting Christian Science down. He proposed to soldier on without her, and Mary expelled him from the association.

Trouble haunted the Eddys as it had the Pattersons. The 1878 printing of *Science and Health* was badly bungled. Gilbert Eddy's nest egg was wiped out in a bank failure. Spofford disappeared, and Gilbert Eddy was arrested for his murder before Spofford reappeared. That winter, Mary Baker Eddy began lecturing in Boston. "I have lectured in parlors 14 years," she wrote. "God calls me now to go before the people in a wider sense."

The Church of Christ, Scientist—an outgrowth of the Christian Scientists' Association—was chartered in Massachusetts in August 1879. At roughly the same time, Eddy laid the groundwork for a school to train Christian Science healers. Her Massachusetts Metaphysical College opened in May 1882. Mary Eddy was the sole instructor on the faculty. Within a month, Gilbert died. A grieving Mary Eddy closed the school and left Boston, trying, as she wrote to a student, "to sever all the chords that bind one to person or things material."

She reopened the school later that summer. Calvin Frye, a former student, began working as Mary Eddy's secretary, a job that he would hold for the next 28

Mary Baker Eddy

BORN

July 16, 1821
Bow, New Hampshire

DIED

December 3, 1910
Chestnut Hill, Massachusetts

TRADITION

Christianity (Christian Science)

ACCOMPLISHMENTS

Founder of Christian Science movement and of the *Christian Science Monitor*; author of several books, including *Science and Health* (1875) and *Manual of the Mother Church* (1895)

years. Eddy was busier than ever. In 1883 she founded a bimonthly (later monthly) periodical, the *Journal of Christian Science,* and brought out the sixth edition of *Science and Health.* This edition included the commentary on the biblical books Genesis and Revelation.

Eddy's church continued to grow, although the services were so simple that a college professor called her "the pantheistic and prayerless Mrs. Eddy," implying that she saw God in all things and ignored traditional Christian practices. Her services usually consisted of readings from the Bible and *Science and Health,* the Lord's Prayer, silent prayer, and a sermon.

Audiences for her lectures swelled, and people clamored for a glimpse or touch of the miraculous Mrs. Eddy. She did not like the attention. "Christian Science is not forwarded by these methods," she rebuked her followers. In the middle of 1889, her movement hugely successful, Mary Baker Eddy retired. She closed the college, resigned as pastor of the Boston Church of Christ, Scientist, handed control of the *Christian Science Journal* over to the National Christian Scientist Association (founded in 1886), and dissolved the Boston Christian Scientists' Association.

By 1890, eight years after she opened her college, Eddy's movement had grown from a single church to 20 churches and 33 teachers. Her *Journal's* circulation exceeded 10,000 readers. Eddy settled in New Hampshire to write. The 50th revision of *Science and Health* came out in 1891. The next year, she bought a farmhouse near Concord, New Hampshire, and

rethought the idea of her church. She centered her new form of church government in a self-perpetuating body, the Christian Science Board of Directors. She gave them land in Boston for the building of a church edifice. The First Church of Christ, Scientist building was dedicated in January 1895. She directed that the Bible and *Science and Health* alone be its pastors, although she agreed to serve as pastor emeritus.

By the turn of the century, Eddy had supervised the founding of the Christian Science Board of Education to train new teachers, and another periodical, the *Christian Science Weekly.* The Boston church continued to grow, and its famous domed building was added in 1906 to hold new worshipers.

But Eddy's fame also brought detractors. As an antidote to the sensational journalism that pervaded American newspapers, she began a newspaper of her own. In July 1908, she ordered the Christian Science Board of Directors to publish the *Christian Science Monitor,* a daily newspaper. They scoured the membership for journalists and published the first issue that November.

By this time, Eddy was withdrawing more and more from the day-to-day activities of her church. Eddy revised her *Manual of the Mother Church* and then, in October 1909, resigned fully from the church. Her written rules would speak for her, she said. A year later, at 89, she died. "God is my life" were the last words that she wrote.

In its dependence on God over conventional medicine for healing,

Christian Science has at times called dramatic attention to itself. The religion is today active in more than 60 countries. There are nearly 2,000 Christian Science churches in the United States alone. Few women in history have built so impressive a structure.

FURTHER READING

Christian Science Publishing Society. *We Knew Mary Baker Eddy.* Boston: Christian Science Publishing Society, 1979.

Eddy, Mary Baker. *The First Church of Christ, Scientist and Miscellany.* Boston: The First Church of Christ, Scientist, 1953.

———. *Science and Health with Key to the Scriptures.* Boston: The First Church of Christ, Scientist, 1994.

Orcutt, William Dana. *Mary Baker Eddy and Her Books.* Boston: Christian Science Publishing Society, 1950.

Peel, Robert. *Mary Baker Eddy.* 3 vols. New York: Holt, Rinehart & Winston, 1966–77.

Smaus, Jewel Spangler. *Mary Baker Eddy: The Golden Days.* Boston: Christian Science Publishing Society, 1966.

Smith, Louise A. *Mary Baker Eddy.* New York: Chelsea House, 1991.

Thomas, Robert David. *"With Bleeding Footsteps": Mary Baker Eddy's Path to Religious Leadership.* New York: Knopf, 1994.

Mohandas Gandhi

"THE GREAT SOUL IN PEASANT GARB"

B ut I have a first-class ticket!" the young man insisted. No matter. As a native of India, Mr. Gandhi, the London-trained lawyer traveling on business, was redirected to the crowded third-class car. He refused to leave the first-class car and was forced off the train. He spent the night in a South African train station, cold, hungry, and deep in thought. A loyal subject of the British Empire, Gandhi had been taught to believe in fairness, but it seemed that all that mattered now was the color of his skin.

Mohandas Gandhi (center) was revered by millions of his fellow Indians. Gandhi adopted the simple dress of common people to express kinship with poorer Indians and to shun foreign-produced fabrics.

Gandhi works at his spinning wheel in public. He used this device to symbolize self-reliance and self-rule. In fighting for Indian independence from Great Britain, Gandhi relied on nonviolent tactics, such as a boycott of British textiles.

Years later, when he was asked to name the most creative moment of his life, Gandhi recalled that night in the train station. By the next morning, he had decided to fight for his right to be treated as a human being. Over the course of his life, his efforts moved millions of people—and the British Empire.

Gandhi was born into the merchant caste, one of the four major social classes in India. His father was an administrator, and his mother was a deeply religious woman who cheerfully and regularly fasted as a kind of prayer.

The family often hosted guests from different religious backgrounds, from Muslim and Parsi friends to Jain monks.

The Jain tradition, with its emphasis on *ahimsa* (nonviolence), would have a great influence on Gandhi's own thinking, although as a boy he found religion uninteresting. Gandhi was married at the age of 13, which was customary at that time. His wife, Kasturbai, never learned to read or write, but she worked alongside Gandhi throughout their 62-year marriage.

Gandhi's school career was checkered. "Good conduct, poor spelling," read one report. After Gandhi's father died, the young man's family arranged for him to study law in London. There, he weathered intense loneliness, finally finding friends through the Vegetarian Society. They introduced him to new ideas, from "voluntary simplicity" (doing without many material comforts) to the teachings of religious books. Gandhi explored India's traditions through the Hindu *Bhagavad Gita* and *The Light of Asia*, which was about the Buddha; he also found himself drawn to the Christian New Testament, especially Jesus' Sermon on the Mount. In the Buddha's teachings about nonviolence and vegetarianism, Gandhi found echoes of the Jain ideas to which he had been exposed as a child. The *Gita* is the story of a prince, Arjuna, forced to lead his army into war. Gandhi rejected the violence but absorbed the *Gita*'s message about the need for self-disciplined action.

Gandhi disputed the Christian belief that Jesus was the son of God ("If God could have one son," he asked, "why not many?") but embraced Jesus' message of peace, similar to the Jain concept of nonviolence.

When Gandhi returned to India from London, he could not find work. Although he had studied law, he was not a very effective lawyer: in front of a crowd, he was tongue-tied. After two years, he finally found work representing an Indian Muslim firm in South Africa. Although he did not intend to stay long, Gandhi soon became involved in the struggle for equal rights for Indians, a significant minority group in South Africa. He stayed 20 years. He began his first experimental community, Phoenix House, there, inspired by the British critic John Ruskin's ideas about communal life and the dignity of all labor. Gandhi published his first magazine, *Indian Opinion*, in South Africa. It was also in South Africa that Gandhi, married and the father of four sons, took a lifelong vow of celibacy.

The roots of Gandhi's religious thinking took hold in South Africa. From the ancient Vedas, India's oldest Hindu texts, Gandhi absorbed the concept of *swaraj*—self-rule and self-restraint. Returning to the *Bhagavad Gita*, he found a philosophy of self-discipline that would prove immensely useful, both in focusing his energies on his mission and in appealing to his Indian followers. "Arming himself with discipline, seeing everything with an equal eye," a passage in the *Gita* reads, the wise man sees "the self in all creatures and all creatures in the self." Drawing on the traditional Indian idea that all living things are connected, Gandhi's philosophy combined *swaraj* with tolerance. Because no one can know the whole truth, he argued, people should practice tolerance and nonviolence—no one should ever harm another person.

In South Africa Gandhi invented the word *satyagraha* (often translated as "soul force") to describe his ideal of nonviolent action. *Satya* is derived from the Sanskrit word meaning "truth," and *agraha* is from a root meaning "holding firmly." Gandhi's goal was not merely the absence of violence but the transformation of conflict. A person who practiced *satyagraha* was known as a *satyagrahi*, someone who acted out of love and tolerance.

The young man who had been so timid that he could not say a word in court became a compelling speaker. In 1907, South Africa's government passed an act requiring Indians—who, like blacks, were not permitted to vote—to carry identity passes, meet a 9 P.M. curfew, and register with the government. Gandhi responded with a massive *satyagraha* campaign, involving at its height more than 50,000

"Non-cooperation with evil is as much a duty as is cooperation with good."

—from 1922 court testimony

> *"Having flung aside the sword, there is nothing except the cup of love which I can offer to those who oppose me. It is by offering that cup that I expect to draw them close to me."*
>
> —from *Young India* (1931)

protesters. Thousands of *satyagrahis*, including Gandhi, were jailed.

Gandhi's tactic was to appeal to his opponent's common sense and decency. His humor and generosity often converted his opponents into friends. Many contemporaries noted his cheerful nature and rapid wit. Huge, adoring crowds met him when he returned to India in 1915 at the age of 45. On the advice of Indian nationalist leader G. K. Gokhale, Gandhi spent a year "with his ears open and his mouth closed." He emerged from silence convinced that India must be freed from British rule.

Britain's presence in India dates back to 1600, when the British East India Company began running India as a kind of vast company store. Under Queen Victoria in the 19th century, India became "the jewel in the British crown." Gandhi was appalled by how this domination by a foreign country seemed to have weakened his fellow citizens.

He set about remaking Indians so they could take their country back. Gandhi did not expect social change to transform people; he expected personal changes to transform society. He had several goals: to raise the people from filth and ignorance, to foster Muslim-Hindu friendship, to seek equal rights for women, and to accept India's Untouchables, members of the lowest caste, as Harijans, or Children of God. His weapon against the British in India, as it had been in South Africa, was *satyagraha*.

The onetime dapper European adopted a simple homespun *dhoti*, or loincloth. He gave away his possessions and refused to travel by anything more luxurious than third-class railway or by foot. Urging Indians to boycott British cloth and other goods, Gandhi took up spinning himself. The spinning wheel became his symbol of Indian independence.

The poet Rabindrath Tagore, who lived and worked with Gandhi, called him "the great soul in peasant garb." The name *Mahatma*, which means "great soul," stuck. Gandhi became a hero to the hundreds of thousands of poor, illiterate people in India. Although they could not read his articles, they could see that he dressed and traveled as they did. Later, when he fasted for religious tolerance, it was as though he were speaking to them directly.

Gandhi waged many campaigns for poor Indians. He investigated the grievances of poor farmers, urged factory workers and others to strike for independence from Britain, and fasted on behalf of Untouchables and in support of Hindu-Muslim friendship. His most startling act in the name of Indian independence was the 1930 Salt March.

Although salt is essential to life, the British taxed it and forbade Indians from harvesting it. In the spring of 1930, Gandhi and 78 companions began walking the 200 miles from his ashram, or retreat center, to the Indian Ocean. He had no plan of what he would do once there, he said. But Gandhi had faith that a higher power existed. Believing that all religions pointed to the same end, he referred variously to the Hindu Ram, the Islamic Allah, the Jewish and Christian God, and often simply, Truth. He trusted that as a self-disciplined seeker of truth, he would know what to do.

Twenty-four days after he began his salt march, Gandhi's entourage had grown to several thousand marchers. The 60-year-old leader waded into the sea. As he walked back to the shore, he scooped up a handful of dried salt. His gesture electrified the Indian people. Gandhi later compared it to the Boston Tea Party, another revolutionary refusal to abide by rules perceived to be unfair. In the following weeks, between 60,000 and 100,000 Indians, including Gandhi, were arrested and jailed without trial. The Indians practiced nonviolence, but the British officials attacked the protesting crowds. Indians gained the moral high ground.

A year later, Gandhi went to London to negotiate for India's independence. His good humor and humane approach captivated the British as it had the Indians. Asked if he felt underdressed in his *dhoti* when he was presented to the British king, Gandhi joked, "The king was wearing enough for both of us." Even English textile workers, the objects of Gandhi's boycott, saw him as a hero.

India was not freed from British rule for 18 more years. World War II intervened, and conflicts within the Indian community—particularly among Hindus, Muslims, and Untouchables—slowed progress. On several occasions, Gandhi fasted as a gesture to encourage Indian peace and order.

The actual day of Indian independence, August 15, 1947, was a dark one for Gandhi. The leader of the country's Muslims, Gandhi's onetime ally Muhammad Ali Jinnah, had wrested a new country, Pakistan, out of India as a condition of independence. Gandhi abhorred the idea of dividing India along religious lines. Hindu-Muslim violence accompanied the partition of India. Gandhi, then in his 70s, went to Bengal and then Delhi, fasting "to death" until people agreed to tolerate differences.

He was finally overcome by the violence sweeping India. A Hindu fundamentalist, convinced that Gandhi's religious tolerance masked pro-Muslim sentiments, shot the hero of nonviolence on his way to evening prayers. Gandhi remained standing for an instant, then fell. A pious Hindu to the end, Gandhi's last words called on Rama (God).

Gandhi's example of political action and spiritual leadership have influenced many people. Chief among those who have applied Gandhi's "soul force" to their own situation was Martin Luther King, Jr., leader of the U.S. civil rights movement.

FURTHER READING

Brown, Judith. *Gandhi: Prisoner of Hope*. New Haven: Yale University Press, 1989.

Bush, Catherine. *Gandhi*. New York: Chelsea House, 1985.

Cheney, Glenn Alan. *Mohandas Gandhi*. New York: Franklin Watts, 1989.

Coolidge, Olivia. *Gandhi*. Boston: Houghton Mifflin, 1971.

Fischer, Louis. *Gandhi: His Life and Message for the World*. New York: NAL-Dutton, 1982.

————. *The Life of Mohandas Gandhi*. New York: Harper, 1950.

Gandhi, Mahatma. *The Collected Works of Mahatma Gandhi*. 92 vols. Canton, Maine: Greenleaf Books, 1983.

Rawding, F. W. *Gandhi*. New York: Cambridge University Press, 1980.

Shankar, R. *Story of Gandhi*. Pomona, Calif.: Auromere, 1979.

Shirer, William L. *Gandhi: A Memoir*. New York: Washington Square Press, 1979.

BELIEVERS

Mohandas Gandhi

BORN

October 2, 1869
Porbandar, India

DIED

January 30, 1948
Delhi, India

FORMAL EDUCATION

Legal training at Lincoln's Inn of the Court, London

TRADITION

Hinduism

ACCOMPLISHMENTS

Political and spiritual leader in South Africa and India; formulator and exponent of *satyagraha*, the ideal of nonviolent action; his writings include "Indian Self-rule" ("Hind Swaraj") (1909), *Autobiography* (1927), and *The History of Satyagraha in South Africa* (1928); founded the weekly papers *Navajivana*, *Young India*, *Harijan*, and *Harijanabandhu*

Pope John XXIII

"TO ENCOMPASS ALL MANKIND"

Angelo Guiseppe Roncalli was 77 years old when, as John XXIII, he became pope, the leader of the world's Roman Catholics. Many people assumed that because of his age, John would be a transitional pope, quietly biding his time. They misread him. John's deepest religious impulse was pastoral, to provide counseling and guidance to his people. As pope, he would be pastor to the world.

Roncalli was born in 1881 in a small village near Bergamo in northeastern Italy. Something of the native son remained in him all his life, making him sympathetic to other people's love for their own lands and customs. His parents were poor, pious sharecroppers, farmers who worked rented land. Angelo was one of 13 children and the oldest boy. He was guided into the priesthood, which was the primary way for bright sons of poor families to receive an education. After his early schooling, Roncalli earned a scholarship to study in Rome and was ordained a priest in 1904. To mark this event, he began keeping a diary, the *Journal of a Soul,* in which he recorded the details of his spiritual struggles. He was interested in history and published two books of church history early in his career.

After his ordination, Roncalli earned a doctorate in theology and became secretary to Giacomo Radini-Tedeschi, the bishop of Bergamo, Italy. Radini was active in Bergamo's political and economic life. Because of these secular, or worldly, activities, Pope Pius X suspected Radini and his secretary Roncalli of modernism during his 1907 campaign against heretics, those who held unorthodox beliefs.

By the beginning of the 20th century, the world had changed a great deal since the first Christians began spreading Jesus' message after his death in about 33 C.E. And that was the issue during Pope Pius X's tenure: should the church adapt to the world and possibly be changed itself, or should it insist that the world adapt to it?

In Italy, this question assumed greater importance in the late 19th century, when the modern Italian nation was born and replaced the church as Italy's central authority. Church leaders turned away from the changing world, discouraging Catholics from voting, joining labor unions, or exploring new ideas. "Modernism" became the new heresy.

The "modernist" label kept Roncalli far from power much of his career. After a tour as a medic during World War I and a turn in the church's missionary office (which oversaw foreign missions) in Rome, he taught at an ultra-conservative Catholic college. His teachings were not

With Vatican City in the background, Pope John XXIII contemplates a morning prayer. His good nature and personification of Christian charity made him one of the most beloved pontiffs of all time.

Under Roncalli's guidance, tensions between Catholic and Eastern Orthodox Christians in Bulgaria eased. He worked hard, organizing a conference of Bulgarian Catholics, encouraged the use of the Bulgarian language in Catholic schools and services, and promoted Bulgarians in the church. Roncalli's warm personality made him popular with Bulgarians of all traditions. Still, he felt hidden from the world.

Church leaders appointed Roncalli as a church delegate to Turkey and Greece in 1934, and he settled in Istanbul. There, he found a sizable Catholic congregation, as well as a noisy clash of religious and political hatreds. Besides the variety of religions represented in the region—Roman Catholicism, Greek Orthodoxy, Eastern Orthodoxy, Islam, and Judaism—Roncalli also had to face the Greek government's dislike of Catholicism and the Turkish government's distrust of religion in general.

Roncalli's motto became, as he put it, to "see everything, ignore a great deal, improve things where possible." By taking small, careful steps, he slowly befriended both the Greek Orthodox and Turkish secular camps. Roncalli introduced the Turkish language into Catholic services and visited the patriarch of the Greek Orthodox Church. Many Greek Orthodox and Turkish leaders came to admire him for the respect he showed them.

During World War II, Turkey became a center of international espionage. Roncalli used his contacts to achieve humanitarian goals. Through his friendship with the German ambassador to Turkey, he gained information that helped many Jews escape persecution in Europe. Active in relief efforts throughout the war, Roncalli helped persuade England to relax its blockade of food and medicine to Greece. After the war, he

traditional enough for church officials, so they removed him after a year and sent him to Bulgaria as apostolic visitor, a minor church official.

Roncalli arrived in Sofia, Bulgaria, in April 1925 with little guidance about what his mission should be. For years, he had recorded in his diary an ongoing struggle against ambition. Far from Rome, in a country with a tiny Catholic population, he prayed often for the strength to obey his orders.

> *"The social progress, order, security and peace of each country are necessarily connected with the social progress, order, security and peace of all other countries."*
>
> —from *Pacem in Terris* (1963)

established an office in Istanbul for prisoners of war and missing persons.

At the close of the war, Pope Pius XII called on Roncalli for another difficult task. The French government had asked Rome to recall the papal nuncio, or diplomat, because he had allied himself with France's Nazi invaders and sympathizers. Pius named Roncalli as his representative to France in December 1944.

Again, Roncalli's tact and sensitivity smoothed a rough way. Working with the French government, he helped ease out of office a small number of bishops who had collaborated with the Nazis and recommended 27 new bishops. He befriended French leaders, including socialists, and initially supported the worker-priest movement, in which priests labored at factory jobs alongside ordinary workers. UNESCO, the United Nations Educational, Scientific and Cultural Organization, secured its first papal representative at Roncalli's behest. When Pope Pius XII condemned Catholic radicals in his 1950 statement *Humani Generis (Of the Human Race)*, Roncalli discreetly suggested that theological controversy had caused enough bloodshed.

At age 71, Roncalli was named a cardinal priest of Rome, joining the body of advisers to the pope, and began to plan his retirement. To his surprise and gratification, he was elected, in 1953, to serve as patriarch of Venice.

Again, Roncalli searched for common ground. Although he opposed socialism and communism, he supported other social and labor movements. Breaking with tradition, he welcomed the huge Venice Biennale arts festival and attended the exhibition himself. Roncalli even addressed the Italian Socialist Congress in 1957, telling the assembly, "My heart is big enough to wish to encompass all mankind."

A year later, still immersed in his pastoral work, Roncalli was called to Rome. Pope Pius XII had died, and a new pope would be elected. On the 11th ballot of the College of Cardinals, Roncalli was selected. A man more different from Pius could not have been chosen.

Roncalli chose John as his papal name, after his father and John the Baptist. His first act was to draw all the assembled cardinals into the church government and call for an ecumenical, or churchwide, council to address church affairs. Bringing more people into decision making would be a hallmark of his papal term.

Although recent popes had waited for the world to return to the church, John preached *aggioranmento,* or adjusting to the modern world. He felt that the world's problems—such as the dangerous uncertainty of the cold war between the United States and the Soviet Union, and the increasing gulf between the world's rich and

poor people—needed the church's guidance.

Rather than greeting visitors from behind a desk, John met with his guests in an easy chair. He wore sturdy shoes instead of the traditional papal slippers, and except for breakfast he never ate alone. Unlike Pius, he toured Rome constantly, leaving his car to talk to people. He visited people in hospitals and prisons, and at one prison told his audience, "Because you cannot come to me, I came to you."

Pope John XXIII spoke out for economic and social justice in two early encyclicals, or papal letters. The *Princeps Pastorum (On the Missions,* 1959) condemned colonialism, or the governing of weak countries by more powerful ones. In *Mater et Magistra (Mother and Teacher,* 1961) he discussed in detail the conditions for social and economic justice.

The Second Vatican Ecumenical Council, the first in almost a century, was held from 1962 to 1965. The council included observers from many Christian faiths, ranging from Russian Orthodox to Quaker. Its purpose, John noted, was not to argue church doctrine but to restore unity among the world's faithful. In his opening speech, John rejected the "prophets of doom," the haters of the modern world who "behave as though history, which teaches us about life, has nothing to teach them." The issue, he said, was to discover the truths of faith in their modern expression. In supporting modern biblical scholarship, he veered, some thought, toward heresy.

John withdrew after his initial statement and let the assembled bishops think and argue for themselves. He intervened only once, to break an impasse over biblical studies. At the close of the session, two months later, he praised the "opening of the church's window" and planned the second session for the following autumn. He would not live to see it; he was diagnosed with a fatal cancer. Still, he remained active.

The Second Vatican Council radically changed the face of Roman Catholicism, overturning the church's former rejection of the modern world with a number of sweeping changes. Latin, for centuries the language of Catholic worship, was replaced by modern languages in the celebration of Mass. Priests had traditionally worshiped in the same direction as the congregation, but Vatican II asked them to face their parishioners and to view the whole church, priest and believers, as "the people of God." With Vatican II, 20th-century art and music began to find their way into Catholic worship. And Roman Catholicism's earlier rigid separation from other Christian traditions began to be more flexible, opening a way for Catholics and Protestants to find common ground. Finally, the council ended a centuries-old bitterness by rejecting the earlier Christian claim that Jews were responsible for the death of Jesus.

The Cuban Missile Crisis between the United States and the Soviet Union erupted during the Vatican Council. In a radio address, Pope John appealed for peaceful negotiations, allowing leaders of the countries to step back from war. The following Easter, John delivered his greatest encyclical, *Pacem in Terris (Peace on Earth*, 1963). Significantly, he ad-

dressed the work to "all men of goodwill," not solely to Catholics.

John was the first pope to address the threat of nuclear war. He advocated a nuclear test ban, global disarmament, and a universal peacekeeping authority. He also confronted the causes of war. *Pacem in Terris* stated the absolute right of each person to worship God according to conscience and to profess his or her religion, both privately and publicly. In the spring of 1963, he accepted the international Balzan Peace Prize for his contributions to "humanity, peace, and brotherhood," although some criticized him because the prize committee included Soviets. But John opened the door even to communists. He received the son-in-law of the Soviet premier Nikita Khrushchev and began to learn Russian in order to speak with Khrushchev himself.

Fearless and optimistic, Pope John XXIII was serene in meeting the world's dangers and uncertainties and served as an inspiration to many people. His death, in June 1963, was widely mourned.

FURTHER READING

Bonnot, Bernard R. *Pope John XXIII: An Astute Pastoral Leader*. Staten Island, N.Y.: Alba House, 1979.

Hebblethwaite, Peter. *Pope John XXIII: Shepherd of the Modern World*. Garden City, N.Y.: Doubleday, 1985.

John XXIII. *Journal of a Soul*. New York: McGraw-Hill, 1965.

Johnson, Paul. *Pope John XXIII*. Boston: Little, Brown, 1974.

Walch, Timothy. *John the Twenty-third*. New York: Chelsea House, 1987.

Wynn, Wilton. *Keepers of the Keys: John XXIII, Paul VI, John Paul II: Three Who Changed the World*. New York: Random House, 1988.

Pope John XXIII

BORN

November 25, 1881
Sotto il Monte, Italy

DIED

June 3, 1963
Rome, Italy

FORMAL EDUCATION

Doctorate, Roman Seminary (Apollinaire), Rome

TRADITION

Christian (Roman Catholic)

ACCOMPLISHMENTS

Pope (1958–63); convened the Second Vatican Council (1962–65); author of several books, including *Journal of a Soul* (1965), a biography of Giacomo Radini-Tedeschi, and three works about church history

Elijah Muhammad

BLACK MUSLIM
PROPHET

One of 13 children born to a Georgia farmer and Baptist preacher, Elijah Poole grew up in poverty. At 16, he left home, made his way north, and for the next 10 years he worked at odd jobs. Then, in 1923, Poole, his wife, Clara, and their two children settled in Detroit, where he found work in an automobile factory.

Six years later, at the beginning of the Great Depression, Poole joined a new religious organization. Known as the Nation of Islam, the movement called on African Americans to recognize their common condition and work to improve it. It taught that the world's nonwhite people belonged to a single nation whose god was Allah and whose truth was Islam.

The Nation of Islam was not the first large movement to mobilize African Americans since legalized slavery in the United States ended in 1865. Marcus Garvey's Universal

Elijah Muhammad remains one of the most controversial homegrown religious leaders in the United States. He taught that Christianity was a tool that whites used to oppress blacks and proposed an alternative: a program of self-discipline and self-sufficiency in which blacks should fear no one but Allah.

Negro Improvement Association (UNIA) and Noble Drew Ali's Moorish Science Temple both preceded the movement. Garvey advocated a separate black nation, encouraged black-owned businesses, and founded the Christian-based African Orthodox Church. He galvanized a generation of African Americans before he was deported to Jamaica in 1923.

Drew Ali formed a black Islamic movement in 1913. Like Garvey, he saw religion in political terms. "Before you can have a God you must have a nationality," he asserted. Ali's movement quickly spread from its origins in Newark, New Jersey, to New York City, Chicago, Philadelphia, Pittsburgh, and Detroit.

Ali died in 1929, and a silk merchant named Wallace D. Fard took up the message of the Nation of Islam. A door-to-door salesman in Detroit, Fard made many converts through personal contact. He had come from Mecca, the holy city of Islam, he said, "to wake the dead Nation of the West, to teach the truth about the white man, and prepare for Armageddon," or the battle of the Last Judgment.

Fard taught that the earth's original people, the tribe of Shabazz, were black and that an insane scientist, Yacub, had created whites out of perverted curiosity. The whites had risen against the blacks, scattering and oppressing them. Many African Americans found this account a powerful tonic. When Elijah Poole met Fard, he dropped his surname, which he called a "slave name," and took the name of Muhammad, after the 7th-century prophet of Islam.

The Nation of Islam initially appealed most strongly to young black men. Most were former Christians and former southerners who had traveled north in the massive exodus of African Americans in the 1920s. Many converts came from black neighborhoods in the North that, in many respects, already resembled a separate nation. The Nation

of Islam also forged a strong presence in U.S. prisons, finding converts among the African-American inmate population.

Muhammad rose quickly in Fard's ranks, and Fard promoted him to head of Temple Number 1, which was located in Detroit. In 1932 Muhammad moved to Chicago and established the Southside Mosque, later known as Temple Number 2. That same year, Fard's life unraveled. Detroit authorities arrested him as an accessory in a cultic murder inspired by his writings. He sought refuge with Muhammad but was arrested again in Chicago. Fard then disappeared.

In the struggle that followed for control of the organization, Elijah Muhammad traveled extensively, fighting off rivals and building up the movement in other cities. He spent the years from 1942 to 1946 in jail for refusing, on the basis of religion and conscience, to serve in the U.S. Army during World War II. Muhammad's prison term gave him heroic standing among many of his followers, and he emerged the undisputed leader of the Nation of Islam. Under his leadership the movement established temples or missions in nearly every U.S. city with a sizable black population. The present Nation of Islam is still centered in his Chicago Temple.

Muhammad viewed Christianity as a tool whites used to oppress blacks; whites approached blacks with a Bible in one hand and a gun in the other, he said. Muhammad wanted to replace Christian values with Black Muslim ones.

> "America is the place where Allah will make himself felt."
>
> —from *The Supreme Wisdom* (1957)

Elijah Muhammad

BORN
October 7, 1897
Sandersville, Georgia

DIED
February 25, 1975
Chicago, Illinois

TRADITION
Islam (Nation of Islam)

ACCOMPLISHMENTS
Leader of the Nation of Islam; author of *The Supreme Wisdom* (1957), *Message to the Blackman in America* (1965), and *How to Eat to Live* (1972)

In a 1955 newspaper statement, Elijah Muhammad spelled out the goals of his movement. It sought to allow African Americans to "discover themselves, elevate their distinguished men and women, give outlets to their talented youth, and assume the contours of a nation." This translated into a message of model behavior and self-respect. He urged his followers to obey a set of principles that included praying regularly, telling the truth regardless of circumstances, maintaining moral and physical hygiene, and fearing no one but Allah. Elijah Muhammad insisted that his followers avoid drinking, smoking, drug use, gluttony, gambling, and other self-destructive acts. He also demanded that the United States set aside territory in the South for an independent black nation.

Elijah Muhammad wanted to replace white institutions with black ones. He called on Black Muslims to shape their own destiny by opening black-owned businesses. The Nation of Islam has itself undertaken business ventures. It operates farms, banks, publishing ventures, restaurants, and schools for both children and adults.

Elijah Muhammad's message of black pride, black nationalism, and black self-reliance attracted many followers. The onetime petty criminal Malcolm Little joined the movement in 1952. Adopting the name Malcolm X, he became instrumental in spreading Elijah Muhammad's teachings.

Malcolm X was Elijah Muhammad's prize disciple for many years, but he began to distance himself from Muhammad when the older man was accused of adultery, a serious violation of Islamic ethics. Muhammad suspended his disciple in 1964, and the two men never reconciled. Black Muslims were implicated in the 1965 assassination of Malcolm X, and the movement began to falter. Elijah Muhammad died in 1975.

Workers inspect copies of *Muhammad Speaks,* the Nation of Islam's official newspaper, as it comes off the press in the 1970s. A photograph of Elijah Muhammad appears on the back page.

His son, Wallace D. Muhammad, took control of the movement after his father's death and shifted it in the direction of orthodox Islam. He rejected some of his father's adamant color consciousness and his father's call for a separate black nation. Perhaps most significantly, he denied that Fard was divine. In the early 1980s, Wallace D. Muhammad changed his name to the Muslim Warith Deen Muhammad and renamed the Nation of Islam the American Muslim Mission. In 1985, he formally dissolved the Nation of Islam to allow Black Muslims to join the larger Islamic community. He continues to be active in Islamic religion and culutre, serving as an imam, or leader, of a Chicago mosque.

Not everyone embraced the younger Muhammad's steps, however. His most important critic has been Louis Farrakhan. In 1978, Farrakhan broke with Muhammad and created a second Nation of Islam, with principles closer to those of Elijah

Muhammad, including dietary and dress restrictions and a harsher view of whites. Although he has attracted controversy, Farrakhan continues many of Elijah Muhammad's social and economic programs. He directs his movement from the former lead temple of the Nation of Islam in Chicago.

FURTHER READING

Halasa, Malu. *Elijah Muhammad.* New York: Chelsea House, 1990.

Lincoln, C. Eric. *The Black Muslims in America.* Boston: Beacon Press, 1973.

Muhammad, Elijah. *Message to the Blackman in America.* Chicago: Muhammad's Temple No. 2, 1965.

Parks, Greg. *Freedom, Justice, and Equality: The Teachings of the Nation of Islam.* Hampton, Va.: United Brothers and Sisters, 1992.

Teresa of Calcutta

THE FACE OF CHARITY

Many Europeans might have found August 1946 a good time to leave India. The eve of Indian independence, it was a time of growing public disorder and violence. But for a young Albanian nun, August 1946 was when she received her "call within a call." God commanded her, she said, to leave her comfortable life as a schoolteacher and seek out "the poorest of the poor."

Mother Teresa was born Agnes Bojaxhiu, the third child and second daughter of an Albanian Catholic family living in Serbian Yugoslavia (now Macedonia). As a girl, she was a distinguished singer and an excellent student. Her father, Nikola, was a generous-spirited businessman and a pro-Albanian political activist. He died at the end of World War I, when Agnes was eight.

Perhaps the world's most recognizable symbol of charity, Mother Teresa won the Nobel Peace Prize in 1979 for her efforts to help sick and suffering people around the world.

Mother Teresa has spent her entire adult life ministering to poor children. Here, on a visit to the Philippines, she meets with some residents of Manila.

Her mother, Drana, supported the family as a dressmaker after her husband died. An extremely devout Roman Catholic, Drana made regular charity visits, frequently accompanied by her children, to people in need. Teresa recalls that her family rarely ate a meal without being joined by a stranger whom their mother had in–vited. The family also prayed together every evening.

When Agnes was in high school, a new Roman Catholic priest came to her town. Although Yugoslavia was then predominantly Eastern (Serbian) Orthodox, the Catholic priest made his church a spiritual and cultural magnet. He was especially enthusiastic about foreign missions, and Agnes absorbed his enthusiasm, reading widely in his missionary magazines.

Agnes decided to become a nun and chose to join the Order of the Loreto Sisters. Based in Ireland, the Loreto Sisters followed the guidelines of Saint Ignatius Loyola's *Spiritual Exercises*, a manual of devotions and prayer. The Loreto Sisters performed their missionary work in Bengal, India.

Agnes's family was surprised when she announced her plans. Her mother retreated to her room for an entire day before she emerged to give Agnes her blessing. Agnes's brother Lazar, away at military school, was harshly critical. She responded: "You think you're important because you are an officer.... But I am serving the King of the whole world! Which of us do you think is in the better place?" Lazar later conceded that she had amazing organizational skills. "You are an officer," he told his sister. "You could have gone to military school."

More than 100 people gathered at the train station to bid the 18-year-old Agnes a safe trip to Ireland. After she received her training there, she traveled to the order's center in Darjeeling, in northern India. There she continued her studies, including learning Indian languages, and began teaching in the Loreto Convent School.

In 1931 Agnes took her first vows as a nun. She changed her name to Teresa, after the 19th-century French saint Teresa, who was known as the Little Flower of Lisieux. Assigned to a convent school, she taught history and geography in Calcutta. By her own account, Teresa loved teaching. But on a train ride to an annual retreat in Darjeeling, Teresa heard a clear message from God to serve Calcutta's poor.

Then the second largest city in the British Empire, Calcutta contained both enormous wealth and appalling poverty. People stepped over the bodies of the ill and dying on their way to work.

In the summer of 1948, Teresa exchanged her dark Loreto habit, or uniform, for a plain, white sari with a blue border. After six months of medical training, she began her new life in Calcutta.

Arranging to live in a nearby convent, she entered the Motijhil slum, gathered a small group of children around her, and simply began teaching. Her only tool was a stick, which she used to write with in the dirt.

After her first year of work in Calcutta, an Indian Catholic family invited Teresa to share their house so that she could be closer to her work. Two of her former Loreto students, one of whom took the name Agnes, soon joined her. Teresa became an Indian citizen, saying, "I feel Indian to the most profound depths of my soul."

In 1948 she founded her own Catholic order, the Missionaries of Charity, which received sanction from Pope Pius XII in 1950. The band of sisters grew to 26, and with help from the Archbishop of India, they bought a building of their own.

Lazar's remark about his sister's organizational skills was indeed confirmed. Like a capable general, she sent help wherever it was needed. Moved by people too poor to die anywhere but on the street, Teresa opened a Hindu shrine called the *Nirmal Hriday*, "Place of the Pure Heart," for them. To local Hindus who complained that a Catholic was using a shrine to the Hindu mother goddess Kali, Teresa's defenders replied, "The temple holds a stone image of Kali. Here we have the living Kali!"

A year later, Mother Teresa opened a home for orphans and set up a food distribution program. To avoid religious conflicts, she invited Hindus one day, Muslims the next. When a group of sufferers from Hanson's disease (leprosy) approached her for help, she organized traveling health-care vans, clinics, and rehabilitation centers. Although the families of the lepers had rejected them, Teresa gave them the same care that she gave everyone else. God does not distinguish among people, she believed; each person has the same worth in God's eyes.

Church rules required Teresa to wait 10 years before expanding her order. When the time had passed, her missions grew rapidly throughout India. She began traveling to raise money and support for her work, although she felt her real gift was love rather than talk. She was nevertheless a very successful fund-raiser.

In the early 1960s, Mother Teresa received permission to expand her order outside India. Her first outpost was in Cocorote, Venezuela, an impoverished village of people descended from African slaves. In the late 1960s the Missionaries of Charity opened a center in Rome itself. Their first American outpost opened in 1971 in the South Bronx, a section of New York City.

Teresa of Calcutta

BORN

August 27, 1910
Skopje, Serbia (present-day Macedonia)

TRADITION

Christianity (Roman Catholic)

ACCOMPLISHMENTS

Founder of the Missionaries of Charity (1948); awarded Nobel Peace Prize (1979)

"How can you love God whom you do not see, if you do not love your neighbor whom you see, whom you touch, with whom you live?"

—from Nobel Peace Prize address (1979)

Other people wished to join Mother Teresa's efforts. An order of priests joined the Missionaries of Charity in 1963. With the help of a British supporter, Ann Blaikie, Teresa started a lay group, the International Association of Co-Workers of Mother Teresa. Because some sick people also wanted to become Co-Workers, Teresa founded the Sick and Suffering Co-Workers. Their work is largely prayer.

As Mother Teresa's missions grew, so did her awards and honors. In 1979 she was awarded the Nobel Peace Prize, the universally recognized award for generosity and courage. The attention made Mother Teresa uneasy. She prefers not to be lionized. "My life or yours, it's still just a life," she says.

Mother Teresa of Calcutta has devoted her life to becoming "the living expression of God's kindness," which is what she instructs her workers to strive for as well. To a world impressed by the ability to achieve things efficiently, she is an insistent reminder that physical care is not enough: "You must give your heart as well."

Near the Missions of Charity building in Calcutta, local people have built a small shrine in a patch of dirt. Leaning against a tree, it holds flowers and candles, small carvings of Jesus and Mary, and photographs torn from magazines of Mother Teresa. Future generations may well regard her as a saint.

FURTHER READING

Clucas, Joan Graff. *Mother Teresa*. New York: Chelsea House, 1988.

Craig, Mary. *Mother Teresa*. Pomfret, Vt.: Trafalgar, 1991.

Doig, Desmond. *Mother Teresa: Her People and Her Work*. New York: Harper & Row, 1976.

Egan, Eileen. *Such a Vision of the Street: Mother Teresa—The Spirit and the Work*. Garden City, N.Y.: Doubleday, 1985.

Giff, Patricia Reilly. *Mother Teresa: Sister to the Poor*. New York: Puffin, 1987.

Lazo, Caroline. *Mother Teresa*. New York: Macmillan, 1993.

Le Joly, Edward. *Mother Teresa of Calcutta: A Biography*. New York: Harper & Row, 1985.

Muggeridge, Malcolm. *Something Beautiful for God*. New York: Harper & Row, 1986.

Porter, David. *Mother Teresa: The Early Years*. Grand Rapids, Mich.: Eerdmans, 1986.

Serrou, Robert. *Teresa of Calcutta: A Pictorial Biography*. New York: McGraw-Hill, 1980.

Tames, Richard. *Mother Teresa*. New York: Franklin Watts, 1991.

Teresa, Mother. *Life in the Spirit: Reflections, Meditations, Prayers*. New York: Harper & Row, 1983.

———. *My Life for the Poor*. New York: Harper & Row, 1985.

———. *Total Surrender*. New York: Walker, 1993.

Malcolm X

"GOD IS BLACK"

A well-meaning reporter once asked Malcolm X to describe the time when he first experienced racial discrimination. "Well," he replied, "I was born in a segregated hospital, of a segregated mother. When I was four, my house was burned down by segregationists. When I was six, my father was murdered by segregationists. Shall I go on?" In Malcolm X, righteous African-American anger found its 20th-century voice.

Malcolm X was born Malcolm Little on May 19, 1925, in Omaha, Nebraska. His father, Earl Little, was a Baptist minister who favored a mixture of Christianity and Garveyism. Garveyism was a popular black nationalist, back-to-Africa movement founded by the Jamaican leader Marcus Garvey. A white racist group attacked Little for both his color and his views and burned down his family's house.

A powerful speaker, Malcolm X was a charismatic leader in the Nation of Islam who urged black Americans to take pride in their origins, identity, and heritage.

The two most prominent leaders of the civil rights movement, Martin Luther King, Jr. (left) and Malcolm X shake hands during a rare face-to-face encounter in Washington, D.C., in March 1964. While King advocated nonviolent protest and resistance, Malcolm X said that blacks should use "any means necessary" to achieve justice.

Resettling in Lansing, Michigan, Earl Little started a grocery business and continued preaching. Two years later, he was found dead, with his head crushed. The family survived on public assistance until Malcolm's mother, Louise Little, collapsed; she spent the rest of her life in a mental institution. Her children dispersed to different homes.

One of the top students in his school, Malcolm joined the debating team and was elected president of his class. But he was badly shaken when he discovered that talent and intelligence were not enough. A teacher whom he admired talked him out of becoming a lawyer. "A lawyer!" Malcolm recalled the teacher's words, "That is not a realistic goal for a nigger.... You're good with your hands.... Why don't you plan on carpentry?"

Disillusioned, Malcolm eagerly accepted an invitation from his half-sister Ella Collins to spend the summer of 1940 in Boston. Mesmerized by Boston's black culture, he left Michigan for good. Although he was fresh out of the eighth grade, Malcolm's size made him look older. The young would-be lawyer now schooled himself in being a hustler who could outwit the system. His teachers were prostitutes, pimps, drug dealers, and other criminals. In the underworlds of Boston and New York, Malcolm made a name for himself—Big Red, after his height and his reddish-colored skin.

In Boston, Malcolm teamed up with his white girlfriend, her sister, and two other black men to form a burglary ring. They were caught. "This will teach you to stay away from white girls," the judge said, handing Malcolm a prison sentence of eight to ten years.

Prison reawakened Malcolm's intellect. Encouraged by another burglar, Bimbi, to read something besides thrillers, Malcolm devoured the prison library. He was drawn especially to philosophy and philology, the study of literature and language. His brother Reginald is credited with introducing him to the Black Muslims, but Malcolm may have already known something of the movement. His sister Ella was once a close friend of its leader, Elijah Muhammad.

The Black Muslim movement, officially called the Nation of Islam, was born in Detroit's black ghetto during the Great Depression of the 1930s. Its founder, Wallace D. Fard, was a silk merchant and probably an Arab. In his homemade version of Islam, Fard preached that God is black and made black people in his image; white people were the result of a terrible experiment gone awry. He declared that Christianity was the "white man's religion."

One early convert to the Nation of Islam was Elijah Poole, an ex-Baptist minister from Georgia. When Fard disappeared and other Black Muslims were found dead, Poole—who had taken the name Elijah Muhammad—took over leadership of the movement. When Malcolm heard Elijah Muhammad preach that the white man was the devil, it had the force of a religious conversion. The world finally made sense to him.

The Black Muslims were a small movement until Malcolm Little joined them after being released from prison. Elijah Muhammad recognized Malcolm's abilities, and the two men forged a strong father-son relationship. Malcolm rose through the movement's ranks. He headed the New York mosque and opened other mosques, or houses of worship, all along the East Coast. With many other Black Muslims, Malcolm discarded his surname as a remnant of slavery. He replaced it with the letter X, to serve as a placeholder for the African name lost during slavery. The X also stood for "ex-smoker, ex-drinker, ex-Christian, ex-slave," he said.

Malcolm X preached the Black Muslim gospel of clean living, strong family life, and total separation from whites. "The only thing I like integrated is coffee," he once said. Two years after joining the movement, he married a nurse, Betty Shabazz, with whom he had six daughters.

A powerful, articulate speaker, Malcolm X regularly drew large crowds when he preached, but he was not well regarded by mainstream black leaders, who thought the Black Muslim message was divisive. Martin Luther King, Jr., refused to debate Malcolm X. Those who did debate him quickly found their pro-integration arguments shredded by his fast wit.

In a sense, Malcolm X became the lawyer that he had wanted to be as a boy. He roamed the country as though it were a courtroom, pleading the case of African Americans. He taught that blacks had been so damaged by racism that they had come to believe that they were inferior. Only strong measures, he said, would free them. Elijah Muhammad forbade his followers from taking political action, however.

Eventually, strains in Malcolm's relationship with Elijah Muhammad began to show. Malcolm had become so successful that he stood in danger of eclipsing the older man. There were signs that Malcolm had reached his limit in the movement. His column in New York's black newspaper, the *Amsterdam News*, was taken over by Elijah Muhammad, and the newspaper that Malcolm had started, *Muhammad Speaks*, was moved to Chicago. He sensed that he was being closely watched.

When Elijah Muhammad finally confirmed rumors that he had fathered several out-of-wedlock children, Malcolm's faith in him plummeted. In his speeches, Malcolm began to focus less on religion and more on politics and economics.

In the end, Elijah Muhammad broke with Malcolm X. Muhammad

Malcolm X

BORN

May 19, 1925
Omaha, Nebraska

DIED

February 21, 1965
New York, New York

TRADITION

Islam (Nation of Islam)

ACCOMPLISHMENT

Black Muslim leader; founded Muslim Mosque, Inc. (1964); author of *The Autobiography of Malcolm X* (1965)

> *"Our God is a live God.... He is walking around here with you, among you, in you...God is black like you."*
>
> —from a sermon in Detroit (1953)

had forbidden his ministers to comment on the assassination of President John F. Kennedy in 1963, but in a question period after a speech, Malcolm referred to Kennedy's death as "chickens coming home to roost." Muhammad immediately suspended him.

When Malcolm's suspension period ended in February 1964, he was not reinstated. He began a group of his own called the Muslim Mosque, Inc. His new role, he said, would be similar to that of Billy Graham, the Protestant evangelist. Traveling around the country, he would preach black nationalism and, this time, take political action. Few followers signed up.

Malcolm traveled abroad, and in Mecca, the holy city of Islam, he experienced a second, momentous religious conversion—to orthodox Sunni Islam. Taking the name el-Hajj Malik el-Shabazz, he embraced orthodox Islam's message of universal brotherhood. On the same trip, he met the African revolutionary leaders Ben Bella of Algeria and Kwame Nkrumah of Ghana. He began dreaming of an international freedom struggle and looked to socialism as a new model of community.

After returning to the United States, Malcolm sorted through his ideas, discarding those that were no longer true for him. He believed that he had been used by Elijah Muhammad and turned sharply away from his earlier black separatist beliefs. The good student turned street hustler turned Black Muslim minister was remaking himself as a man of tolerance.

Old enemies, however, had their own plans. Malcolm's house was bombed. He told his biographer Alex Haley that he knew he was a marked man. Still, he was driven to speak out. In one of his last speeches, before the Afro-American Broadcasting Company, Malcolm made his final case. "You can't hate your origin and not end hating yourself," he reminded his audience who, like other Americans, had absorbed images of black inferiority alongside those of white achievement.

"How could you think you're an American when you haven't ever had any kind of an American treat over here? Just being at the table with others who are dining doesn't make me a diner. Let us practice brotherhood among ourselves," he said, "then if others want to practice brotherhood with us, we're for practicing it with them also. But I don't think we should run around trying to love somebody who doesn't love us." He predicted, correctly, that racial unrest loomed ahead for American cities in the summer of 1965.

Malcolm's last appearance was a speech at the Audubon Ballroom in New York. He had invited other prominent blacks to join him that day, but he walked onto an empty stage. "*Wa-salaam alaikum*" (Peace be upon you), he greeted his audience in Arabic. "*Wa-alaikum-salaam*" (And upon you, too), they replied. Then a scuffle broke out. Three black men in the front row stood up, raised their guns, and fired. The apostle of black pride was dead. His killers appeared to be Black Muslims, but controversy over whether they were connected with that movement still rages.

Malcolm X overcame extremely difficult circumstances to cast himself as a voice for black consciousness. His ideas were central to the Black Power movement of the 1960s and 1970s and have influenced all subsequent discussions of race in the United States.

FURTHER READING

Davies, Mark. *Malcolm X: Another Side of the Movement*. Englewood Cliffs, N.J.: Silver Burdett Press, 1990.

Goldman, Peter. *The Death and Life of Malcolm X*. New York: Harper & Row, 1973.

Grimes, Nikki. *Malcolm X: A Force for Change*. New York: Fawcett, 1992.

Haskins, Jim. *One More River to Cross: The Stories of Twelve Black Americans*. New York: Scholastic, 1992.

Malcolm X. *Malcolm X Speaks*. 2nd ed. New York: Pathfinder, 1993.

Malcolm X with Alex Haley. *The Autobiography of Malcolm X*. New York: Random House, 1964.

Myers, Walter Dean. *Malcolm X: By Any Means Necessary*. New York: Scholastic, 1993.

Rummel, Jack. *Malcolm X*. New York: Chelsea House, 1989.

Strickland, William, with Cheryl Y. Greene. *Malcolm X: Make It Plain*. New York: Viking, 1994.

Williams, Todd. *The Sayings of Malcolm X*. New York: Dell, 1992.

Martin Luther King, Jr.

FREEDOM MARCHER

I n December 1955, Rosa Parks, a black seam-
stress in Montgomery, Alabama, refused to give
up her bus seat to a white rider and set off a
revolution. A key figure in this revolution was
Martin Luther King, Jr., a young Baptist minister. In the 12 years before an assassin took his life, King
would take the cause of civil rights for African Americans
from the buses of Montgomery to countless cities, to the
front pages of newspapers, and into the halls of Congress.

The origins of this revolution date to the beginnings of
slavery in the Americas in the early 16th century. Ratifica-
tion of the 13th Amendment to the Constitution ended legal
slavery in the United States in 1865. For nearly another
century, however, racially biased laws, such as the one that
denied Rosa Parks a front seat on a bus, kept many African
Americans from full citizenship. The U.S. Supreme Court
began to overturn these laws with its decision in *Brown* v.
Board of Education (1954). In that landmark case, the Court
declared that segregation in public schools was unconstitu-
tional because separate facilities are inherently unequal; such

As a leader of the black civil rights movement, apostle of
nonviolence, and the youngest recipient of the Nobel Peace
Prize, Martin Luther King, Jr., offered a profound moral vision for
America that drew both black and white supporters.

a system denied black students the equal protection of the laws of the state.

Martin Luther King, Jr., was 25 when the Court decided the *Brown* case. He had spent his childhood under the punishing segregation laws of his native Atlanta, Georgia. These laws required blacks and whites to use separate facilities, from water fountains to store entrances.

King was named for his father, a stern, hard-working Baptist minister and civil rights activist who had begun his life as a sharecropper. Alberta, his mother, was the daughter of a preacher. Martin, Jr., his older sister, Christine, and their younger brother, A. D., grew up in middle-class comfort, and their father hoped his oldest son would follow him into the ministry. But Martin wanted no part of a church that offered comfort, not change, to black people. Young King decided to become a lawyer.

Extremely bright, King entered Atlanta's Morehouse College at age 15. There, an old friend of his father's, the Reverend Benjamin Mays, served as King's mentor and guided him back to the church. The summer before he graduated, at age 18, King was named associate pastor of his father's church, Ebenezer Baptist.

His intellectual curiosity was too strong, and perhaps his father's influence too great, for King to return home so soon. In 1949 he entered Crozer Theological Seminary, located near Philadelphia. Crozer was an integrated college where the Social Gospel—a movement within American Prostantism which applied Christian ethics to modern social problems—was a strong influence. Other seminary students nicknamed King "Tweed" because he seemed so buttoned-down. Though King tempered his conservative image with a reputation as a pool shark and ladies' man, he nevertheless graduated at the top of his class.

During his time at Crozer, King studied the works of Mohandas Gandhi, the Indian revolutionary and apostle of nonviolence. King also began reading Karl Marx, the German economist and revolutionary.

After Crozer, King went on to earn a doctorate in theology at Boston University. He wrote his dissertation on the conceptions of God held by two Protestant theologians, Paul Tillich and Nelson Wieman. King was also shaping his own ideas about God. He favored a "personalist" theology, one in which God, far from being abstract, is "responsive to the deepest yearnings of the human heart," he wrote. The theology King worked out in his life owed debts to such Protestant ideas as the Social Gospel and to the ideals of nonviolence espoused by Gandhi, but he also drew from strong black American traditions as well. The abolitionist Frederick Douglass and the 20th-century philosopher W. E. B. Du Bois helped shape King's commitment to an integrated society. And the African-American church tradition he grew up in played a vital role in King's thinking.

Theologian James Cone has described this tradition as rooted in the Bible and focused on the values of justice, mercy (the turning away from vengeance for wrongs done to blacks), and hope—the idea that, as King said, "God can make a way out of no way." King believed that the black community had been called by God to "save the soul of America," and he drew often on the biblical prophets, such as Amos and Hosea, who called on their societies to remember their highest values.

When King finished graduate school, he accepted a position preaching at the Dexter Avenue Baptist Church in Montgomery, Alabama. He left Boston with his new wife and fellow southerner, Coretta Scott King. She was the daughter of an Alabama businessman whose stores had been repeatedly burned out by white racists.

King (front row, second from left) helps lead the March on Washington for Jobs and Freedom in August 1963. The occasion of his "I Have a Dream" speech, the march was the largest nonviolent gathering in the nation's history.

She had gone to Boston to train as a singer and had planned to stay in the North, but King convinced her to marry him and give up her career.

Once in Montgomery, King opened his somewhat stuffy, middle-class church to everyone and urged his people to join the National Association for the Advancement of Colored People (NAACP), an organization formed in 1910 to advance political and social equality for American blacks. Fellow minister Ralph Abernathy persuaded King to become involved in a proposed boycott of Montgomery's buses to protest the arrest of Rosa Parks.

As someone new in town who had not yet made any enemies, King was voted president of the boycott commission. The commission was still debating the merits of a boycott when several thousand people showed up for a rally in its favor. Delivering a hastily organized speech, King sealed his role as the country's most eloquent, passionate voice for civil rights. "We are not wrong in what we are doing," he told the overflow crowd in his rich baritone. "If we are wrong, the Supreme Court of this nation is wrong. If we are wrong, God Almighty is wrong!" The crowd thundered its approval as King invoked the biblical prophet Amos: "We are determined here in Montgomery to work and fight until justice runs down like water, and righteousness like a mighty stream!"

As he tested the institution of segregation, King found himself tested, too. Threatening phone calls—as many as 40 a day—became commonplace. One January night, unable to sleep after such a call, King sat in his kitchen, thinking. He thought about the theology and philosophy he had studied, trying to understand evil. He later wrote, "But the answer didn't quite come there.... I discovered then that religion had to become real to me and I had to know God for myself.... And I

bowed down over that cup of coffee.... And I prayed out loud that night, I said, 'Lord, I'm down here trying to do what's right.'" But, he confessed in his prayer, he could feel himself losing courage. In response, he heard assurance: "Martin Luther," a voice told him, "stand up for righteousness. Stand up for justice. Stand up for truth. And lo, I will be with you, even until the end of the world." Like the prophets of ancient Israel, King felt certain that he was doing God's work.

The Montgomery boycott lasted a year. The bus company lost money; so did local merchants. King's house was bombed, and he was arrested. But the black community, in Montgomery and elsewhere, had its first victory. The original, fairly modest demands had grown into an ambitious program. Demands by African Americans now ranged from desegregating public facilities to guaranteeing voting rights for all African Americans.

King spent his next years in a fever of activity and acclaim. In 1957, King, Abernathy, and other black ministers formed the Southern Christian Leadership Conference (SCLC) to promote the use of nonviolent action to combat other injustices in the South. King went to the African nation of Ghana to celebrate that country's independence from Great Britain. In Washington, D.C., he led a civil rights prayer pilgrimage of 30,000 people.

The same year, with a thousand federal soldiers standing by, Central High School in Little Rock, Arkansas, was integrated. Congress passed a Civil Rights Act, and although it was too weak to please civil rights leaders, it was a start. King began receiving honors, and he wrote a book, *Stride Toward Freedom*.

The first attempt on King's life occurred when he was in Harlem, an African-American neighborhood in New York City, on a trip to promote his book. A deranged woman stabbed him with a sharpened letter opener. The perils of outspoken public life, however, did not daunt him. He quit his pastorate at Dexter Avenue, moved his family to Atlanta, and dedicated himself full-time to the civil rights struggle.

Inspired by King and the air of change in the South, black college students held the first sit-in at a dime store counter in Greensboro, North Carolina, in January 1960. As the sit-in movement grew, the Student Nonviolent Coordinating Committee, or SNCC, was born. SNCC had King's early blessing but was not part of the SCLC.

That fall, John F. Kennedy won the 1960 Presidential election, and King and others began pressing for a civil rights bill. In the summer of 1961—Freedom Summer, as it became known—black and white students tried to travel by bus through the segregated South to register voters. Their first bus was stopped and set afire; riders on the second were badly beaten at the bus terminal in Birmingham, Alabama. Each act of violence shocked the nation.

A failed attempt to desegregate public facilities in Albany, Georgia, where white violence prompted black violence, led King to plan his next action with supreme care. In the spring of 1963, he went to Birmingham. He wanted to test desegregation efforts in the city he called "the most viciously segregated in the country." Three hundred people were arrested. King, Abernathy, and Wyatt Walker, director of the SCLC, were legally forbidden to march. They marched anyway. King was jailed in solitary confinement. In response to criticism from some religious leaders, he wrote his *Letter from a Birmingham Jail*.

In the *Letter* King asks: When is it right for someone to disobey a law he believes to be unjust? His answer frames his philosophy of nonviolence. It is right to disobey an unjust law, he wrote, when the cause is just, when all avenues of negotiation have been exhausted,

and when the disobedient are committed to nonviolence. "My friends," he addressed the clergymen, "we have not made a single gain in civil rights without determined legal and nonviolent pressure.... Freedom is never voluntarily given by the oppressor; it must be demanded by the oppressed."

King was released in April 1963. The next month, despite the presence of television cameras, Birmingham's police chief, Eugene "Bull" Connor, unleashed dogs and fire hoses on some 3,000 children marching in the cause of freedom. Leading them was the black minister Charles Billups, who told Connor, "We are not turning back. We have done nothing wrong. All we want is our freedom.... Bring on your dogs." Connor called for the hoses again, but the police and fire fighters, many of them weeping, refused his order. An agreement to let blacks enter a whites-only park was reached five days later.

The struggle was far from over, even in Birmingham. In June, Medgar Evers, head of the Mississippi chapter of the NAACP, was shot to death standing in the doorway of his home. King led a 125,000-strong march in Detroit to protest the murder of Evers. That summer, more than 250,000 people marched on Washington for civil rights. It was the largest public gathering in U.S. history. King closed the ceremonies with an electrifying speech. In the "I Have a Dream" speech, as it is now known, he asked the United States to cash the check of freedom it had written to all Americans in the Declaration of Independence. King reminded his listeners that "white destiny is bound up with black." Whites needed to free blacks as badly as blacks needed to be freed. He ended by recalling the dream once held by slaves: "Free at last."

More than 900 public demonstrations for civil rights took place in 1963. Then, in September, Birm-

Martin Luther King, Jr.

BORN

January 15, 1929
Atlanta, Georgia

DIED

April 4, 1968
Memphis, Tennessee

FORMAL EDUCATION

B.A., Morehouse College; M.A., Crozer Theological Seminary; Ph.D., Boston University

TRADITION

Christianity (Protestant)

ACCOMPLISHMENTS

American civil rights leader; awarded Nobel Peace Prize (1964); cofounder of the Southern Christian Leadership Conference (1957); his writings include *Stride Toward Freedom: The Montgomery Story* (1958), *Letter from a Birmingham Jail* (1963), *Strength to Love* (1963), *Why We Can't Wait* (1963), *Trumpet of Conscience* (1967), *Where Do We Go from Here? Chaos or Community* (1967), and *The Measure of a Man* (1968)

> *"Oppressed people cannot remain oppressed forever."*
>
> —from Nobel Peace Prize acceptance speech (1964)

ingham's 16th Street Baptist Church was bombed during services. Four black girls died in the blast. Two more children were killed in the riots that followed. The "fierce urgency of now" King had spoken of in Washington assumed still greater urgency. In an unrelated violent episode, President Kennedy was assassinated in November. The following spring, the bodies of three missing civil rights workers were found buried in a Mississippi dam.

On December 10, 1964, Martin Luther King, Jr., was awarded the Nobel Peace Prize. In his acceptance speech, King put the world on notice that the civil rights issue was not only an American problem.

King also broadened his message to include economic justice. African Americans had streamed into northern cities during the Great Depression of the 1930s. Although they enjoyed many rights denied to blacks in the South, northern blacks had so few economic opportunities that their rights seemed hollow to them. King moved his family to a Chicago ghetto but soon had to send his children home to their grandparents. They had all too quickly adopted the ghetto mask of despair and hopelessness.

In 1967, further broadening his ministry, King joined the antiwar movement, speaking out at churches, and marching in large demonstrations. Although President Lyndon Johnson embraced civil rights, shepherding the Voting Rights Act through Congress in 1965, he turned against King over the Vietnam War.

King began work on a second major march on Washington, a Poor People's March. This would bring poor whites, northern blacks, and other minorities into his cause. Political equality had been only the first step; economic justice was his next goal.

King's struggle came to a tragic end in Memphis, Tennessee, where he had gone to support striking black sanitation workers. Financed by a still-unknown backer, a drifter and escaped convict shot King on the balcony of his hotel. King had been preparing to leave for dinner. His last words were to a musician: "Be sure to play 'Precious Lord.'"

People have called Martin Luther King, Jr., a prophet and have compared him to Moses, who led his people out of slavery. King even echoed Moses on the eve of his death, when he told a church congregation that he was not afraid. He had been "to the mountaintop," he said, "and seen the promised land."

FURTHER READING

Bishop, Jim. *The Days of Martin Luther King, Jr.* New York: Putnam, 1971.

Branch, Taylor. *Parting the Waters: America in the King Years, 1954–1963.* New York: Simon & Schuster, 1988.

Faber, Doris, and Harold Faber. *Martin Luther King, Jr.* North Bellmore, N.Y.: Marshall Cavendish, 1986.

Garrow, David. *Bearing the Cross: Martin Luther King, Jr. and the Southern Christian Leadership Conference.* New York: Morrow, 1986.

Haskins, James. *The Life and Death of Martin Luther King, Jr.* New York: Lothrup, 1977.

Jakoubek, Robert. *Martin Luther King, Jr.* New York: Chelsea House, 1990.

King, Martin Luther, Jr. *Letter from a Birmingham Jail.* San Francisco: Harper, 1994.

———. *Stride Toward Freedom: The Montgomery Story.* San Francisco: Harper, 1987.

———. *Trumpet of Conscience.* New York: HarperCollins, 1988.

———. *Why We Can't Wait.* New York: NAL-Dutton, 1993.

———. *Where Do We Go from Here: Chaos or Community.* Boston: Beacon Press, 1989.

Kosof, Anna. *The Civil Rights Movement & Its Legacy.* New York: Franklin Watts, 1989.

Patrick, Diane. *Martin Luther King, Jr.* New York: Franklin Watts, 1990.

Patterson, Lillie. *Martin Luther King, Jr. and the Freedom Movement.* New York: Facts on File, 1989.

Peck, Ira. *The Life and Words of Martin Luther King, Jr.* New York: Scholastic, 1991.

Washington, James Melvin, ed. *A Testament of Hope: The Essential Writings of Martin Luther King, Jr.* San Francisco: Harper & Row, 1986.

Witherspoon, William Roger. *Martin Luther King, Jr.: To the Mountaintop.* Garden City, N.Y.: Doubleday, 1985.

Desmond Tutu

PEACE WITH JUSTICE

As a young boy in South Africa in the 1930s, Desmond Tutu endured racial discrimination and the pain of watching his father produce an identity pass on demand. But he did not become outraged by apartheid until the Bantu Education Act became law in 1956. Apartheid—the official separation of blacks and whites in South Africa—is a 20th-century institution. It was intended to formalize the historical *basskap* (boss-ship) of whites over blacks.

Basskap had developed over more than three centuries. Europeans first claimed Africa's southern Cape of Good Hope around 1600. In 1800, the native African Xhosa people lost the battle for their land to Dutch and French settlers. The British overthrew the Boers, as European South Africans became known 100 years later, but did not extend political rights to the Xhosa or other African peoples.

Inspired by the teachings of Mohandas Gandhi and Martin Luther King, Jr., and by the religious creed of his Anglican faith, Bishop Desmond Tutu worked to bring a peaceful end to South Africa's system of apartheid.

Like other religious leaders before him, Tutu found a prescription for social justice in the doctrines of his faith. He also found that injustice destroys faith: "Apartheid can cause a child of God to doubt that he or she is a child of God," he wrote. Here, Tutu leads the funeral procession of four blacks who were killed by police in 1985.

South Africa's Nationalist Party rose to power in 1948 and ruled the entire population along racial lines. Blacks were required always to carry identity passes. The state's Homelands policy removed Africans from desirable areas, known as black spots, and relocated them to places designated as tribal homelands. From these homelands they could no longer participate in South African life.

Blacks were not permitted to vote, own property or live in white areas, move about freely, protest, or marry whites. All public facilities, such as restaurants and rest rooms, were segregated. Education was also segregated.

Desmond Tutu's father, Zachariah, was the principal of a primary school for black children. His mother, Aletta, supplemented the family's income by taking in laundry. The Tutu family was unusual in black South Africa because the father lived at home. Many black fathers had to live away from home, near the mines or cities where they worked. As a boy, Desmond recognized the unfairness of racial segregation, noting that white schoolchildren received free lunches, while most blacks did not. He chafed under the racial bias of his education, which taught that white explorers had "discovered" Africa and that the native Xhosa people were thieves. But Desmond grudgingly accepted segregation as a way of life.

Young Tutu decided to become a preacher, inspired by his local *umfundisi,* or preacher. By the time he finished high school, however, in 1950, he had recently recovered from tuberculosis and wanted to become a doctor. Because his family could not afford his school fees, Tutu chose to be a teacher instead. He attended Pretoria Bantu Normal College, a segregated teachers' college for black Africans. Working as a student teacher in Pretoria, Tutu met—and was greatly impressed by—Nelson Mandela, a leader, with Oliver Tambo, of the new African National Congress (ANC).

Tutu received a correspondence degree from the University of Johannesburg in 1954 and married his fellow schoolteacher Leah Shenzane that July. Three years later, although they were parents of a young child, Tutu and his wife resigned their teaching positions to protest the Bantu Education Act. This act offered an inferior, nonscientific, non-English education for all black children of South Africa. In a step Tutu later

Desmond Tutu

"Reconciliation is only possible between equals."

—from a letter to P. W. Botha (May 1976)

BORN

October 7, 1931
Klerksdorp, Transvaal, South Africa

FORMAL EDUCATION

Teaching certificate, Pretoria Bantu Normal College; correspondence degree, University of Johannesburg; B.A., M.A., Kings College, London

TRADITION

Christianity (Protestant)

ACCOMPLISHMENTS

Anglican dean of Johannesburg (1975); general secretary of South African Council of Churches (1978–84); awarded Nobel Peace Prize (1984); archbishop of Cape Town, South Africa (1986–present)

called being "grabbed by God by the scruff of the neck in order to spread His word, whether it is convenient or not," he entered the Anglican ministry.

Tutu already knew the Anglican Church as a place of humane treatment and respect. When he was 12, his family had moved to Sophiatown, Johannesburg's only multiracial neighborhood. There, the Anglican priest, Trevor Huddleston, was a champion of equal rights for all people. He raised money to buy food for his parishioners, built the only swimming pool in an area of close to a million black people, and started a jazz band. Inside his church, Jesus was depicted as black. Tutu was startled one day to see Huddleston doff his hat to Tutu's mother.

While Tutu was training for the ministry, the newly organized anti-apartheid movement grew. The government detained ANC leader Nelson Mandela on a charge of treason, but other anti-apartheid voices arose to take his place. In 1960, Robert Sobukwe, head of the Pan-Africanist Congress (PAC), called for a national strike and protest against the pass laws. When a huge protest crowd gathered in Sharpeville, a black area south of Johannesburg, police opened fire without warning. Hundreds were wounded; 67 people were killed. The government declared a state of emergency and banned both the ANC and the PAC.

Ordained an Anglican priest in 1961, Tutu continued his education away from the turmoil of South Africa, at King's College in London. There he earned a bachelor's degree in divinity and a master's in theology. From 1962 to 1966

he and his family experienced the joy of life in a land without passes or overt racism. He was astounded by London's Speaker's Corner, a corner of Hyde Park where anyone can speak publicly and no subject is banned. Tutu was elated: "You would see a policeman next to [a speaker] not to arrest him for what appeared to be such subversive statements but actually to protect him from people who could get incensed. Incredible!"

In London, Tutu learned to disagree with whites, to overthrow the "self-disgust, self-contempt, and self-hatred" that apartheid had instilled in him. He drew inspiration from two Americans, Jackie Robinson, who had broken the color barrier in professional baseball, and the civil rights leader Martin Luther King, Jr.

Armed with his degrees in theology, Tutu returned to South Africa in 1966. By then the father of four children, he became a lecturer at the Federal Theological Seminary (FEDSEM), where he began speaking out, arguing that Christianity had a role to play in black independence. At a nearby all-black university, the journalist Steve Biko and others began laying the foundation of South Africa's Black Consciousness movement. Government attitudes changed little, however.

In 1972, after teaching at the University of Lesotho, an independent nation inside South Africa, Tutu went back to England to serve on the World Council of Churches (WCC). Traveling extensively for the WCC, Tutu saw people of color around the world taking leadership roles; the church *could* address social problems. "You brought us the Bible and we are taking it seriously," he told whites.

"If we want peace...let us work for justice."

—from the Nobel Peace Prize acceptance speech (1984)

Three years later, Tutu was named Anglican dean of Johannesburg. He refused an exception as an "honorary white" that would have let him live in the Johannesburg deanery. Tutu and his wife lived instead in Soweto, the *South West Township*, one of the world's most underdeveloped urban areas.

Tutu appealed to Prime Minister Balthazar Vorster to undo some of apartheid's worst evils. "There can be no racial reconciliation without justice," he warned. Vorster did not reply. On June 16, 1976, 15,000 Soweto students marched to protest the Bantu education system. The police fired on them, killing a 13-year-old black student. In the clashes with police that followed, some 600 blacks were killed. An anguished Tutu raised his voice: "For goodness' sake, somebody listen to us."

Increasingly, Tutu found himself speaking at the only forums available to blacks—funerals. In early 1977 he spoke at the funeral of Steve Biko, aged 30, who had been beaten to death in jail. Six months later, he appeared at the funeral of Robert Sobukwe. Tutu accepted a position as the first black director of the South African Council of Churches. He swore to work "for justice and peace and reconciliation—in that order." He openly compared the Nationalist government to Nazism and promised "to destroy this diabolical system, whatever the cost to me."

Tutu met with Prime Minister P. W. Botha in 1980 and asked him to end white rule. Botha asked Tutu to denounce black liberation movements such as the ANC. Neither backed down. Within the year, the South African government revoked Tutu's passport.

Tutu had for some time been advocating economic sanctions against South Africa, a boycott of his country's goods. The government tried to discredit Tutu, even convening an official commission to investigate his South African Council of Churches. They could find no wrongdoing, but attacks on him continued. Of his poor image in the press, Tutu has said that if he walked on water, South African papers would report, "Tutu Can't Swim."

In 1984 the Nobel committee awarded Tutu its annual Peace Prize. South African blacks were overjoyed. Tutu reminded his audience in his acceptance speech that "if we want peace...let us work for justice." He took his award as a sign that "justice is going to win." In the same year, he was appointed bishop of Johannesburg, and two years later, he was named archbishop of Cape Town.

Frankly appalled that South Africa's rulers regard themselves as Christians, Tutu argues that Christ is the Christ of all people. To deny someone's humanity, he says, is blasphemy, showing contempt for God.

Through the efforts of many courageous people in South Africa, Bishop Tutu among them, the walls of apartheid are falling. In April 1994, South Africa held its first democratic election among all citizens, black and white. Nelson Mandela, who had spent 27 of his adult years in prison, was elected president.

FURTHER READING

Bentley, Judith. *Archbishop Tutu of South Africa*. Hillside, N.J.: Enslow, 1988.

Du Boulay, Shirley. *Tutu: Voice of the Voiceless*. Grand Rapids, Mich.: Eerdmans, 1988.

Tutu, Desmond. *Hope and Suffering: Sermons and Speeches*. Compiled by Mothobi Mutloatse and edited by John Webster. Grand Rapids, Mich.: Eerdmans, 1984.

———. *The Words of Desmond Tutu*. Selected by Naomi Tutu. New York: Newmarket, 1989.

Wepman, Dennis. *Desmond Tutu*. New York: Franklin Watts, 1989.

Tenzin Gyatso

THE DALAI LAMA: LEADER IN EXILE

O n November 17, 1950, after rising well before dawn and participating in a long ceremony, a 15-year-old boy became the leader of a country under attack by a powerful neighbor. The besieged country was the mountainous, desert nation of Tibet. Its powerful neighbor was the People's Republic of China.

The leader of Tibet's 2 million inhabitants was born Lhama Thondup to a family of farmers living in a house made of stone and mud. He was discovered by a search party when he was only three. Signs and visions had identified him as the next (14th) incarnation of the bodhisattva Avalokitesvara. Bodhisattvas are Buddhist men and women who reach enlightenment, or supreme under-

A political as well as a religious leader, Tenzin Gyatso, the Dalai Lama, symbolizes Tibet's hopes for independence.

"Only the thought of my responsibility to the six million Tibetans kept me going.... I reminded myself constantly of the Buddha's teaching that our enemy is in a sense our greatest teacher."

—from *Freedom In Exile: The Autobiography of the Dalai Lama* (1990)

standing, but who forego the experience of nirvana, or freedom from life's pain and misery, in order to help free others from suffering.

Once he was identified as the Dalai Lama, the boy and most of his family moved to Lhasa, the capital of Tibet, to begin training for his future life. Lhama Thondup was given a new, official name—Jetsun Jamphel Ngawang Lobsang Yeshe Tenzin Gyatso—which is usually shortened to Tenzin Gyatso.

The Dalai Lama serves both as Tibet's spiritual and political ruler, in a form of government known as a theocracy. As many as one-fourth of all Tibetan men are Buddhist monks; the country contains more than 2,500 monasteries.

Chinese and Indian missionaries introduced Buddhism to Tibet in the 7th century. For some centuries, it coexisted uneasily with Tibet's native Bon religion, which was primarily concerned with keeping a range of spirits and demons at peace through magic and rituals. Tibetan Buddhism assumed its present form in the 14th century, after a further influence from Mongolian religion. (*Dalai* is a Mongolian word meaning "ocean." *Lama*, which means "teacher," is Tibetan.)

Popular Tibetan Buddhism involves chanting, using prayer wheels, and meditating on thangkas, or mandalas (sacred circles) in order to reach enlightenment. But perhaps Tibetan Buddhism's most striking contribution to the faith is the *Bardol Thodol* (*Tibetan Book of the Dead*). Based, as all Buddhist teachings are, on the core ideas of *karma* (consequences), *samsara* (liberation), and *karma-samsara* (the idea that right living will free one from an endless cycle of rebirths), the *Bardol Thodol* is a guide to the soul's journey after death, describing what will happen. It is also a way to approach living. Because Buddhists believe that all

reality is contained within the self, its accounts of the various and strange worlds of the dead suggest that the world of the living is full of unimaginable possibilities.

Many teachers helped Tenzin Gyatso prepare for his extraordinary role. In his early years, he studied drama, music and dance, astrology, poetry, and composition. Later, he studied medicine, Sanskrit, logic, fine arts, metaphysics, and the philosophy of religion. During his years of study, Tibet was ruled by a regent, or governor, until the Dalai Lama was old enough to take charge.

As a boy, one of the Dalai Lama's amusements had been to melt down lead soldiers and recast them as monks. Political events eventually mocked his boyhood game. In June 1950, the People's Liberation Army (PLA) of Mao Tse-Tung's new People's Republic of China invaded Tibet to free it from what the Chinese called "foreign influences." Ironically, the most recent foreign influence had been China, which ruled Tibet from 1720 until 1912, when the British freed the mountain state. Tibet's standing army numbered only 10,000 people, and the PLA easily captured Tibetan territory. The 15-year-old Dalai Lama was invested with political power five months later, three years earlier than customary. His training, though extensive, had not prepared him to lead a country in crisis.

Although Tibet sought help, notably from India and the United States, no nation came to its defense. In May 1951, a stunned Tenzin Gyatso heard Tibet's emissary to China announce over the radio that Tibet had "returned to the Chinese motherland." The Chinese modernized parts of Tibet, built roads and hospitals, and redistributed farmland to poor Tibetans. But they also dismantled Tibet's religious and cultural life, robbing and destroying monasteries and forbidding

With China still in control of Tibet, the Dalai Lama works from this compound in Dharamsala in northern India to raise consciousness about Tibetan Buddhism and the plight of his homeland.

In *Freedom in Exile,* the Dalai Lama writes that "suffering is caused by ignorance, and that people inflict pain on others in pursuit of their own happiness or satisfaction. Yet true happiness comes from a sense of inner peace and contentment, which in turn must be achieved through cultivation of altruism, of love, of compassion, and through the elimination of anger, selfishness, and greed."

worship of the Dalai Lama. Rape and torture were common.

In 1956, the Dalai Lama went to India for celebrations honoring the 2500th anniversary of the Buddha's birth. Although people advised him to stay in India, he returned to Tibet, hoping to soften the Chinese presence with his own gentleness.

The situation in Tibet worsened. In March 1959, thousands of Tibetans

went to Lhasa for the Dalai Lama's 15-hour ceremonial examination. Tensions did not ease after he passed the exam. Consulting his family and the Tibetan oracle, the Dalai Lama finally agreed to leave his homeland. Late one evening, wearing ordinary clothing and carrying a rifle and a prayer book, he slipped through the crowds and headed for India. Two days later, the Chinese fired on the crowds in Lhasa. The Dalai Lama estimates that some 87,000 Tibetans, excluding suicides and starvation victims, died in the uprising and Chinese retaliation.

Losing his country and many of his countrymen tested Tenzin Gyatso's nerves but not his faith. Citing the Buddha, he noted in his account of leaving Tibet, *Freedom in Exile*, that "suffering is the first step to liberation." His own ideal, he has said, is to follow the example of the bodhisattvas. From the Sanskrit words *bodhi* (wisdom) and *sattva* (compassion), a bodhisattva is a being who dedicates himself entirely to helping free all other beings from suffering.

Although Tibet had been overrun, the Dalai Lama did not cease to be the leader of his people. In Dharamsala in

"Religion is essential, especially for those engaged in politics."

—from Freedom In Exile: The Autobiography of the Dalai Lama (1990)

Tenzin Gyatso

BORN

July 6, 1935
Taktser, Tibet

TRADITION

Buddhism (Tibetan)

ACCOMPLISHMENTS

Leader in exile of the Tibetan people; awarded Nobel Peace Prize (1989); author of *My Land and My People* (1962), *The Buddhism of Tibet* (1975), *The Path to Enlightenment* (1982), *Tantra in Tibet* (1987), *Freedom in Exile: The Autobiography of the Dalai Lama* (1990), and *My Tibet* (1990)

northern India, he and his officials established a Tibetan government in exile. It was the first full democracy in Tibet's history. Eventually, more than 100,000 Tibetan refugees settled in India.

While the Dalai Lama and other Tibetan refugees were re-creating Tibetan culture in India, China's grasp on Tibet tightened. In 1965, the Chinese renamed Tibet the Xizang Province and began to govern it directly. During the Chinese Cultural Revolution of the late 1960s and early 1970s—which was aimed at destroying artistic and intellectual opposition to Mao Tse-tung's communist regime—much Tibetan art and architecture was destroyed. When Mao died in 1976, Tenzin Gyatso wrote that he saw "an enormous, beautiful rainbow."

Today, Tibet remains firmly under Chinese control, with more than 300,000 Chinese soldiers stationed there. One-third of China's nuclear arsenal is situated in Tibet, and mining in the uranium-rich country continues to pollute Tibetan land. Tenzin Gyatso has traveled the world to promote human rights in Tibet, and in 1989 he was awarded the Nobel Peace Prize. His message is rooted in his philosophy of "universal responsibility," a concern for the sacredness of all life, plant and animal as well as human.

Some Tibetans believe an ancient prophecy that the 14th, or present, Dalai Lama will be Tibet's last. Tenzin Gyatso does not believe he is the last Dalai Lama, but he does believe another ancient prophecy: that one day the Tibetan people will recover their country.

FURTHER READING

Dalai Lama. *The Buddhism of Tibet.* London: George Allen & Unwin, 1975.

———. *Freedom in Exile: The Autobiography of the Dalai Lama.* New York: HarperCollins, 1990.

———. *My Land and My People.* New York: Potala, 1983.

———. *The Path to Enlightenment.* Ithaca, N.Y.: Snow Lion, 1982.

———. *Tantra in Tibet.* Ithaca, N.Y.: Snow Lion, 1987.

Freise, Kai. *Tenzin Gyatso, the Dalai Lama.* New York: Chelsea House, 1989.

Further Reading

Each of the major entries in *Believers* includes a list of readings; refer to the index for page references.

Although the following books vary in level of difficulty, none of them are technical; nearly all are written for a general audience. Books preceded by an asterisk (*) are especially appropriate for younger readers.

General References

Armstrong, Karen. *A History of God*. New York: Knopf, 1993.

Boraks, Lucius. *Religions of the West*. Kansas City, Mo.: Sheed & Ward, 1988.

Bowden, Henry Warner. *Dictionary of American Religious Biography*. Westport, Conn.: Greenwood, 1977.

*Brownstone, David M., and Irene M. Franck. *Scholars and Priests*. New York: Facts on File, 1992.

*Cairns, Trevor, ed. *Barbarians, Christians, and Muslims*. Minneapolis: Lerner, 1975.

Eliade, Mircea, ed. *The Encyclopedia of Religion*. New York: Macmillan, 1987.

Gaer, Joseph. *What the Great Religions Believe*. New York: Dodd, Mead, 1963.

Hinnells, John, ed. *Who's Who of World Religions*. New York: Simon & Schuster, 1992.

Hopfe, Lewis. *Religions of the World*. 5th ed. New York: Macmillan, 1994.

Hutchinson, John A. *Paths of Faith*. New York: McGraw-Hill, 1991.

Melton, J. Gordon. *Religious Leaders of America: A Biographical Guide to Founders and Leaders of Religious Bodies, Churches, and Spiritual Groups in North America*. Detroit, Mich.: Gale, 1991.

*Morris, Scott, ed. *Religions of the World*. Using and Understanding Maps series. New York: Chelsea House, 1993.

Parrinder, Geoffrey. *Mysticism in the World's Religions*. New York: Oxford University Press, 1976.

Rosten, Leo, ed. *Religions of America: Ferment and Faith in an Age of Crisis*. New York: Simon & Schuster, 1975.

Smith, Huston. *The Illustrated World's Religions: A Guide to Our Wisdom Traditions*. San Francisco: Harper San Francisco, 1994.

Wolcott, Leonard, and Carolyn Wolcott. *Religions around the World*. New York: Abingdon, 1967.

Buddhism

Burland, C. A. *Way of the Buddha*. Chester Springs, Pa.: Dufour, 1988.

Connolly, Holly, and Peter Connolly. *Buddhism*. Edited by W. Owen Cole. Chester Springs, Pa.: Dufour, 1992.

Ling, Trevor. *A Dictionary of Buddhism*. New York: Scribners, 1972.

*Morgan, Peggy. *Being a Buddhist*. North Pomfret, Vt.: Trafalgar, 1989.

*Wangu, Madhu Bazaz. *Buddhism*. New York: Facts on File, 1992.

Christianity

Attwater, Donald. *A Catholic Dictionary*. New York: Macmillan, 1949.

*Brown, Alan, and Judy Perkins. *Christianity*. Pomfret, Vt.: Trafalgar, 1989.

*Brown, Stephen F. *Christianity*. New York: Facts on File, 1991.

Farmer, David Hugh, ed. *The Oxford Book of Saints*. New York: Oxford University Press, 1992.

Frankfurter, A. Daniel. *A History of the Christian Movement*. Chicago: Nelson Hall, 1978.

Johnson, Paul. *A History of Christianity*. New York: Atheneum, 1976.

McManners, John, ed. *The Oxford Illustrated History of Christianity*. New York: Oxford University Press, 1992.

Nelson, Yvette. *Celebrating the Eucharist*. Winona, Minn.: St. Mary's Press, 1992.

New Catholic Encyclopedia. New York: McGraw-Hill, 1967.

Confucianism

Creel, H. G. *Chinese Thought from Confucius to Mao Tse Tung*. Chicago: University of Chicago Press, 1953.

*Hoobler, Thomas. *Confucianism*. New York: Facts on File, 1993.

Hinduism

*Aggarwal, Manju. *I Am a Hindu*. New York: Franklin Watts, 1985.

Banerjee, Mrityunjoy. *Invitation to Hinduism*. New York: Arnold-Heinemann, 1978.

*Edmonds, I. G. *Hinduism*. New York: Franklin Watts, 1979.

Embree, Ainslie T. *Sources of Indian Tradition*. 2nd ed. New York: Columbia University Press, 1988.

Kanitakara, Hemanta. *Hinduism*. New York: Bookwright Press, 1985.

Kinsley, David R. *Hinduism: A Cultural Perspective*. Englewood Cliffs, N.J.: Prentice Hall, 1982.

Radhakrishnan, Sarvepalli. *The Hindu View of Life*. New York: Macmillan, 1976.

Singh, Bhagat. *The Story of Krishna*. Pomona, Calif.: Auromere, 1976.

*Wangu, Madhu Bazaz. *Hinduism*. New York: Facts on File, 1991.

*Yogeshananda, Swami. *Way of the Hindu*. Chester Springs, Pa.: Dufour, 1980.

Islam

Bakhtiar, Laleh. *History of Islam*. 2 vols. Chicago: Kazi, 1993.

Bassiouni, M. Cherif. *Introduction to Islam*. Skokie, Ill.: Rand McNally, 1988.

Bosworth, L. E., Evan Donzel, W. P. Heinrichs, and C. Pellat. *The Encyclopedia of Islam*. New York: E. J. Brill, 1993.

Christopher, John B. *The Islamic Tradition*. New York: Harper & Row, 1972.

Doray, S. J. *Gateway to Islam*. Chicago: Kazi, n.d.

El-Amin, Mustafa. *The Religion of Islam and the Nation of Islam: What is the Difference?* Newark, N.J.: El-Amin Productions, 1991.

*Gordon, Matthew S. *Islam*. New York: Facts on File, 1991.

Haddad, Yvonne Yazbeck, ed. *The Muslims of America*. New York: Oxford University Press, 1991.

Hayes, K. H. *Stories of Great Muslims*. Chicago: Kazi, n.d.

*Hood, Abdul Latif Al. *Islam*. New York: Franklin Watts, 1987.

*Iqbal, Muhammad. *Way of the Muslim*. Chester Springs, Pa.: Dufour, 1983.

*Keene, Michael. *Being a Muslim*. Pomfret, Vt.: Trafalgar, 1987.

Siddiqui, A. A. *Elementary Teachings of Islam*. Chicago: Kazi, n.d.

Jainism

Jain, Jyoti P. *The Jain Sources of the History of Ancient India.* Columbia, Mo.: South Asia Books, 1964.

Jaini, Padmanbh. *The Jaina Path of Purification.* Berkeley: University of California Press, 1979.

Judaism

Bamberger, David. *Judaism and the World's Religions.* New York: Behrman House, 1987.

Borowitz, Eugene, and Naomi Patz. *Explaining Reform Judaism.* New York: Behrman House, 1985.

Einstein, Stephen J., and Lydia Kirkoff. *Every Person's Guide to Judaism.* New York: Union of American Hebrew Congregations, 1989.

Fields, Harvey J. *A Torah Commentary for Our Times.* New York: Union of American Hebrew Congregations, 1991.

Ganz, Yaffa. *The Jewish Fact-Finder: A Bookful of Important Jewish Facts and Handy Information.* Spring Valley, N.Y.: Feldheim, 1988.

*Gates, Fay C. *Judaism.* New York: Facts on File, 1991.

Isaacson, Ben, and Deborah Wigoder. *The International Jewish Encyclopedia.* Englewood Cliffs, N.J.: Prentice Hall, 1973.

Jacobs, Louis. *The Book of Jewish Practice.* New York: Behrman House, 1987.

————. *Hasidic Prayer.* Washington, D.C.: B'nai B'rith Books, 1993.

Johnson, Paul. *A History of the Jews.* New York: Harper & Row, 1987.

Kipper, Lenore, and Homard Bogot. *Alef-Bet of Jewish Values: Code Words of Jewish Life.* New York: Union of American Hebrew Congregations, 1987.

*Pasachoff, Naomi. *Basic Judaism for Young People.* New York: Behrman House, 1987.

*Shamir, Ilana, and Schlomo Sharit, eds. *The Young Reader's Encyclopedia of Jewish History.* New York: Viking, 1987.

Singer, Ellen. *Our Sacred Texts: Discovering the Jewish Classics.* New York: Union of American Hebrew Congregations, 1992.

Wigoder, Geoffrey. *Dictionary of Jewish Biography.* New York: Simon & Schuster, 1991.

Mormonism

*Bernotas, Bob. *Brigham Young.* New York: Chelsea House, 1993.

*Cannon, Elaine. *Turning Twelve or More: Living by the Articles of Faith.* Salt Lake City, Utah: Bookcraft, n.d.

Edwards, Paul M. *Our Legacy of Faith: A Brief History of the Reorganized Church of Jesus Christ of Latter Day Saints.* Independence, Mo.: Herald House, 1991.

Madsen, Susan A. *The Lord Needed a Prophet.* Salt Lake City, Utah: Deseret Books, 1990.

Native American Traditions

Clark, Ella. *Guardian Spirit Quest.* Billings, Mont.: Council for Indian Education, 1974.

*Hirschfelder, Arlene, and Paulette Molin. *Encyclopedia of Native American Religions.* New York: Facts on File, 1992.

*Liptak, Karen. *North American Indian Ceremonies.* New York: Franklin Watts, 1992.

Sikhism

*Danihal, Beryl. *Sikhism*. Pomfret, Vt.: Trafalgar, 1987.

*McLeod, W. H. *Way of the Sikh*. Chester Springs, Pa.: Dufour, 1986.

*Singh, Nikky-Guinder Kaur. *Sikhism*. New York: Facts on File, 1992.

Taoism

*Brown, Stephen F. *Taoism*. New York: Facts on File, 1992.

McNaughton, William. *The Taoist Vision*. Ann Arbor: University of Michigan Press, 1971.

Zoroastrianism

Avesta. [Selections] Introduction to Ancient Iranian Religion. Minneapolis: University of Minnesota Press, 1983.

Duchesne-Guillemin, Jacques. *Symbols and Values in Zoroastrianism: Their Survival and Renewal*. New York: Harper & Row, 1966.

Index of Religious Leaders by Tradition

Buddhism
Aśoka Maurya
Tenzin Gyatso
Siddhārtha Gautama

Christian Science
Mary Baker Eddy

Confucianism
Confucius
Mencius

Hinduism
Mohandas Gandhi

Islam
Muhammad
Rābi'ah of Basra

Jainism
Mahavira

Judaism
Isaac Luria
Moses Maimonides
Moses
Isaac Mayer Wise

Manichaeism
Mani

Mormonism
Joseph Smith

Nation of Islam
Malcolm X
Elijah Muhammad

Native American
Handsome Lake

Protestantism
Richard Allen
John Calvin
Anne Hutchinson
Jesus
Martin Luther King, Jr.
Ann Lee
Martin Luther
Cotton Mather
William Penn
Desmond Tutu

Roman Catholicism
Augustine of Hippo
Francis of Assisi
Hildegard of Bingen
Ignatius of Loyola
Jesus
Joan of Arc
Pope John XXIII
Mary
Thomas More
Paul of Tarsus
Junípero Serra
Elizabeth Ann Seton
Teresa of Calcutta

Sikhism
Guru Nānak

Taoism
Chuang Tzu
Lao Tzu

Zoroastrianism
Zarathushtra

Index of Religious Leaders by Place of Birth

Author's note: People are indexed under the names of present-day countries.

Algeria
Augustine of Hippo

Bohemia, Czech Republic
Isaac Mayer Wise

China
Chuang Tzu
Confucius
Lao Tzu
Mencius

Egypt
Moses

France
John Calvin
Joan of Arc

Germany
Hildegard of Bingen
Martin Luther

Great Britain
Anne Hutchinson
Ann Lee
Thomas More
William Penn

India
Aśoka Maurya
Mohandas Gandhi
Mahavira
Guru Nānak
Siddhārtha Gautama

Iran
Mani
Zarathushtra

Iraq
Rābi'ah of Basra

Israel
Jesus
Isaac Luria
Mary

Italy
Francis of Assisi
Pope John XXIII

Macedonia
Teresa of Calcutta

Saudi Arabia
Muhammad

South Africa
Desmond Tutu

Spain
Ignatius of Loyola
Moses Maimonides
Junípero Serra

Tibet
Tenzin Gyatso

Turkey
Paul of Tarsus

United States
Richard Allen
Mary Baker Eddy
Martin Luther King, Jr.
Handsome Lake
Malcolm X
Cotton Mather
Elijah Muhammad
Elizabeth Ann Seton
Joseph Smith

Index

References to main biographical entries are indicated by **bold** page numbers; references to illustrations are indicated by *italics*.

Aaron (brother of Moses), *12*
Abernathy, Ralph, 168
Adam and Eve, *15*, 41, 62, 97-98
Address to Those Who Keep Slaves and Approve the Practice (Allen), 124
Ādi Granth (Guru Nānak), 81, 82
African Colonization Society (ACS), 124
African Methodist Episcopal (AME) Church, 124-25
African National Congress (ANC), 172-73, 174
Ahimsa (nonviolence), 9, 20, 146
Ahura Mazda, 16-17
Ali, Drew, 155
Allah, 58. *See also* Islam
Allen, Richard, **122-25**
American Israelite, The, 139
American Sisters of Charity, 128
American Society of Free Persons of Color, 125
Amyraut, Moise, 107
Analects (Conversations) (Confucius), 30
Angels of Bethesda, The (Mather), 112
Anglican Church, 86
Apartheid, 171-74
Apostles of Christ, 49
Aristotle, 89, 95
Asceticism, 18, 20, 23, 45
Aśoka Maurya, **37-39**
Assertion of the Seven Sacraments, An (More), 86
Atonement, 108
Augustine of Hippo, 53, **54-57**, 89, 98
Avestas (Zarathushtra), 17

Baptists, 165-70
Bardol Thodol (Tibetan Book of the Dead), 176
Benedictines, 66
Bethel African Methodist Episcopal (AME) Church, 124, *125*
Bible. *See* Hebrew Bible; New Testament
Biblia Americana (Mather), 112-13
Black Muslims, 154-56, 161-64
Black Rock (Ka'aba), 58, 60-61
Bojaxhiu, Agnes. *See* Teresa of Calcutta
Book of Abraham, The (Smith), 134
Book of Light (Maimonides), 71
Book of Mormon, The (Smith), 133, *134*
Book of Sermons, The (Mahavira), 20
Botha, P. W., 174

Brahmanism, 18, 22, 23, 39
Buddha. *See* Siddhārtha Gautama
Buddhism, 8, 21-24, 37-39, 175-79

Calvin, John, **95-98**, 102, 140
Canticle of Brother Sun (Francis of Assisi), 75
Caste system (India), 18, 23-24, 82, 146
Catholicism, 42, 53, 54-57, 66-69, 73-75, 76-79, 83-86, 90, 91-94, 114-17, 126-28, 150-53, 157-60
Cauchon, Pierre (bishop of Beauvais), 78-79
Christianity, 40-51. *See also* Catholicism; Christian Science; Mormonism; Protestantism; Quakers
Christian Science, 140-44
Christian Science Monitor, 144
Christian Science Weekly, 144
Chuang Tzu, 27, **34-36**
Church of England, 86, 102
Church of Jesus Christ of Latter-Day Saints. *See* Mormonism
City of God (Augustine), 56-57
Code of Handsome Lake, The (Handsome Lake), 131
Confessions (Augustine), 55, 56, 57
Confucianism, 28-33
Confucius, **28-31**
Cooper, Samuel, 128
Cotton, John, 102-5
Cowdery, Oliver, 132-33, 136
Cynicism, 49

Dalai Lama. *See* Tenzin Gyatso
Dead Sea Scrolls, 44
Dialogue Concerning Heresies (More), 86
Disciples of Jesus, 46
Donatism, 56
Douglass, Frederick, 166
Dualistic monotheism, 15
Du Bois, W. E. B., 166

Eddy, Asa Gilbert, 143
Eddy, Mary Baker, **140-44**
Egoism, 32-33
Enchiridion (The Handbook of a Christian Soldier) (Erasmus), 96
Erasmus, Desiderius, 83-84, 96
Essay Toward the Present and Future Peace of Europe, An (Penn), 109
Essenes, 45
Evil. *See* Good versus evil

Fard, Wallace D., 154, 163
Farel, Guillaume, 97
Farewell Address (Calvin), 98
Five Pillars of Islam, 62
Ford, Philip, 109
Fox, George, 108
Francis of Assisi, **73-75**
Franciscans, 75, 114-17
Free African Society, 123
Free will, 23, 56
Frye, Calvin, 144

Gandhi, Mohandas, **145-49**
Garvey, Marcus, 154, 161
Gathas (Zarathushtra), 17
Gnosticism, 44
Golden Legend (Jacobus de Voragine), 92
Good versus evil, 15-17, 52-53, 56
Guide for the Perplexed (Maimonides), 71, 72
Guru Nānak. *See* Nānak, Guru

Handsome Lake, **129-31**
Hebrew Bible, 11, 12, 53, 70
Hebrew Union College, 139
Hildegard of Bingen, **66-69**
Hinduism, 80, 82
Hocknell, John, 120
Huddleston, Trevor, 173
Huguenots, 98
Humanism, 86, 95-96
Hutchinson, Anne, **102-5**
Hutchinson, William, 102, 105

Ignatius of Loyola, **91-94**
Imitation of Christ, The (Thomas à Kempis), 92
India Christiana (Mather), 112
Indulgences, 88, 89
Inquisition, 93
Institutes of the Christian Religion (Calvin), 96, 102
Islam, 8, 58-63, 64-65, 82

Jainism, 9, 18, 146-47
Jerusalem, *100*
Jesuits, 91-94
Jesus of Nazareth, 41, 42, **43-47**, 53
Joan of Arc, **76-79**
John the Baptist, 45
John XXIII (pope), **150-53**
Journal of a Soul (Pope John XXIII), 150
Judaism, 13-14, 70-72, 99-101, 137-39

Kabbalah, 99, 100-101
Karma, 20
Khadija (wife of Muhammad), 58-60, 61
King, Coretta Scott, 166, 168
King, Martin Luther, Jr., 162, **165-70**
Knox, John, 98
Koran, 61, 62, 65

Lao Tzu, **25-27,** 34, 35, 36
Law, William, 136
Lee, Ann, **118-21**
Letter from a Birmingham Jail (King), 169
Liber divinorum operum (Book of Divine Works) (Hildegard of Bingen), 67, 69
Life of Our Lord Jesus Christ (Ludolph of Saxony), 92
Little, Earl, 161-62
Little, Malcolm. *See* Malcolm X
Loe, Thomas, 106, 107-8
Loreto Sisters, 158-59
Luria, Isaac, **99-101**
Luther, Martin, 86, **87-90,** 96-98

Magnalia Christi Americana (Mather), 112
Mahavira, 9, **18-20**
Maimonides, Moses **70-72**
Malcolm X, 156, **161-64**
Mandela, Nelson, 172, 173, 174
Mani, **52-53,** 55
Manichaeism, 52-53, 54, 55, 56
Manual of the Mother Church (Eddy), 144
Marbury, Francis, 102
Mary (mother of Jesus), **40-42,** 43
Mary Magdalene, 45
Mather, Cotton, **110-13**
Mather, Increase, 113
Memorable Providences (Mather), 111
Mencius, **32-33**
Mencius (collected writings of Mencius), 32, 33
Methodism, 122-25
Minhag America (American Ritual) (Wise), 139
Mishneh Torah (Maimonides), 71-72
Missionaries of Charity, 159-60
Mithraism, 17
Moism, 32-33
Monica (mother of Augustine), 54, 56, 57
Monotheism, 9, 15, 108
More, Thomas, **83-86**
Mormonism, 132-36
Moroni (angel), 132
Moses, **11-14**
Moses ben Maimon. *See* Maimonides, Moses

Mother Teresa. *See* Teresa of Calcutta
Muhammad, **58-63**
Muhammad, Elijah, **154-56,** 163-64
Muhammad, Wallace D., 156
Muslims, 61-63, 154-56
Mysticism, 64-65, 99-101

Nānak, Guru, **80-82**
National Association for the Advancement of Colored People (NAACP), 168
Nation of Islam, 154-56, 161-64
Nazarenes, 47
New Learning. *See* Humanism
New Testament, 53
    English translation, 86
    epistles of Paul, 43-44, 50-51
    Gospels, 41, 46-47
Nietzsche, Friedrich, 17
Nirvana, 20, 23
Nobel Peace Prize, 159, 169, 174
Noble Truths (Buddhism), 23
No Cross, No Crown (Penn), 108, 109
Nonviolence, 9, 169-70. *See also* Ahimsa; Pacifism

Old Testament. *See* Hebrew Bible
Owen, John, 106-7

Pacem in Terris (Peace on Earth) (Pope John XXIII), 153
Pacifism, 145-49. *See also* Ahimsa
Palou, Francisco, 114
Pan-Africanist Congress (PAC), 173
Parks, Rosa, 165, 168
Passover, 13
Patterson, Daniel, 141
Paul of Tarsus, **48-51**
    letters of, 43-44, 50-51
Pelagianism, 56
Penn, William, **106-9**
Pharisees, 45, 47
Plotinus, 55
Polytheism, 9
Predestination, 98, 140
Presbyterians, 98, 132
Prophet's Mosque (Medina), 60
Protestantism, 86, 87-90, 95-98, 102-5, 110-13, 171-74. *See also* Baptists; Methodism; Presbyterians, Puritans; Quakers; Shakers
Puritans, 102-5, 106

Quakers, 106-9, 130-31
Quimby, Phineas P., 141, 143

Rābi'ah of Basra, **64-65**
Rationalism, 99-100
Reformation, Protestant, 89, 96
Reform Judaism, 137-39
Reglamento Echeveste (Serra), 115
Religion of the Everlasting Maxim (Mather), 112
Reminiscences (Wise), 139
Respectful relationships, 29
Revivalism, 134
Rigdon, Sidney, 133
Rishabhanatha (Jainist saint), *19*
Rituals and ceremonies, 29-30
    baptism, **45**
    death, 16-17
    Eucharist, 97
    of the Jews, 50, 138
    of Mormonism, 135
    washing, 52
Roman Catholic Church. *See* Catholicism
Rush, Benjamin, 124

Sadducees, 45, 47
Salem witch trials, 110
Sandy Foundation Shaken, The (Penn), 108, 109
Science and Health (Eddy), 143, 144
Scivias (Know the Ways of the Lord) (Hildegard of Bingen), 66-67, 68
Serra, Junípero, **114-17**
Seton, Elizabeth Ann, **126-28**
Seton, William Magee, 126
Shakers, 118-21
Short Address to the Friends of Him Who Hath No Helper, A (Allen), 124
Siddhārtha Gautama, **21-24,** *26*
    birth of, *21*
Sikhism, 80-82
Smith, Hyrum, 136
Smith, Joseph, **132-36**
Sobukwe, Robert, 173, 174
Society of Friends. *See* Quakers
Society of Jesus, 91-94
Spanish missionaries, 114-17
Speaking in tongues, 51
Spiritual Exercises (Ignatius of Loyola), 92-94
Sufis (Muslims), 64
Sunnis (Muslims), 63

Talmud, 12, 70
Tambo, Oliver, 172
Taoism, 25-27, 34-36
Tao Te Ching (Book of the Way and Power) (Lao Tzu), 26-27
Ten Commandments, 13-14

Tenzin Gyatso, **175-79**
Teresa of Calcutta, **157-60**
Theocracy, 9, 135
Thus Spake Zarathushtra (Nietzsche), 17
Tibetan Buddhism, 175-79
Torah, 11, 45, 70
To the People of Color (Allen), 124
Transfiguration, 15, 16
Transubstantiation, 97
Trinity, 112
Tutu, Desmond, **171-74**
Tyndale, William, 86

Unitarian Church, 112
Universal Negro Improvement Association
  (UNIA), 154-55
Utopia (More), 84, 85

Vardhamāna, Nataputta. *See* Mahavira
Vedas, 18, 38, 147

Wesley, John, 123
Winthrop, John, 104-5
Wise, Isaac Mayer, **137-39**
Witchcraft (Salem trials), 110, 111
Wonders of the Invisible World (Mather),
  111

Word of Wisdom, The (Smith), 134
Words of Understanding (Mather), 112
Wu Ching (Confucius), 31

YHWH (Yahweh), 13
Yin and yang, 35
Young, Brigham, 134, 135, 136

Zarathushtra, **15-17**
Zealots, 45
Zoroaster. *See* Zarathushtra
Zoroastrianism, 16-17

Acknowledgments

Many thanks to Laura Brown of Oxford University Press and to the Press's Young Adult editorial staff, especially Tara Deal. Thank you to the many academic readers, especially Barbara Sproul of Hunter College. Thanks to my readers, particularly Tyler Child, Ben Clark, Jacob Cohen-Holmes, Rabbi Jonathan Gerard, Katie Krumm, Jane Morse, and Monica Wood, and to my students at New Hampshire College. Ellen Barnett listened to many of the ideas here during walks around our town; Jane Morse's support and counsel, informed by years of friendship, both encouraged and improved this book. Finally, special thanks to my husband, Patrick L. Clary, and our sons, Gabriel and Jacob Clary, who welcomed this rich parade of religious figures as it passed through our daily lives and conversations.

Picture Credits

Elizabeth Goldman is a freelance writer who has also worked as an editor and book publicist. She earned her master's degree in religious studies at Indiana University, where she received the D. J. Bowden Religion Essay Award and an Academy of American Poets Prize. She has also received a New York State Creative Artists Fellowship. Ms. Goldman lives in Dover, New Hampshire, where she divides her time between writing and teaching.